It Just Got Easier to Keep Slim, Healthy, and Fit by the Numbers.

Now it's simple to gain a healthier life and a sleeker image through calorie control. This slim, handy guide lets you navigate the supermarkets, order your favorite fast foods, buy name brands, and dine out without doubts.

Here are handy calorie counts for thousands of foods with many new listings, including:

Frusen Glädjé Ice Cream
Stouffer's Mexican Entrees
Contadina Fresh Pastas
Mrs. Smith's Pie in Minutes
And More

WHETHER DINING IN OR EATING OUT, YOU'RE IN CONTROL.

The Corinne T. Netzer 1991 Calorie Counter

Carry It with You Wherever You Go!

THE
Corinne T. Netzer
1991
Calorie
Counter

A DELL BOOK

Published by
Dell Publishing
a division of
Bantam Doubleday Dell Publishing Group, Inc.
666 Fifth Avenue
New York, New York 10103

ISBN: 0-440-20738-X

Printed in the United States of America

Published simultaneously in Canada

February 1991

10 9 8 7 6 5 4 3 2 1

RAD

Introduction

The 1991 Corinne T. Netzer Calorie Counter has been compiled with a two-fold purpose: as an annual, to keep you up-to-date with many of the changes made by the food industry, and to provide a slim, handy, put-in-purse-or-pocket volume.

My books The Brand-Name Calorie Counter, The Complete Book of Food Counts, and The Encyclopedia of Food Values are much larger in size and scope, and are therefore much less portable. However, THIS BOOK CONTAINS MORE PRODUCTS THAN ANY OTHER BOOK OF ITS SIZE!

To keep this book concise yet comprehensive, I have grouped together listings of the same manufacturer whenever possible. Many brand-name yogurts, for example, are listed as "all fruit flavors." Therefore, instead of three pages filled with individual flavors of yogurt—all with identical calorie counts—I have been able to use the extra space for many other products. And for many basic foods and beverages (such as butter, oil, and liquor) I have used the generic listing, rather than include the numerous brands with the same or similar caloric values. Also in the interest of saving space, you will generally find only one description of a food—usually in the form it is most commonly eaten.

This book contains data derived from individual producers and manufacturers and from the United States Department of Agriculture. It contains the most current information available as we go to press.

Good luck—and good eating.

C.T.N.

Abbreviations

diam. . . . . diameter
fl. . . . . fluid
lb. . . . . pound(s)
oz. . . . . ounce(s)
pkg. . . . . package
pkt. . . . . packet
tbsp. . . . . tablespoon
tsp. . . . . teaspoon

Symbols

" . . . . inch
< . . . . less than
* . . . . prepared according to package directions

A

Food and Measure	Calories

Abalone, meat only, dipped in flour, salted and fried, 4 oz. 214
Acorn squash:
baked, 4 oz. 64
boiled, mashed, ½ cup 41
Albacore, see ''Tuna, canned''
Alfredo sauce:
(*Contadina Fresh*), 6 oz. 540
mix (*French's* Pasta Toss), 2 tsp. 25
mix (*Lawry's* Pasta Alfredo), 1 pkg. 226
Allspice, ground (*Spice Island*), 1 tsp. 6
Almond, shelled:
all varieties (*Planters*), 1 oz. 170
dried, sliced or diced, 1 cup 554
Almond butter:
raw, regular or blanched (*Hain*), 2 tbsp. 190
toasted, blanched (*Hain*), 2 tbsp. 210
Almond paste, 1 oz. 127
Amaranth, whole grain, 1 oz. 106
Anchovies, meat only:
fresh, European, raw, 1 oz. 37
canned in olive oil, drained, 5 medium, approx. .7 oz. 42
Anise seed, 1 tsp. 7
Apple:
fresh, with peel, 1 medium, 2¾" diam. 81
fresh, with peel, sliced, ½ cup 32
fresh, peeled, 1 medium, 2¾" diam. 72
fresh, peeled, sliced, ½ cup 31
canned, baked style (*White House*), 3.5 oz. 118
canned, sliced (*White House*), 4 oz. 54
canned, spiced rings (*White House*), 3.5 oz. 180

9

Apple (cont.)
dried, chunks (*Sunmaid/Sunsweet*), 2 oz.	150
dried, slices (*Del Monte*), 2 oz.	140
Apple, escalloped, frozen (*Stouffer's*), 4 oz.	130
Apple butter, all varieties (*Smucker's*), 1 tsp.	12

Apple cider:
(*Indian Summer*), 6 fl. oz.	80
(*Tree Top*), 6 fl. oz.	90
cinnamon (*Indian Summer*), 6 fl. oz.	90
Apple crisp, frozen (*Pepperidge Farm* Berkshire), 1 ramikin	250
Apple danish, see "Danish pastry"	
Apple dumpling, frozen (*Pepperidge Farm*), 3-oz. piece	260
Apple fritter, frozen (*Mrs. Paul's*), 2 pieces	270
Apple fruit square, frozen (*Pepperidge Farm*), 1 piece	220

Apple juice, 6 fl. oz., except as noted:
(*Campbell's* Juice Bowl)	110
(*Kraft* Pure 100%)	80
(*Mott's* Natural Style)	76
(*Red Cheek* 100% Pure/Natural)	97
(*Tree Top*)	90
(*Veryfine*), 8 fl. oz.	107
blend (*Libby's Juicy Juice*)	90
chilled or frozen* (*Minute Maid*)	91
Apple pie, see "Pie"	
Apple-cherry juice (*Red Cheek*), 6 fl. oz.	113
Apple-cranberry drink (*Mott's*), 10-oz. bottle	176

Apple-cranberry juice, 6 fl. oz.:
(*Mott's*)	83
canned or frozen* (*Tree Top*)	100

Apple-grape juice, 6 fl. oz.:
(*Libby's Juicy Juice*)	90
(*Mott's*)	86
(*Red Cheek*)	109
canned or frozen* (*Tree Top*)	100
cocktail, bottled (*Welch's* Orchard)	110
cocktail, frozen* (*Welch's* Orchard)	90
Apple-raspberry juice (*Mott's*), 6 fl. oz.	83

Applesauce:
(*Del Monte*), ½ cup	90
(*Hunt's* Snack Pack), 4.25 oz.	80
(*Mott's*), 6 oz.	150
(*Mott's* Natural), 6 oz.	80
cinnamon (*Mott's*), 6 oz.	152
with peach (*Musselman's* Fruit 'n Sauce), 4 oz.	90
with pineapple (*Musselman's* Fruit 'n Sauce), 4 oz.	110
with strawberry (*Musselman's* Fruit 'n Sauce), 4 oz.	100

Apricot:
fresh, 3 medium, approx. 12 per lb. 51
fresh, pitted, halves, ½ cup 37
canned, whole or halves (*Del Monte*), ½ cup 100
canned, in heavy syrup, peeled, whole (*S&W*), ½ cup 100
canned, in heavy syrup, unpeeled, halves (*S&W*), ½ cup 110
dried (*Del Monte*), 2 oz. 140
Apricot nectar (*Del Monte*), 6 fl. oz. 100
Arby's:
sandwiches:
　beef 'n cheddar, 7 oz. 455
　chicken breast, 6.5 oz. 493
　ham 'n cheese, 5.5 oz. 292
　roast beef, regular, 5.2 oz. 353
　roast beef, super, 8.3 oz. 501
　roast chicken club, 8.3 oz. 610
　turkey deluxe, 7 oz. 375
French fries, 2.5 oz. 246
potato cakes, 3 oz. 204
shake, Jamocha, 11.5 oz. 368
Artichoke, globe or French:
fresh, boiled, 1 medium, approx. 11.3 oz. raw 60
fresh, boiled, fully trimmed or hearts, 4 oz. 57
canned, hearts, marinated (*S&W*), 3.5 oz. 225
frozen, hearts (*Birds Eye* Deluxe), 3 oz. 30
Arugula (*Frieda's* of California), 2 oz. 14
Asparagus:
fresh, boiled, 4 medium, ½″ at base 15
fresh, boiled, cuts and spears, ½ cup 22
canned, all varieties (*Del Monte*), ½ cup 20
canned, cuts and spears (*Green Giant*), ½ cup 20
frozen, spears (*Southern*), 3.5 oz. 27
frozen, spears or cuts (*Birds Eye*), 3.3 oz. 25
Asparagus pilaf (*Green Giant* Microwave Garden Gourmet), 1 pkg. .. 190
Au jus gravy:
canned (*Franco-American*), 2 oz. 10
mix* (*French's*), ¼ cup 10
Avocado:
California, 8 oz. or 1 medium 306
California, puree, 1 cup 407
Florida, 1 lb. or 1 medium 339
Florida, puree, 1 cup 257
Avocado dip (*Kraft*), 2 tbsp. 50

B

Food and Measure   **Calories**

Bacon, cooked:
(*Black Label* Sliced), 2 slices	60
(*Oscar Mayer*), 1 slice, approx. .2 oz.	35
(*Oscar Mayer* Center Cut), 2 slices, approx. .3 oz.	48
(*Range Brand* Sliced), 2 slices	110
(*Red Label*), 3 slices	110
thick sliced (*Oscar Mayer*), 1 slice, approx. .4 oz.	64

Bacon, Canadian style:
(*Hormel* Sliced), 1 oz.	45
(*Oscar Mayer*), 1-oz. slice	35
unheated (*Jones Dairy Farm*), 1 slice	25

Bacon, substitute, cooked:
beef (*Oscar Mayer* Lean 'n Tasty), 1 strip	46
beef (*Sizzlean*), 2 strips	70
pork (*Oscar Mayer* Lean 'n Tasty), 1 strip	54
pork (*Sizzlean*), 2 strips	90
brown-sugar cured (*Sizzlean*), 2 strips	110

Bacon bits:
(*Bac*Os*), 2 tsp.	25
real bacon (*Hormel*), 1 tbsp.	30
real bacon (*Oscar Mayer*), ¼ oz.	21

Bacon-horseradish dip:
(*Kraft*), 2 tbsp.	60
(*Kraft* Premium), 2 tbsp.	50

Bacon-onion dip (*Kraft* Premium), 2 tbsp.   50

Bagel, frozen:
plain, egg, or rye (*Lender's*), 2-oz. piece	150
plain or onion (*Lender's* Bagelettes), .9-oz. piece	70
plain, onion, or poppy seed (*Sara Lee*), 3.1-oz. piece	230
cinnamon-raisin (*Sara Lee*), 3.1-oz. piece	240

Bagel (cont.)

egg (*Sara Lee*), 3-oz. piece 250
garlic, onion, pumpernickel, poppy, or sesame seed
   (*Lender's*), 2-oz. piece 160
raisin 'n honey (*Lender's*), 2.5-oz. piece 200
sesame seed (*Sara Lee*), 3.1-oz. piece 260
wheat 'n raisin (*Lender's*), 2.5-oz. piece 190
Baking powder (*Davis*), 1 tsp. 8
Bamboo shoots, canned (*La Choy*), 1.5 oz. 8
Banana, 1 medium, 8¾" long 105
Banana, baking, see "Plantain"
Banana nectar, canned (*Libby's*), 6 fl. oz. 110
Barbecue loaf (*Oscar Mayer* Bar-B-Q), 1-oz slice. .. 47
Barbecue sauce, 2 tbsp., except as noted:
all varieties (*French's Cattleman's*), 1 tbsp. 25
all varieties (*Heinz* Thick and Rich), 1 tbsp. 20
all varieties, except onion bits and hickory with onion (*Kraft*) 40
(*Hunt's* Original), 1 tbsp. 20
chunky (*Kraft* Thick 'N Spicy) 60
honey or Kansas City (*Kraft* Thick 'N Spicy) 60
onion bits or hickory with onion (*Kraft*) 50
regular or hickory smoke (*Kraft* Thick 'N Spicy) 50
Oriental (*La Choy*), 1 tbsp. 16
Barley, pearled, dry (*Quaker Scotch*), approx. ¼ cup .. 172
Basil, dried, ground, 1 tsp. 4
Bass, fresh, raw:
sea, see "Sea bass"
smallmouth and largemouth, meat only, 4 oz. 118
striped, meat only, 4 oz. 109
Bay leaves, dried (*Spice Island*), 1 tsp. 5
Bean curd, see "Soybean curd"
Bean dip, see specific listings
Bean mix*:
Cajun, and sauce (*Lipton*), ½ cup 160
chicken, and sauce (*Lipton*), ½ cup 150
Bean salad, canned, ½ cup:
four-bean (*Joan of Arc/Read*) 100
three-bean (*Green Giant*) 70
three-bean or German green bean (*Joan of Arc/Read*) .. 90
Bean sprouts:
fresh, mung, raw, 1 cup 32
fresh, soy, raw, 1 cup 90
canned (*La Choy*), 2 oz. 6
Beans, adzuki, boiled, ½ cup 147
Beans, baked, canned (see also specific listings):
(*Allens*), ½ cup 170
(*Campbell's* Home Style), 8 oz. 230

Beans, baked (cont.)
(*Campbell's* Ranchero), 7¾ oz. 180
(*Grandma Brown's*), 1 cup 301
(*Grandma Brown's* Saucepan), 1 cup 307
(*S&W* Brick Oven), ½ oz. 160
Boston (*Health Valley*), 4 oz. 213
brown sugar (*Van Camp's*), 1 cup 284
and franks (*Van Camp's Beanee Weenee*), 1 cup 326
molasses and brown sugar (*Campbell's* Old Fashioned), 8 oz. ... 230
and pork:
  (*Hormel* Micro-Cup), 7.5-oz. cup 254
  (*Hunt's*), 4 oz. 140
  (*S&W*), ½ cup 130
  (*Van Camp's*), 1 cup 216
  in tomato sauce (*Campbell's*), 8 oz. 190
  in tomato sauce (*Joan of Arc/Green Giant*), ½ cup .. 90
vegetarian or plain (*Allens*), ½ cup 110
vegetarian or plain (*B&W*), 8 oz., ⅞ cup 280
Western style (*Van Camp's*), 1 cup 207
Beans, barbecue, canned:
(*B&M*), 8 oz., ⅞ cup 310
(*Campbell's*), 7⅞ oz. 210
Beans, black:
boiled, ½ cup 113
turtle, canned (*Progresso*), 8 oz. 205
Beans, black-eyed, see "Black-eyed peas"
Beans, broad, see "Broad beans"
Beans, butter, canned (*Green Giant/Joan of Arc*), ½ cup 80
Beans, chili, canned:
(*Hunt's*), 4 oz. 102
(*Green Giant/Joan of Arc* Caliente Style), ½ cup 100
(*Van Camp's* Mexican Style), 1 cup 210
in chili gravy (*Dennison's*), 7.5 oz. 180
in sauce (*Hormel*), 5 oz. 130
Beans, great northern, canned:
(*Allens*), ½ cup 105
(*Green Giant/Joan of Arc*), ½ cup 80
Beans, green:
fresh, raw, 1 lb. 123
fresh, boiled, drained, ½ cup 22
canned, all varieties, except Italian cut (*Del Monte*), ½ cup ... 20
canned, all varieties (*Green Giant*), ½ cup 20
canned, dilled (*S&W*), ½ cup 60
canned, Italian cut (*Del Monte*), ½ cup 25
frozen:
  (*Green Giant*), ½ cup 14

Beans, green, frozen **(cont.)**
whole, cut or French style (*Birds Eye/Birds Eye* Deluxe), 3 oz. 25
cut (*Green Giant Harvest Fresh*), ½ cup 16
Italian (*Birds Eye*), 3 oz. 30
in butter sauce (*Green Giant* One Serving), 5.5 oz. 60
in butter sauce, cut (*Green Giant*), ½ cup 30
Beans, green, combinations, frozen:
Bavarian, with spaetzle, sauce (*Birds Eye* International), 3.3 oz. .. 100
French, with toasted almonds (*Birds Eye* Combinations), 3 oz. .. 50
mushroom casserole (*Stouffer's*), 4.75 oz. 160
and mushroom, creamy (*Green Giant* Garden Gourmet), 1 pkg. 220
Beans, kidney, canned:
red, dark, or light (*Green Giant/Joan of Arc*), ½ cup 90
red, light (*Van Camp's*), 1 cup 184
white (*Progresso* Cannellini), 8 oz. 180
Beans, lima:
canned (*Green Giant/Joan of Arc*), ½ cup 80
canned, green, with liquid, (*Del Monte*), ½ cup 70
canned, and ham (*Dennison's*), 7½ oz. 250
frozen (*Green Giant*), ½ cup 100
frozen (*Green Giant Harvest Fresh*), ½ cup 60
frozen, baby (*Birds Eye*), 3.3 oz. 130
frozen, in butter sauce (*Green Giant*), ½ cup 100
frozen, Fordhook (*Birds Eye*), 3.3 oz. 100
Beans, navy, canned (*Allens*), ½ cup 160
Beans, pinto, canned:
(*Green Giant/Joan of Arc*), ½ cup 90
(*Progresso*), 8 oz. 165
baked style, with pork (*Luck's*), 7.5 oz. 220
picante style (*Green Giant/Joan of Arc*), ½ cup 100
Beans, red, canned:
(*Green Giant/Joan of Arc*), ½ cup 90
(*Van Camp's*), 1 cup 194
Beans, refried, 4 oz.:
canned (*Rosarita*) 130
canned, regular or spicy (*Del Monte*) 130
canned or bottled, plain, or with green chiles (*Old El Paso*) 100
canned or bottled, with sausage (*Old El Paso*) 360
canned or bottled, vegetarian (*Old El Paso*) 90
frozen (*Patio* Boil-in-Bag) 190
mix* (*Fantastic Foods*) 207
Beans, Roman, canned (*Progresso*), 8 oz. 210
Beans, yellow or wax:
fresh, see "Beans, green"
canned, (*Allens*), ½ cup 15
canned, golden, cut, or French style (*Del Monte*), ½ cup 20

Beans and frankfurters dinner, frozen:

(*Banquet*), 10 oz.	520
(*Swanson*), 10½ oz.	440
Beechnuts, shelled, 4 oz.	656

Beef, choice grade, retail trim to ¼″ fat (except as noted), meat only:

brisket, whole, braised, lean with fat, 4 oz.	437
brisket, whole, braised, lean only, 4 oz.	274
chuck, arm pot roast, braised, lean with fat, 4 oz.	395
chuck, arm, braised, lean only, 4 oz.	255
chuck, blade roast, braised, lean with fat, 4 oz.	412
chuck, blade roast, braised, lean only, 4 oz.	298
flank steak, trimmed to 0″ fat, braised, lean only, 4 oz.	298
ground, lean, broiled, medium, 4 oz.	308
ground, regular, broiled, medium, 4 oz.	328
porterhouse steak, broiled, lean with fat, 4 oz.	346
porterhouse steak, broiled, lean only, 4 oz.	247
rib, whole, roasted, lean with fat, 4 oz.	426
rib, whole, roasted, lean only, 4 oz.	276

round:

bottom, braised, lean with fat, 4 oz.	322
bottom, braised, lean only, 4 oz.	249
eye of, roasted, lean with fat, 4 oz.	273
eye of, roasted, lean only, 4 oz.	198
tip, roasted, lean with fat, 4 oz.	280
tip, roasted, lean only, 4 oz.	213
top, broiled, lean with fat, 4 oz.	254
top, broiled, lean only, 4 oz.	214
short ribs, braised, lean with fat, 4 oz.	534
short ribs, braised, lean only, 4 oz.	335
sirloin, top, broiled, lean with fat, 4 oz.	305
sirloin, top, broiled, lean only, 4 oz.	229
T-bone steak, broiled, lean with fat, 4 oz.	338
T-bone steak, broiled, lean only, 4 oz.	243
tenderloin, broiled, lean with fat, 4 oz.	345
tenderloin, broiled, lean only, 4 oz.	252
top loin, broiled, lean with fat, 4 oz.	338
top loin, broiled, lean only, 4 oz.	243

Beef, corned:

(*Eckrich* Slender Sliced), 1 oz.	40
(*Healthy Deli*), 1 oz.	35
(*Hillshire Farm*), 1 oz.	31
(*Oscar Mayer*), .6-oz. slice, 10 per 6-oz. pkg.	16
canned (*Dinty Moore*), 2 oz.	130
Beef, corned, hash, canned (*Mary Kitchen*), 7½ oz.	360
Beef, corned, spread (*Hormel*), ½ oz.	35

Beef, roast, see "Beef" and "Beef luncheon meat"

Beef, roast, spread (*Hormel*), 1 oz.   31
Beef dinner, frozen:
(*Banquet Extra Helpings*), 16 oz.   870
(*Swanson*), 11¼ oz.   340
in barbeque sauce (*Swanson*), 11 oz.   460
chopped (*Banquet*), 11 oz.   420
chopped sirloin (*Le Menu*), 12¼ oz.   440
chopped sirloin (*Swanson*), 11 oz.   370
chopped steak (*Swanson Hungry-Man*), 16¾ oz.   640
enchilada, see "Enchilada dinner"
Mexicana (*The Budget Gourmet*), 12.8 oz.   560
patty, charbroiled (*Freezer Queen*), 10 oz.   300
pepper steak (*Healthy Choice*), 11 oz.   290
pepper steak (*Le Menu*), 11½ oz.   370
pot roast, Yankee (*Armour Classics*), 10 oz.   310
pot roast, Yankee (*The Budget Gourmet*), 11 oz.   380
pot roast, Yankee (*Healthy Choice*), 11 oz.   260
pot roast, Yankee (*Le Menu*), 11 oz.   370
Salisbury steak:
(*Armour Classics*), 11¼ oz.   350
(*Banquet*), 11 oz.   500
(*Banquet Extra Helping*), 18 oz.   910
(*Healthy Choice*), 11.5 oz.   300
(*Swanson*), 10¾ oz.   410
(*Swanson Hungry Man*), 18¼ oz.   680
with gravy and mushrooms (*Stouffer's Dinner Supreme*), 11⅝ oz.   400
parmigiana (*Armour Classics*), 11.5 oz.   410
sirloin (*The Budget Gourmet*), 11.5 oz.   410
short ribs, boneless (*Armour Classics*), 9.75 oz.   380
sirloin tips (*Armour Classics*), 10.25 oz.   230
sirloin tips (*Healthy Choice*), 11.75 oz.   290
sirloin tips (*Le Menu*), 11½ oz.   400
sirloin tips, in Burgundy sauce (*The Budget Gourmet*), 11 oz.   310
sliced (*Swanson Hungry-Man*), 15¼ oz.   450
sliced, gravy and (*Freezer Queen*), 10 oz.   210
Stroganoff (*Le Menu*), 10 oz.   450
Swiss steak (*The Budget Gourmet*), 11.2 oz.   450
Swiss steak (*Swanson*), 10 oz.   340
Beef enchilada, see "Enchilada"
Beef entree, canned (see also specific listings):
chow mein (*La Choy* Bi-Pack), ¾ cup   70
stew (*Dinty Moore*, 24-oz. can), 8 oz.   220
stew (*Hormel/Dinty Moore Micro-Cup*), 7.5-oz. cup   190
stew (*Wolf*), 7½ oz.   179
Beef entree, frozen:
(*Banquet Platters*), 10 oz.   460

Beef entree, frozen **(cont.)**

and broccoli w/rice (*La Choy Fresh & Lite*), 11 oz.	260
casserole (*Pillsbury Microwave Classic*), 1 pkg.	430
champignon (*Tyson Gourmet Selection*), 10.5 oz.	330
cheeseburger (*MicroMagic*), 4.75 oz.	450
chop suey, with rice (*Stouffer's*), 12 oz.	300
creamed, chipped (*Banquet Cookin' Bags*), 4 oz.	100
creamed, chipped (*Stouffer's*), 5½ oz.	230
Oriental (*The Budget Gourmet* Slim Selects), 10 oz.	290
patty, mushroom gravy and (*Banquet Family Entrees*), 8 oz.	290
patty, onion gravy and (*Banquet Family Entrees*), 8 oz.	300
pepper Oriental (*Chun King*), 13 oz.	310
pepper steak (*Healthy Choice*), 9.5 oz.	250
pepper steak (*Tyson Gourmet Selection*), 11.25 oz.	330
pepper steak, green, with rice (*Stouffer's*), 10½ oz.	330
pepper steak, with rice, vegetables (*La Choy Fresh & Lite*), 10 oz.	280
pie (*Banquet*), 7 oz.	510
pie (*Stouffer's*), 10 oz.	500
pie (*Swanson* Pot Pie), 7 oz.	380
pie (*Swanson* Hungry Man Pot Pie), 16 oz.	700
pot roast, homestyle (*Right Course*), 9¼ oz.	220
ragout, with rice pilaf (*Right Course*), 10 oz.	300
Salisbury steak (*Swanson* Homestyle Recipe), 10 oz.	480
Salisbury steak, in gravy (*Stouffer's*), 9⅞ oz.	250
Salisbury steak, sirloin (*The Budget Gourmet* Slim Selects), 9 oz.	280
Salisbury steak supreme (*Tyson Gourmet Selection*), 10 oz.	430
short ribs (*Tyson Gourmet Selection*), 11 oz.	470
short ribs, in gravy (*Stouffer's*), 9 oz.	350
sirloin, in herb sauce (*The Budget Gourmet* Slim Selects), 10 oz.	290
sirloin, roast (*The Budget Gourmet*), 9.5 oz.	560
sirloin tips, in Burgundy sauce (*Swanson* Homestyle), 7 oz.	270
sirloin tips, with vegetables (*The Budget Gourmet*), 10 oz.	310
sliced, barbecue sauce or gravy and (*Banquet Cookin' Bags*), 4 oz.	100
sliced, gravy and (*Freezer Queen Deluxe Family Suppers*), 7 oz.	130
steak, breaded (*Hormel*), 4 oz.	370
stew (*Banquet Family Entrees*), 7 oz.	140
stew (*Freezer Queen Family Suppers*), 7 oz.	150
Stroganoff, with parsley noodles (*Stouffer's*), 9¾ oz.	390
Szechuan (*Chun King*), 13 oz.	340
teriyaki (*Chun King*), 13 oz.	380
teriyaki (*Stouffer's*), 9¾ oz.	290
teriyaki, with rice and vegetables (*La Choy Fresh & Lite*), 10 oz.	240

Beef entree, packaged:

pepper steak, Oriental (*Hormel Top Shelf*), 1 serving	290
roast, tender (*Hormel Top Shelf*), 1 serving	240
Salisbury steak with potatoes (*Hormel Top Shelf*), 10 oz.	254
Stroganoff (*Hormel Top Shelf*), 1 serving	320

Beef entree mix*:
Oriental (*Hunt's Minute Gourmet*), 7.6 oz. 271
stew, hearty (*Lipton Microeasy*), ¼ pkg. 370
Beef gravy, canned:
(*Franco-American*), 2 oz. 25
with chunky beef (*Hormel Great Beginnings*), 5 oz. 136
Beef luncheon meat:
(*Eckrich* Slender Sliced), 1 oz. 35
corned, see "Beef, corned"
loaf, jellied (*Hormel* Perma-Fresh), 2 slices 90
oven roasted, cured (*Hillshire Farm* Deli Select), 1 oz. 31
oven roasted, top round (*Boar's Head*), 1 oz. 40
roast (*Healthy Deli*), 1 oz. 30
smoked (*Hillshire Farm* Deli Select), 1 oz. 31
smoked (*Oscar Mayer*), .5-oz. slice, 12 per 6-oz. pkg. 14
smoked, cured (*Hormel*), 1-oz. slice 50
smoked, cured, dried (*Hormel*), 1 oz. 45
Beef pie, see "Beef entree, frozen"
Beef stew, see "Beef entree"
Beef stew seasoning mix (*Lawry's*) 1 pkg. 131
Beer:
regular, 12 fl. oz. 150
light, 12 fl. oz. 95
Beerwurst, see "Salami, beer"
Beet:
fresh, raw, 1 medium, 2" diam. 36
fresh, boiled, sliced, ½ cup 26
canned, ½ cup:
  all cuts (*S&W*) 40
  whole, tiny or sliced (*Del Monte*) 35
  Harvard (*Stokely*) 70
  pickled (*Stokely*) 100
  pickled, extra small or red wine vinegar (*S&W*) 70
  pickled, crinkle (*Del Monte*) 80
Beet greens, fresh, boiled, drained, 1" pieces, 1 cup 40
Berliner, pork and beef, 1 oz. 65
Biscuit:
(*Awrey's*), 2-oz. piece 160
(*Wonder*), 1 piece 80
Biscuit, refrigerator, 1 piece, except as noted:
(*Pillsbury* Big Premium Heat 'n Eat), 2 pieces 280
(*Pillsbury* Country) 50
all varieties (*Ballard Ovenready*) 50
all varieties (*Big Country/1869 Brand*) 100
butter (*Pillsbury*) 50
buttermilk (*Hungry Jack* Extra Rich) 50
buttermilk (*Pillsbury*) 50

Biscuit, refrigerator (cont.)

buttermilk (*Pillsbury* Heat 'n Eat), 2 pieces	170
buttermilk (*Pillsbury* Tender Layer)	60
buttermilk, fluffy (*Hungry Jack*)	90
flaky (*Hungry Jack*)	80
flaky (*Hungry Jack Butter Tastin'*)	90
fluffy (*Pillsbury* Good 'n Buttery)	90
Blackberry, fresh, ½ cup	37
Blackberry cobbler, see "Cobbler"	
Black-eyed peas, canned (*Green Giant/Joan of Arc*), ½ cup	90
Blood sausage, 1 oz.	107
Blueberry:	
fresh, 1 cup	82
canned, in heavy syrup (*S&W*), ½ cup	111
Bluefish, raw, meat only, 4 oz.	140
Bockwurst, 1 link, approx. 2.3 oz.	200
Bok Choy, see "Cabbage, Chinese"	
Bologna:	
(*Eckrich*), 1-oz. slice	100
(*Ekrich* German Brand), 1 oz.	80
(*Eckrich* Thick Slice, 12-oz. pkg.), 1.7-oz. slice	160
(*Hillshire Farm* Large), 1 oz.	90
(*Hormel* Fine Ground), 2 oz.	170
(*Hormel* Perma-Fresh), 2 slices	180
beef:	
(*Boar's Head*), 1 oz.	74
(*Eckrich*), 1-oz. slice	90
(*Eckrich* Thick Slice), 1.5-oz. slice	130
(*Hebrew National* Original Deli Style), 1 oz.	90
(*Kahn's/Kahn's* Giant), 1 slice	90
(*Oscar Mayer*), 1-oz. slice	90
Lebanon (*Oscar Mayer*), .8-oz. slice, 10 per 8-oz. pkg.	49
beef or regular (*Hormel* Coarse Ground), 2 oz.	160
beef and cheddar (*Kahn's*), 1 slice	90
beef and pork (*Healthy Deli*), 1 oz.	41
cheese (*Oscar Mayer*), .8-oz. slice, 10 per 8-oz. pkg.	74
cheese or garlic (*Eckrich*), 1 slice	90
chicken, see "Chicken bologna"	
ham (*Boar's Head*), 1 oz.	40
pork and beef (*Boar's Head*), 1 oz.	80
turkey, see "Turkey bologna"	
Bolognese sauce, refrigerated (*Contadina Fresh*), 7.5 oz.	230
Bonito, raw, meat only, 1 oz.	37
Bouillon (see also "Soup"):	
beef (*Steero* Cube or Instant), 1 serving	6
brown, regular or kosher (*G. Washington's*), .14 oz.	6

Bouillon (cont.)
chicken (*Steero* Cube or Instant), 1 serving 8
onion flavor, instant (*Wyler's*), 1 tsp. 10
vegetable flavor, instant (*Wyler's*), 1 tsp. 6
Boysenberry, fresh, see "Blackberry"
Bran (see also "Cereal"), unprocessed (*Quaker*), 2 tbsp., ¼ oz. 8
Bratwurst:
(*Eckrich*), 1 link 310
(*Hickory Farms* Brotwurst), 1 oz. 90
(*Kahn's*), 1 link 190
cooked (*Hillshire Farm*), 2 oz. 170
hot (*Hickory Farms* Hot Brots), 1 oz. 96
smoked (*Hillshire Farm*), 2 oz. 190
smoked (*Oscar Mayer International Sausages*), 2.7-oz. link 237
Braunschweiger:
(*Hormel*), 1 oz. 80
(*JM*), 1-oz. slice 80
(*Oscar Mayer* German Brand), 1 oz. 94
(*Oscar Mayer* Slices or Tube), 1 oz. 96
Brazil nuts, shelled, 1 oz., 6 large or 8 medium 186
Bread, 2 slices, except as noted:
apple walnut (*Arnold*) 128
(*Arnold Bran'nola* Original) 170
bran, whole (*Brownberry* Natural) 116
(*Brownberry* Health Nut) 142
cinnamon oatmeal (*Oatmeal Goodness*) 180
cinnamon raisin (*Arnold*) 134
cinnamon swirl (*Pepperidge Farm*) 180
corn and molasses (*Pepperidge Farm* Thin Sliced) 140
date walnut swirl (*Pepperidge Farm*) 180
French (*DiCarlo* Parisian) 140
French (*Pepperidge Farm*), 2 oz. 150
garlic (*Colombo* Brand), 2 oz. 185
grain, nutty (*Arnold Bran'nola*) 170
granola, oat and honey (*Pepperidge Farm*) 120
honey bran (*Pepperidge Farm* 1½ lb.) 180
Italian (*Arnold Francisco International*), 1-oz. slice 72
Italian (*Pepperidge Farm*) 140
Italian (*Wonder* Family) 140
multi-grain (*Pepperidge Farm* Very Thin) 80
oat (*Arnold Bran'nola* Country) 180
oat, crunchy (*Pepperidge Farm*) 190
oat bran (*Awrey's*) 100
oatmeal (*Pepperidge Farm*) 140
oatmeal (*Pepperidge Farm*, 1½ lb.) 180
oatmeal with raisins (*Pepperidge Farm*) 140

Bread (cont.)

pita (*Sahara* Mini), 1-oz. piece	79
pita, oat bran (*Sahara*), ½ piece	66
pita, whole wheat (*Sahara*), 1 piece, approx. 2 oz.	150
pumpernickel (*Arnold*)	140
pumpernickel (*Pepperidge Farm*)	160
pumpernickel, small (*Pepperidge Farm Party*), 4 slices	60
raisin cinnamon swirl (*Pepperidge Farm*)	180
rye, all varieties (*Beefsteak*)	140
rye, Dijon (*Pepperidge Farm*)	100
rye, Dijon (*Pepperidge Farm* Thick Sliced)	140
rye, dill (*Arnold*)	142
rye, with seeds (*Pepperidge Farm* Family)	160
rye, seedless (*Pepperidge Farm*)	160
rye, small (*Pepperidge Farm Party*), 4 slices	60
sesame wheat (*Pepperidge Farm*)	190
seven grain (*Pepperidge Farm*)	180
sourdough (*DiCarlo*)	140
Vienna (*Pepperidge Farm* Thick Sliced)	140
wheat:	
(*Arnold* Brick Oven)	114
(*Arnold* Bran'nola Hearty)	176
(*Home Pride* Butter Top/7 Grain)	140
(*Pepperidge Farm* 1½ lb.)	180
(*Pepperidge Farm* Family)	140
all varieties (*Wonder* Family)	140
cracked (*Pepperidge Farm*)	140
germ (*Pepperidge Farm*)	120
honey (*Arnold* Wheatberry)	154
honey (*Pepperidge Farm* Wheat Berry)	140
sprouted (*Pepperidge Farm*)	140
whole (*Arnold* Stoneground 100%)	96
whole (*Pepperidge Farm* Very Thin)	70
whole (*Wonder* 100%/Soft 100%)	140
white:	
(*Arnold* Brick Oven)	102
(*Arnold* Country)	196
(*Home Pride* Butter Top)	140
(*Pepperidge Farm/Pepperidge Farm* Family)	140
(*Pepperidge Farm* Country)	190
(*Pepperidge Farm* Sandwich)	130
(*Pepperidge Farm* Thin Sliced)	140
(*Pepperidge Farm* Toasting)	180
(*Pepperidge Farm* Very Thin)	80
extra fiber (*Arnold* Brick Oven)	110
plain or buttermilk (*Wonder*)	140

Bread, brown and serve:
Austrian or French (*du Jour*), 1 slice 70
Italian (*Pepperidge Farm*), 1 oz. 80
Bread crumbs:
plain (*Devonsheer*), 1 oz. 108
Italian style (*Devonsheer*), 1 oz. 104
Bread dough:
frozen, white (*Rich's*), 2 slices 120
refrigerator, cornbread twists (*Pillsbury*), 1 twist 70
refrigerator, French (*Pillsbury*), 1" slice 60
refrigerator, wheat or white (*Pipin' Hot*), 1" slice 80
Breadfruit, ¼ small, approx. 3.4 oz. 99
Breadsticks:
plain (*Stella D'oro*), 1 piece 41
onion (*Stella D'oro*), 1 piece 40
refrigerator, soft (*Pillsbury*), 1 piece 100
sesame (*Stella D'oro*), 1 piece 51
wheat (*Stella D'oro*), 1 piece 42
Broad beans, boiled, drained, 4 oz. 64
Broccoli:
fresh, raw, 1 spear, approx. 8.7 oz. 42
fresh, boiled, 1 spear, approx. 6.3 oz. 51
fresh, boiled, chopped, ½ cup 22
frozen:
  spears (*Green Giant Harvest Fresh*), ½ cup 20
  spears, baby (*Birds Eye* Deluxe), 3.3 oz. 30
  spears, in butter sauce (*Green Giant*), ½ cup 40
  spears or florets (*Birds Eye/Birds Eye* Deluxe), 3.3 oz. . 25
  cuts (*Green Giant* Polybag), ½ cup 12
  cuts (*Green Giant Harvest Fresh*), ½ cup 16
  in butter sauce (*Birds Eye* Combinations), 3.3 oz. .. 45
  in butter sauce (*Green Giant* One Serving), 4.5 oz. .. 45
  with cheese sauce (*Birds Eye* Combinations), 5 oz. .. 130
  in cheese flavor sauce (*Green Giant*), ½ cup 60
Broccoli combinations, frozen:
and carrots, baby whole and chestnuts (*Stokely Singles*), 3 oz. . 30
carrot fanfare (*Green Giant Valley Combination*), ½ cup . 20
carrots and water chestnuts (*Birds Eye* Farm Fresh), 4 oz. ... 45
and cauliflower:
  medley (*Green Giant Valley Combination*), ½ cup ... 30
  supreme (*Green Giant Valley Combination*), ½ cup .. 20
and cauliflower and carrots:
  (*Birds Eye* Farm Fresh), 4 oz. 35
  in butter sauce (*Green Giant*), ½ cup 30
  in cheese sauce (*Birds Eye For One*), 5 oz. 110
  in cheese sauce (*Green Giant* One Serving), 5 oz. .. 70

Broccoli combinations, cauliflower and carrots (cont.)

and corn, red peppers (*Birds Eye* Farm Fresh), 4 oz. 60
fanfare (*Green Giant Valley Combination*), ½ cup 70
green beans, pearl onions, and red pepper (*Birds Eye* Farm Fresh),
   4 oz. 35
red peppers, bamboo shoots, and straw mushrooms (*Birds Eye*
   Farm Fresh), 4 oz. 30
rotini, in cheese sauce (*Green Giant* One Serving), 5.5 oz. 120

Brown gravy:
canned, with onions (*Franco-American*), 2 oz. 25
in jars (*McCormick/Schilling*), ⅓ cup 30
mix* (*Lawry's*), ¼ cup 24
mix* (*McCormick/Schilling*), ¼ cup 23
mix* (*Pillsbury*), ¼ cup 15

Brownie (see also "Cookies"):
fudge walnut (*Tastykake*), 3-oz. piece 373
frozen:
   chocolate chip, double (*Nestlé* Toll House Ready to Bake), 1.4 oz. 150
   hot fudge chocolate chunk (*Pepperidge Farm* Monterey) 1 ramikan 480
   hot fudge or peanut butter (*Pepperidge Farm* Malibu/Newport),
     1 ramikan 400
mix*:
   (*Duncan Hines* Gourmet Truffle), 1 piece 280
   caramel fudge chunk (*Pillsbury*), 2" square 170
   chocolate, milk or fudge (*Duncan Hines*), 1 piece 160
   fudge (*Pillsbury/Pillsbury* Family), 2" square 150
   fudge (*Pillsbury* Microwave), 1 piece 190
   fudge, double (*Pillsbury*), 2" square 160
   fudge, triple or rocky road (*Pillsbury*), 2" square 170
   walnut (*Pillsbury*), 2" square 150
   white, Vienna (*Duncan Hines*), 1 piece 240
refrigerated, fudge, with chocolate flavored chips
   (*Pillsbury* Ready to Microwave), 1 piece 180

Brussels sprouts:
fresh, boiled, ½ cup 30
frozen (*Frosty Acres*), 3.3 oz. 35
frozen (*Green Giant* Polybag), ½ cup 25
frozen, in butter sauce (*Green Giant*), ½ cup 40
frozen, baby, with cheese sauce (*Birds Eye*), 4.5 oz. 110
Buckwheat flour, 1 cup 402
Buckwheat groats, roasted, cooked, 1 cup 182
Bulgur, cooked, 1 cup 152
Burbot, raw, meat only, 1 oz. 26
Burger King:
breakfast, 1 serving:
   bagel sandwich 387
   bagel sandwich with bacon 438

Burger King, breakfast **(cont.)**

bagel sandwich with ham	418
bagel sandwich with sausage	731
Croissan'wich	304
Croissan'wich with bacon	354
Croissan'wich with ham	335
Croissan'wich with sausage	538
French toast sticks	449
Great Danish	500
scrambled egg platter	468
scrambled egg platter with bacon	536
scrambled egg platter with sausage	702

sandwiches, 1 serving:

bacon double cheeseburger	510
bacon double cheeseburger deluxe, 6.9 oz.	592
barbeque bacon double cheeseburger, 6.1 oz.	536
BK Broiler chicken sandwich, 5.9 oz.	379
cheeseburger	317
chicken Specialty Sandwich	688
double cheeseburger, 6.1 oz.	483
ham and cheese Specialty Sandwich	471
hamburger	275
mushroom swiss double cheeseburger, 6.2 oz.	473
Whaler	488
Whopper	628
Whopper with cheese	711
Whopper Jr.	322
Whopper Jr. with cheese	364
tenders, chicken, 6 pieces	236
tenders, fish, 6 pieces	267

salads, 1 serving:

chef salad	180
chicken salad	140
garden salad	90
side salad	20

dressings and sauces: 1 full packet:

bleu cheese dressing	300
French dressing	280
house dressing	260
Italian dressing, reduced calorie	30
Ranch dipping sauce, 1 oz.	171
sweet & sour sauce, 1 oz.	45
tartar dipping sauce, 1 oz.	174
Thousand Island	240

side dishes, 1 serving:

french fries, regular	227
onion rings	274

Burger King, side dishes **(cont.)**

tater tenders, 2.5 oz. 213

"Burger," vegetarian:

frozen (*Morningstar Farm Grillers*), 2.25-oz. piece 180

mix (*Loveburger*), 2 oz. mix or 4-oz. burger 245

Burrito, frozen, 1 piece, except as noted:

(*Hormel* Burrito Grande), 5½ oz. 380

beef (*Hormel*) 205

beef and bean (*Patio Britos*), 3.63 oz. 250

beef and bean, green chili (*Patio*), 5-oz. pkg. 330

beef and bean, red chili (*Patio*), 5-oz. pkg. 340

beef nacho (*Patio Britos*), 3.63 oz. 270

cheese (*Hormel*) 210

cheese, nacho, spicy chicken, green chili (*Patio Britos*), 3.63 oz. ... 250

chicken and rice (*Hormel*) 200

chili, red (*Patio Britos*), 3.63 oz. 240

chili, red hot (*Patio*), 5-oz. pkg. 360

chili, hot (*Hormel*) 240

Burrito dinner, frozen:

(*Patio*), 12 oz. 517

beef and bean (*Old El Paso* Festive Dinners), 11 oz. 470

Burrito dinner mix:

(*Tio Sancho* Dinner Kit):

seasoning mix, 3.25 oz. 265

1 tortilla 125

Burrito entree, frozen:

bean and cheese or beef and hot bean (*Old El Paso*), 1 pkg. 340

beef and bean, medium or mild (*Old El Paso*), 1 pkg. 330

Burrito filling mix, beans (*Del Monte*), ½ cup 110

Butter, salted or unsalted:

regular, 4 oz., 1 stick or ½ cup 813

regular, 1 tbsp. 102

whipped, ½ cup or 1 stick 542

whipped, 1 tbsp. 67

Butterfish, raw, meat only, 4 oz. 164

Butternut, dried, shelled, 1 oz. 174

Butternut squash, baked, cubed, ½ cup 41

Butterscotch, baking, chips (*Nestlé* Toll House Morsels), 1 oz. 150

Butterscotch topping (*Kraft*), 1 tbsp. 60

C

Food and Measure	Calories
Cabbage, fresh:	
raw, 1 head, 5¾″ diam.	215
raw, shredded, 1 cup	16
boiled, shredded, 1 cup	32
Cabbage, Chinese, fresh:	
bok-choy, raw, whole, 1 lb.	52
bok-choy, boiled, shredded, 1 cup	20
pe-tsai, raw, whole, 1 lb.	68
pe-tsai, boiled, shredded, 1 cup	16
Cabbage, red:	
fresh, raw, shredded, 1 cup	19
fresh, boiled, shredded, 1 cup	32
Cabbage, savoy, fresh:	
raw, whole, 1 lb.	100
boiled, drained, shredded, 1 cup	35
Cake (see also "Cake, frozen" and "Cake, snack"):	
apple streusel (*Awrey's*), 2″ x 2″ piece	160
Black Forest torte (*Awrey's*), 1/14 cake	350
carrot supreme, iced (*Awrey's*), 2″ x 2″ piece	210
chocolate, double, two layer (*Awrey's*), 1/12 cake	250
chocolate, double, three layer (*Awrey's*), 1/12 cake	310
chocolate, German, iced (*Awrey's*), 2″ x 2″ piece	160
chocolate, German, three layer (*Awrey's*), 1/12 cake	350
chocolate, white iced, two layer (*Awrey's*), 1/12 cake	270
pound, golden (*Awrey's*), 1/14 loaf	130
yellow, white iced (*Awrey's*), 2″ x 2″ piece	150
Cake, frozen, 1 slice or piece:	
banana, iced (*Sara Lee*), 1/8 cake	170
Black Forest (*Sara Lee*), 1/8 cake	190
Boston cream (*Pepperidge Farm*), 2⅞ oz.	290

Cake, frozen (cont.)

carrot, iced (*Sara Lee*), ⅛ cake	260
carrot, cream cheese icing (*Pepperidge Farm*), ½ oz.	150
cheese (*Sara Lee* Classic Snacks), 1 piece	200
cheese, French (*Sara Lee* Light), ⅒ cake	200
cheese, strawberry, French (*Sara Lee* Light), ⅒ cake	200
chocolate (*Pepperidge Farm* Supreme), 2⅞ oz.	300
chocolate fudge or German layer (*Pepperidge Farm*), 1⅝ oz.	180
chocolate fudge stripe layer (*Pepperidge Farm*), 1⅝ oz.	170
chocolate mousse (*Sara Lee* Light), ⅒ cake	200
coconut layer (*Pepperidge Farm*), 1⅝ oz.	180
coffee, all butter cheese (*Sara Lee*), ⅛ cake	210
coffee, all butter pecan or streusel (*Sara Lee*), ⅛ cake	160
devil's food layer (*Pepperidge Farm*), 1⅝ oz.	180
golden layer (*Pepperidge Farm*), 1⅝ oz.	180
lemon coconut (*Pepperidge Farm* Supreme), 3 oz.	280
peach Melba (*Pepperidge Farm* Supreme), 3⅛ oz.	270
pineapple cream (*Pepperidge Farm* Supreme), 2 oz.	190
pound (*Pepperidge Farm* Cholesterol Free), 1 oz.	110
pound, all butter (*Sara Lee* Original), ⅒ cake	130
pound, butter (*Pepperidge Farm*), 1 oz.	130
strawberry cream (*Pepperidge Farm* Supreme), 2 oz.	190
strawberry shortcake (*Sara Lee*), ⅛ cake	190
strawberry stripe layer (*Pepperidge Farm*), 1½ oz.	160
vanilla layer (*Pepperidge Farm*), 1⅝ oz.	190

Cake, snack (see also "Cake, snack, frozen" and "Pie, snack"):

apple spice (*Little Debbie*), 2.2-oz. piece	270
banana (*Hostess Suzy Q's*), 1 piece	240
banana (*Tastykake* Banana Treat), 1.1-oz. piece	138
chocolate:	
(*Hostess Ding Dongs/King Dons*), 1 piece	170
(*Hostess Ho Hos*), 1 piece	120
(*Hostess Suzy Q's*), 1 piece	250
(*Little Debbie*), 2.5-oz. piece	320
(*Little Debbie* Choco-Cake), 2.17-oz. piece	270
cream-filled (*Drake's Devil Dog*), 1 piece	160
fudge round (*Little Debbie*), 1.19-oz. piece	150
roll, cream-filled (*Drake's Yodel*), 1 piece	170
coconut (*Tastykake* Juniors), 3.3-oz. piece	317
coconut covered (*Hostess Sno Balls*), 1 piece	140
coffee (*Tastykake* Koffee Kake Juniors), 2.5-oz. piece	317
coffee, cinnamon crumb (*Drake's*), 1 piece, 1.33 oz.	150
crumb cake (*Hostess*), 1 piece	160
cupcake:	
chocolate (*Hostess*), 1 piece	170
chocolate (*Tastykake*), 1.1-oz. piece	113

Cake, snack, cupcake (cont.)

chocolate, cream-filled (*Drake's Ring Ding*), 1 piece	100
creme (*Tastykake* Kreme Kup), .9-oz. piece	104
orange (*Hostess*), 1 piece	150
devil's food (*Little Debbie* Devil Cremes), 1.3-oz. piece	160
(*Drake's Funny Bone*), 1 piece, approx. 1¼ oz.	150
fig (*Little Debbie* Figaroos), 1.5-oz. piece	160
fruit (*Hostess Fruit Loaf*), 1 piece	400
(*Hostess Lil' Angels*), 1 piece	90
(*Hostess Twinkies*), 1 piece	140
peanut butter (*Tastykake* Kandy Kakes), .7-oz. piece	103
vanilla (*Tastykake* Creamie), 1.5-oz. piece	182
vanilla, cream filled (*Tastykake* Krimpets), 1.1-oz. piece	139

Cake, snack, frozen:

carrot cake (*Sara Lee* Deluxe), 1.8-oz. cake	180
cheese, classic (*Sara Lee*), 2-oz. cake	200
cheese, strawberry (*Pepperidge Farm* Manhattan), 1 ramikin	300
chocolate fudge (*Sara Lee*), 1.6-oz. cake	190
coffee:	
apple cinnamon (*Sara Lee* Individual Wrap), 2.9-oz. cake	290
apple crumb (*Pepperidge Farm* Amherst), 1 ramikin	220
butter streusel (*Sara Lee* Individual Wrap), 2-oz. cake	230
pecan (*Sara Lee* Individual Wrap), 2.2-oz. cake	280
pound, all butter (*Sara Lee*), 1.6-oz. cake	200
shortcake, peach Melba (*Pepperidge Farm* Charleston), 1 ramikin	220

Candy:

all varieties (*Charleston Chew!*), 1 oz.	120
butterscotch (*Callard & Bowser*), 1 oz.	115
(*Baby Ruth*), 1 oz.	130
(*Butterfinger*), 1 oz.	130
caramel:	
(*Kraft*), 1 piece	35
(*Sugar Babies*), 1⅝-oz. pkg.	180
(*Sugar Daddy*), 1⅜-oz. pop	150
chocolate coated (*Pom Poms*), 1 oz.	100
chocolate coated, with cookies (*Twix*), 2-oz. piece	140
chocolate (see also "Chocolate, baking"):	
candy coated (*M&M's*), 1.69-oz. pkg.	250
candy coated, with peanuts (*M&M's*), 1.74 oz.	250
with caramel (*Caramello*), 1.6 oz.	220
dark (*Hershey's Special Dark*), 1.45-oz.	220
fudgie (*Kraft*), 1 piece	35
milk chocolate:	
(*Hershey's*), 1.55-oz.	240
(*Hershey's Kisses*), 9 pieces or 1.46 oz.	220
(*Nestlé*), 1.45 oz.	220

Candy, chocolate (cont.)

with almonds (*Hershey's*), 1.45-oz. bar	230
with almonds (*Nestlé*), 1.45-oz.	230
with crisps (*Nestlé Crunch*) 1.4 oz.	210
with crisps and peanuts (*Nestlé 100 Grand*), 1.5 oz.	200
with fruit and nuts (*Chunky*), 1.4 oz.	210
white, with almonds (*Nestlé Alpine*), 1.25 oz.	170
coconut, dark/milk chocolate coated (*Bounty*), 1.05-oz. bar	150
cough drops (*Beech-Nut*), 1 piece	10
fruit flavored (*Skittles*), 2.3 oz.	265
fruit flavored, chews, all flavors (*Bonker's!*), 1 piece	20
fruit flavored, chews, all flavors (*Starburst*), 2.07 oz.	240
gum, 1 piece:	
(*Beech-Nut*)	10
(*Big Red/Juicy Fruit/Doublemint/Wrigley's Spearmint*)	<10
bubble (*Bubble Yum*)	25
bubble, sugarless, all flavors (*Bubble Yum*)	20
candy coated, all flavors (*Beechie's*)	6
fruit flavored, all flavors (*Care*Free*)	8
hard candy, all flavors (*Life Savers*), 1 piece	8
honey (*Bit-O-Honey*) 1.7 oz.	200
(*Hot Tamales*), 1 piece	9
(*Jolly Joes*), 1 piece	9
licorice, strawberry (*Y&S Twizzlers*), 1 oz.	100
lollipops, all flavors (*Life Savers*), 1 piece	45
(*Mars*), 1.76-oz. bar	240
marshmallow:	
(*Campfire*), 2 large or 24 mini pieces	40
(*Funmallows*), 1 piece	30
(*Kraft* Jet-Puffed), 1 piece	25
bunnies (*Just Born*), 1 large piece	111
peeps (*Just Born*), 1 piece	27
(*Mike & Ike*), 1 piece	9
(*Milky Way*), 2.15-oz. bar	280
(*Milky Way* Dark), 1.76 oz.	220
mint (*Junior Mints*), 1 oz. approx. 12 pieces	120
mint (*Kraft* Butter or Party Mints), 1 piece	8
mint, dark chocolate coated (*After Eight*), 1 piece	35
nonpareils (*Nestlé Sno-Caps*), 1 oz.	140
peanut, chocolate coated (*Goobers*), 1⅜ oz.	220
peanut brittle (*Kraft*), 1 oz.	130
peanut butter (*PB Max*), 1.48 oz.	240
popcorn, caramel, with peanuts (*Cracker Jacks*), 1 oz.	120
raisin, chocolate coated (*Raisinets*), 1⅜ oz.	180
(*Snickers*), 2.07-oz. bar	280
(*3 Musketeers*), 2.13-oz. bar	260

Candy (cont.)
toffee (*Callard & Bowser*), 1 oz. 135
toffee (*Kraft*), 1 piece 30
toffee, English (*Heath Bar*), 2 pieces, 1³⁄₁₆ oz. 180
(*Tootsie Roll*), 1 oz. 112
Cannelloni, canned, mini (*Chef Boyardee*), 7.5 oz. 230
Cannelloni entree, frozen, Florentine (*Celentano*), 12 oz. . 350
Cantaloupe, fresh, ½ melon, 5″ diam. 94
Capocollo (*Hormel*), 1 oz. 80
Capon, see "Chicken"
Caramel topping (*Kraft*), 1 tbsp. 60
Caraway seeds (*Spice Islands*), 1 tsp. 8
Cardamom seeds (*Spice Islands*), 1 tsp. 6
Cardoon, fresh, boiled, drained, 4 oz. 25
Carrot:
fresh, raw, 1 medium, 7½″ x 1⅛″ diam. 31
fresh, boiled, drained, sliced, 1 cup 70
canned, diced, sliced, or whole (*Del Monte*), ½ cup 30
frozen, baby, whole (*Birds Eye* Deluxe), 3.3 oz. 40
frozen, and peas, pearl onions (*Birds Eye* Deluxe), 3.3 oz. . 50
Carrot juice, canned, (*Hain*), 6 fl. oz. 80
Casaba melon, cubed, 1 cup 45
Cashew, 1 oz.:
dry-roasted or salted (*Planters*) 160
oil-roasted (*Flavor House*) 180
Cashew butter, raw or toasted (*Hain*), 2 tbsp. 190
Catfish:
fresh, channel, raw, meat only, 4 oz. 132
frozen, breaded (*Mrs. Paul's Light*), 1 fillet, 4½ oz. .. 250
Catsup:
(*Del Monte/Del Monte* No Salt Added), ¼ cup 60
(*Heinz*), 1 tbsp. 16
(*Hunt's*), 1 tbsp. 16
Cauliflower:
fresh, raw, cuts, 1 cup 24
fresh, boiled, drained, 1 cup 30
frozen, cuts (*Green Giant*), ½ cup 12
frozen, in cheese sauce (*Birds Eye* Combinations), 5 oz. . 130
frozen, in cheese flavor sauce (*Green Giant*), ½ cup ... 60
Cauliflower combinations, frozen:
and broccoli and carrots in cheese sauce (*Freezer Queen* Family
    Side Dishes), 5 oz. 60
baby whole carrots, and snow pea pods (*Birds Eye* Farm Fresh),
    4 oz. 40
zucchini, carrots, and red pepper (*Birds Eye* Farm Fresh), 4 oz. ... 30
Caviar (see also "Roe"), black and red, granular, 1 oz. .. 71

Celery, fresh:

raw, 1 stalk, 7½ " x 1¼" diam.	6
raw, diced, ½ cup	10
boiled, drained, diced, ½ cup	13
Celery seed (*Spice Islands*), 1 tsp.	11

Cereal, ready-to-eat, 1 oz. except as noted:

bran:

(*All-Bran*)	70
(*Bran Buds*)	70
(*Kellogg's* 40 + Bran Flakes)	90
(*Kellogg's Heartwise*)	90
(*Post* Natural Bran Flakes)	90
with fruit (*Kellogg's Fruitful Bran*)	110
with fruit and nuts (*Müeslix*)	140
with raisins (*Kellogg's* Raisin Bran)	120
with raisins (*Post* Natural Raisin Bran)	120
with raisins (*Total Raisin Bran*), 1.5 oz.	140

corn:

(*Kellogg's* Corn Flakes)	100
(*Kellogg's* Frosted Flakes)	110
(*Nutri-Grain*)	100
(*Post Toasties*)	110
(*Total* Corn Flakes)	110
with nuts and honey (*Nut & Honey Crunch*)	110

granola or natural style:

(*C.W. Post* Hearty)	130
with almonds (*Sun Country* 100% Natural)	130
with raisins (*Sun Country*)	125
with raisins and dates (*Sun Country* 100% Natural)	123

mixed grain:

(*Kellogg's Crispix*)	110
(*Kellogg's Just Right*)	100
(*King Vitaman*)	110
(*Product 19*)	100
(*Quaker 100% Natural*)	127
(*Special K*)	110
cinnamon and raisin (*Nature Valley* 100% Natural)	120
with fruit (*Kellogg's Apple Raisin Crisp*)	130
with fruit and nuts (*Kellogg's Just Right*)	140
with fruit and nuts (*Müeslix* Five Grain)	140
with fruit and nuts (*Nature Valley* 100% Natural)	130
with raisins and almonds (*Nutri-Grain*)	140
oat bran (*Common Sense*)	100
oat bran (*Cracklin'* Oat Bran)	110
oat bran, with raisins (*Raisin Oat Bran*), 1.5 oz.	150
oats (*General Mills* Oatmeal Crisp)	110

Cereal, ready-to-eat (cont.)

oats (*Life*/Cinnamon *Life*) 101
rice (*Kellogg's Rice Krispies*/Frosted Krispies) 110
rice (*Quaker* Puffed Rice), ½ oz. 54
wheat:
   (*Honey Smacks*) 110
   (*Nutri-Grain*) 100
   (*Quaker* Puffed Wheat), ½ oz. 50
   (*Total*) 100
   (*Wheaties*) 100
   with raisins (*Nutri-Grain*) 130
   raisin filled (*Kellogg's Raisin Squares*) 90
   shredded (*Nabisco*), 1 piece, ⅚ oz. 80
   shredded (*Nutri-Grain*) 90
   shredded (*Quaker*) 2 pieces, 1.4 oz. 132

Cereal, cooking:

bran (*H-O Brand* Super Bran), ⅓ cup dry 110
farina (*H-O Brand* Instant), 1 pkt. 110
oat bran (*Quaker/Mother's*), ⅓ cup dry, ⅔ cup cooked 92
oat bran (*3-Minute Brand* Regular or Instant), 1 oz. 90
oatmeal and oats:
   (*H-O Brand* Quick), ½ cup dry 130
   (*H-O Brand* Instant), 1 pkt. 110
   (*Maypo* 30 Second), 1 oz. 100
   (*Quaker* Quick/Old Fashioned), ⅓ cup dry 99
   regular (*Instant Quaker*), 1 pkt. 94
   apple and cinnamon (*H-O Brand* Instant), 1 pkt. 130
   apple and cinnamon (*Instant Quaker*), 1 pkt. 118
   with fiber, raisin and bran (*H-O Brand* Instant), 1 pkt. . 150
   maple flavored (*Maypo* Vermont Style), 1 oz. 105
   maple and brown sugar (*Instant Quaker*), 1 pkt. 152
   peach or strawberry and cream (*Instant Quaker*), 1 pkt. . 129
wheat (*Wheatena*), 1 oz. 100
wheat, whole (*Quaker/Mother's* Hot Natural), ⅓ cup dry 92
wheat and barley (*Maltex*), 1 oz. 105

Cervelat, see "Thuringer cervelat"

Champagne, see "Wine"

Chard, Swiss, fresh, boiled, drained, chopped, 1 cup 35

Cheddarwurst (*Hillshire Farm*), 2-oz. link 190

Cheese (see also "Cheese food" and "Cheese spread"), 1 oz.,
  except as noted:

American, processed (*Kraft Deluxe/Old English*) 110
American, processed, hot pepper (*Sargento*) 110
asiago, wheel (*Frigo*) 110
(*Bel Paese* Imported) 90
(*Bel Paese* Medallion Processed) 71

Cheese (cont.)

blue (*Kraft*)	100
blue, crumbled, ½ cup not packed	239
Bonbel (*Laughing Cow*)	100
brick (*Kraft*)	110
Brie (*Sargento*)	100
Cajun (*Sargento*)	110
Camembert (*Sargento*)	90
caraway (*Kraft*)	100
cheddar (*Kraft*)	110
cheddar, mild, reduced fat (*Kraft* Light Naturals)	80
cheddar, shredded, ½ cup not packed	228
colby (*Kraft*)	110
colby or colby jack (*Sargento*)	110
cottage cheese, creamed:	
(*Breakstones* Smooth & Creamy), 4 oz.	110
(*Crowley* 4% fat), ½ cup	120
with peaches or pineapple (*Crowley* 4%), ½ cup	140
cottage cheese, pot style, large curd, lowfat 2%	
(*Friendship*), ½ cup	100
cream cheese:	
plain, regular, soft or whipped (*Philadelphia Brand*)	100
with chives or pimentos (*Philadelphia Brand*)	90
soft, all varieties, except plain, chives and onion, or honey	
(*Philadelphia Brand*)	90
soft, chives and onion, or honey (*Philadelphia Brand*)	100
whipped, all varieties, except plain (*Philadelphia Brand*)	90
Edam (*Kraft*)	90
Edam (*Sargento*)	100
farmer (*Friendship*), ½ cup	160
farmer's (*Sargento*)	100
feta (*Churny* Natural)	75
fontina (*Sargento*)	110
gjetost (*Sargento*)	130
Gouda (*Kraft*)	110
Gouda (*Sargento*)	100
Gruyere	117
havarti (*Casino*)	120
hot pepper (*Hickory Farms*)	106
Jarlsberg (*Norseland*)	97
limburger (*Mohawk Valley* Little Gem)	90
Monterey Jack, all varieties (*Kraft*)	110
Monterey Jack, reduced fat (*Kraft* Light Naturals)	80
mozzarella (*Casino*)	90
mozzarella (*Polly-O Fior di Latte*)	80
mozzarella, whole milk (*Polly-O*)	90

Cheese (cont.)

mozzarella, part skim (*Polly-O*)	80
mozzarella, part skim, plain or jalapeño (*Kraft*)	80
Muenster (*Alpine Lace*)	100
Muenster (*Kaukauna*)	110
Parmesan (*Kraft*)	110
Parmesan, grated (*Kraft*)	130
Parmesan and Romano, grated (*Frigo*)	130
pizza, shredded (*Frigo*)	90
Port du Salut	100
port wine (*Hickory Farms*)	97
pot cheese (*Sargento*)	25
provolone, regular or smoked (*Sargento*)	100
ricotta (*Polly-O* Lite), 2 oz.	80
ricotta, whole milk (*Crowley*), 2 oz.	100
ricotta, whole milk (*Polly-O*), 2 oz.	100
ricotta, part skim (*Crowley*), 2 oz.	80
ricotta, part skim (*Polly-O*), 2 oz.	90
Romano (*Sargento*)	110
Romano, grated (*Kraft*)	130
Roquefort	105
smoked (*Sargento* Smokestik)	100
string cheese, regular or smoked (*Sargento*)	80
Swiss (*Alpine Lace Swiss-Lo*)	100
Swiss (*Kraft* Regular or Aged)	110
Swiss Lorraine (*Hickory Farms Light Choice*)	110
Swiss, processed (*Kraft Deluxe*)	90
Swiss, smoked (*Dorman's*)	100
taco cheese, shredded (*Kraft*)	110
Tilsit (*Sargento*)	100
tybo (*Sargento* Red Wax)	100
Cheese blintz, frozen (*King Kold*), 2.5-oz. piece	113

Cheese food, 1 oz.:

all varieties (*Cracker Barrel*)	90
all varieties (*Velveeta*)	100
all varieties, except sharp (*Kraft* Singles)	90
American, regular or sharp (*Borden Singles*)	90
sharp (*Kraft* Singles)	100
Cheese nuggets, frozen (*Banquet* Cheese Hot Bites), 2.63 oz.	240

Cheese nut ball or log, 1 oz.:

all varieties (*Cracker Barrel*)	90
all varieties (*Kaukauna*)	100
Cheese sauce, four cheese (*Contadina Fresh*), 6 oz.	470

Cheese, spreads (see also "Cheese"), 1 oz.:

all varieties (*Cheez Whiz/Squeez-A-Snak*)	80
all varieties, except slices (*Velveeta*)	80

Cheese, spreads (cont.)
(*Velveeta* Slices) 90
American, plain, bacon or with garlic (*Kraft*) 80
blue (*Roka Brand*) 70
brick (*Sargento* Cracker Snacks) 95
Cheese dip:
blue (*Kraft* Premium), 2 tbsp. 45
nacho (*Kraft* Premium), 2 tbsp. 50
Cherimoyas, fresh, 1 medium, approx. 1.9 lb. 515
Cherry:
fresh, sour, trimmed, ½ cup 39
fresh, sweet, trimmed, ½ cup 52
fresh, sweet, 10 medium, approx. 2.6 oz. 49
canned, red sour, in liquid (*A&P*), ½ cup 50
canned, sweet, dark, with pits or pitted (*Del Monte*), ½ cup 90
canned, sweet, light, with pits (*Del Monte*), ½ cup 100
packaged (*Mott's* Cherry Fruit Pak), 3.75 oz. 72
Cherry, maraschino, in jars, with liquid, 1 oz. 33
Cherry cobbler, see "Cobbler"
Cherry fruit square, frozen (*Pepperidge Farm*), 1 piece 230
Cherry juice, blend (*Libby's Juicy Juice*), 6 fl. oz. 90
Chestnuts:
Chinese, boiled or steamed, shelled, 4 oz. 176
Chinese, dried, peeled, 1 oz. 105
European, boiled or steamed, peeled, 4 oz. 148
European, roasted, 4 oz. 280
European, dried, peeled, 1 oz. 105
Japanese, boiled or steamed, 4 oz. 64
Japanese, dried, 1 oz. 102
Chestnuts, Chinese water, see "Water chestnuts"
Chicken, fresh:
broilers or fryers, roasted:
  with skin, ½ chicken or 10.5 oz. 715
  meat only, 4 oz. 215
  dark meat only, 4 oz. 232
  light meat only, 4 oz. 196
  breast, with skin, ½ breast or 3.5 oz. 193
  drumstick, with skin, 1 drumstick or 1.8 oz. 112
  thigh, with skin, 1 thigh or 2.2 oz. 153
  wing, with skin, 1 wing or 1.2 oz. 99
capon, roasted, with skin, ½ capon or 1.4 lb. 1457
capon, roasted, meat with skin, 4 oz. 260
roaster, roasted:
  with skin, ½ chicken or 1 lb. 1071
  meat only, 4 oz. 189
  meat only, chopped or diced, 1 cup, not packed 233

Chicken, roaster, roasted **(cont.)**

dark meat, 4 oz.	202
light meat, 4 oz.	174

stewing, stewed:

with skin, ½ chicken or 9.2 oz.	744
meat only, 4 oz.	269
meat only, chopped or diced, 1 cup, not packed	332
dark meat, 4 oz.	293
light meat, 4 oz.	242

Chicken, boneless and luncheon meat:

breast, oven-roasted (*Oscar Mayer*), 1-oz. slice	29
breast, oven-roasted, deluxe (*Louis Rich*), 1-oz. slice	30
white meat, oven-roasted (*Louis Rich*), 1-oz. slice	40

Chicken, canned:

breast, chunk (*Hormel*), 6¾ oz.	350
chunk style (*Swanson* Mixin'), 2½ oz.	130
white or white and dark (*Swanson*), 2½ oz.	100
white and dark, chunk (*Hormel*), 6¾ oz.	340

Chicken dinner, frozen:

a la king (*Armour Classics*), 11.25 oz.	290
in barbeque sauce (*Swanson*), 11¾ oz.	460
barbecue style (*Stouffer's Dinner Supreme*), 10.5 oz.	390
boneless (*Swanson Hungry-Man*), 17¾ oz.	700
breast, baked, with gravy (*Stouffer's Dinner Supreme*), 10 oz.	300
cacciatore (*The Budget Gourmet*), 11 oz.	300
casserole (*Pillsbury Microwave Classic*), 1 pkg.	400
and cheese casserole (*Pillsbury Microwave Classic*), 1 pkg.	480
cordon bleu (*Le Menu*), 11 oz.	470
fettuccini (*Armour Classics*), 11 oz.	260
Florentine (*Le Menu*), 10¾ oz.	340
Florentine (*Stouffer's Dinner Supreme*), 11 oz.	430

fried:

(*Banquet*), 10 oz.	400
(*Banquet Extra Helping*), 16 oz.	570
(*Stouffer's Dinner Supreme*), 10⅝ oz.	450
barbecue flavored (*Swanson*), 10 oz.	520
dark meat (*Swanson*), 9¾ oz.	560
platter (*Swanson*), 7¾ oz.	340
white meat (*Swanson*), 10¼ oz.	560
white meat (*Swanson Hungry-Man*), 14¼ oz.	870
glazed (*Armour Classics*), 10.75 oz.	300
herb roasted (*Healthy Choice*), 11 oz.	260
mesquite (*Armour Classics*), 9.5 oz.	370
mesquite (*Healthy Choice*), 10.5 oz.	310
nuggets (*Freezer Queen* Platter), 6 oz.	410
nuggets (*Swanson*), 8¾ oz.	460

Chicken dinner (cont.)

nuggets, with barbecue sauce (*Banquet Extra Helping*), 10 oz.	640
Oriental (*Healthy Choice*), 11.25 oz.	220
parmigiana (*Armour Classics*), 11.5 oz.	370
parmigiana (*Stouffer's Dinner Supreme*), 11.5 oz.	360
and pasta divan (*Healthy Choice*), 11.5 oz.	310
roast (*The Budget Gourmet*), 11.2 oz.	280
with Supreme sauce (*Stouffer's Dinner Supreme*), 11⅜ oz.	360
sweet and sour (*Healthy Choice*), 11.5 oz.	280
sweet and sour (*Swanson*), 12 oz.	380
teriyaki (*The Budget Gourmet*), 12 oz.	360
with wine and mushroom sauce (*Armour Classics*), 10.75 oz.	280

Chicken entree, canned:

a la king (*Swanson*), 5¼ oz.	180
chow mein (*La Choy* Bi-Pack), ¾ cup	80
and dumplings (*Swanson*), 7½ oz.	220
Oriental (*La Choy* Bi-Pack), ¾ cup	240
stew (*Swanson*), 7⅝ oz.	170

Chicken entree, frozen:

a la gratin (*Myers*), 3.5 oz.	129
a la king, with rice (*Stouffer's*), 9½ oz.	290
almond, with rice and vegetables (*La Choy Fresh & Light*), 9.75 oz.	270
a l'orange (*Healthy Choice*), 9 oz.	260
a l'orange (*Tyson Gourmet Selection*), 9.5 oz.	300
au gratin (*The Budget Gourmet* Slim Selects), 9.1 oz.	260
and beef luau (*Tyson Gourmet Selection*), 10.5 oz.	330
breast, barbecue marinated (*Tyson*), 3.75 oz.	120
breast, lemon pepper marinated (*Tyson*), 3.75 oz.	120
breast, tenders (*Banquet* Chicken Hot Bites), 2.5 oz.	150
cacciatore (*Swanson* Homestyle), 11 oz.	260
cashew, in sauce, with rice (*Stouffer's*), 9½ oz.	380
with cheddar (*Tyson* Chick' n Cheddar), 2.6 oz.	220
chow mein (*Chun King*), 13 oz.	370
chow mein (*Healthy Choice*), 8.5 oz.	220
chunks (*Country Pride*), 3 oz.	240
chunks, Southern fried (*Country Pride*), 3 oz.	280
cordon bleu (*Swift* International), 6 oz.	360
creamed (*Stouffer's*), 6½ oz.	300
Dijon (*Tyson Gourmet Selection*), 8.5 oz.	310
dipsters or drumsnackers (*Swanson* Plump & Juicy), 3 oz.	220
divan (*Stouffer's*), 8½ oz.	320
and dumplings (*Banquet Family Entrees*), 7 oz.	280
escalloped, and noodles (*Stouffer's*), 10 oz.	420
with fettuccine (*The Budget Gourmet*), 10 oz.	400
fiesta (*Healthy Choice*), 8.5 oz.	250
Francais (*Tyson Gourmet Selection*), 9.5 oz.	280

Chicken entree, frozen (cont.)
fried, breast portions (*Banquet*), 5.75 oz. 220
fried, regular or hot 'n' spicy (*Banquet* Platter), 6.4 oz. 330
fried, white meat, regular or hot 'n spicy (*Banquet* Platter), 9 oz. 430
glazed (*Healthy Choice*), 8.5 oz. 220
Kiev (*Swift* International), 6 oz. 420
Kiev (*Tyson Gourmet Selection*), 9.25 oz. 520
Mandarin (*The Budget Gourmet Slim Selects*), 10 oz. 290
Marsala (*Tyson Gourmet Selection*), 10.5 oz. 300
mesquite (*Tyson Gourmet Selection*), 9.5 oz. 520
nibbles (*Swanson* Homestyle Recipe), 4¼ oz. 340
and noodles, homestyle (*Stouffer's*), 10 oz. 310
nuggets (*Banquet* Chicken Hot Bites), 2.63 oz. 210
nuggets, with cheddar or hot 'n' spicy (*Banquet* Chicken Hot Bites),
  2.63 oz. 250
nuggets, microwave (*Tyson*), 3.5 oz. 220
Oriental (*Tyson Gourmet Selection*), 10.25 oz. 270
Oriental, spicy (*La Choy Fresh & Lite*), 9.75 oz. 270
parmigiana (*Celentano*), 9 oz. 330
parmigiana (*Tyson Gourmet Selection*), 11.25 oz. 380
patties (*Banquet* Platters), 7.5 oz. 380
patties (*Tyson/Tyson* Thick & Crispy), 2.6 oz. 220
picatta (*Tyson Gourmet Selection*), 9 oz. 240
pie (*Stouffer's*), 10 oz. 530
pie (*Swanson*), 7 oz. 370
pie (*Swanson* Homestyle Recipe), 8 oz. 380
pie (*Swanson* Hungry-Man), 16 oz. 740
primavera (*Celentano*), 11.5 oz. 270
sesame (*Right Course*), 10 oz. 320
sticks (*Banquet* Chicken Hot Bites), 2.63 oz. 220
sweet and sour (*Tyson Gourmet Selection*), 11 oz. 420
sweet and sour, with rice (*The Budget Gourmet*), 10 oz. 350
sweet and sour, with rice and vegetables (*La Choy Fresh & Lite*),
  10 oz. 260
tenders, microwave (*Tyson*), 3.5 oz. 230
and vegetables primavera (*Banquet Family Entrees*), 7 oz. 140
walnut, crunchy (*Chun King*), 13 oz. 310
Chicken entree, packaged:
Acapulco (*Hormel Top Shelf*), 1 serving 390
breast, glazed (*Hormel Top Shelf*), 1 serving 210
sweet and sour (*Hormel Top Shelf*), 1 serving 270
Chicken entree, refrigerated, 5 oz. serving:
bleu cheese, Italian (*Chicken By George*) 190
Cajun (*Chicken By George*) 200
lemon herb (*Chicken By George*) 150
mesquite barbecue (*Chicken By George*) 170

Chicken entree, refrigerated (cont.)
mustard, country, dill or teriyaki (*Chicken By George*)	180
tomato herb and basil (*Chicken By George*)	190

Chicken frankfurter:
(*Longacre*), 1 oz.	63
batter-wrapped (*Tyson* Corn Dogs), 3.5 oz.	280

Chicken gravy:
canned (*Franco-American*), 2 oz.	50
canned, giblet (*Franco-American*), 2 oz.	30
mix* (*French's*), ¼ cup	25
mix* (*Lawry's*), ¼ cup	25

Chicken pie, see ''Chicken entree, frozen''

Chicken spread, canned:
(*Hormel*), ½ oz.	30
chunky (*Swanson*), 1 oz.	60
chunky (*Underwood*), ½ can or 2.4 oz.	150

Chickpeas (garbanzos), canned:
(*Allens*), ½ cup	110
(*Green Giant/Joan of Arc*), ½ cup	90
Chicory greens, fresh, untrimmed, 1 lb.	87
Chicory root, fresh, 1 root, approx. 2.6 oz.	44

Chili, canned:
with beans (see also ''Beans, chili''):
(*Dennison's* Cook-Off), 7½ oz.	340
(*Hormel*, 15 oz. can), 7½ oz.	310
(*Hormel Micro-Cup*), 7½ oz. container	250
(*Van Camp's*), 1 cup	352
(*Wolf*), 1 cup	345
hot (*Gebhardt*), 4 oz.	189
hot (*Hormel*), 7½ oz.	310
regular, chunky or hot (*Dennison's*), 7½ oz.	310

without beans:
(*Dennison's*), 7½ oz.	300
(*Hormel*), 10½-oz. can	540
(*Hormel*, 15 oz. can), 7½ oz.	370
(*Van Camp's*), 1 cup	412
(*Wolf*), 1 cup	387
extra spicy (*Wolf*), 7½ oz.	363
hot (*Hormel*), 7½ oz.	370
and franks (*Van Camp's Chilee Weenee*), 1 cup	309
vegetarian (*Gebhardt*), 4 oz.	219
vegetarian, regular, spicy or tempeh (*Hain*), 7½ oz.	160

Chili pepper, see ''Pepper, chili''
Chili powder, 1 tbsp.	24

Chili sauce:
(*Gebhardt*), 2 tbsp.	20

Chili sauce (cont.)

(*Heinz*), 1 tbsp.	17
(*S&W Chili Makins'*), ½ cup	100
green, mild (*El Molino*), 2 tbsp.	10
hot dog sauce (*Wolf*), ⅙ cup	44
tomato (*Del Monte*), ¼ cup	70

Chili seasoning mix:

(*Lawry's* Seasoning Blends), 1 pkg.	143
mix (*Tio Sancho*), 1.23 oz.	109

Chives, fresh or freeze-dried, chopped, 1 tbsp. ... 1

Chocolate, see "Candy"

Chocolate, baking:

(*Nestlé Choco-Bake*), 1 oz.	190
bars, semi-sweet (*Nestlé*), 1 oz.	160
bars, semi-sweet or unsweetened (*Baker's*), 1 oz.	140
bars, unsweetened (*Nestlé*), 1 oz.	180
bars, white (*Nestlé* Premier), ½ oz.	80
chips, semi-sweet (*Baker's*), ¼ cup	200
chips or pieces, all varieties (*Nestlé* Toll House), 1 oz.	150
pieces, white (*Nestlé* Toll House Premier *Treasures*), 1 oz.	160
vanilla milk (*Hershey's*), 1.5 oz. or ¼ cup	240

Chocolate milk:

(*Hershey's*), 1 cup	210
(*Meadow Gold*), 1 cup	210
lowfat, 2% (*Borden* Dutch Brand), 1 cup	180
lowfat, 2% (*Darigold*), 1 cup	190

Chocolate mousse, frozen (*Pepperidge Farm* San Francisco),
1 ramikin ... 490

Chocolate topping and syrup:

(*Kraft*), 1 tbsp.	60
(*Hershey's* Syrup), 2 tbsp. or 1 oz.	80
(*Nestlé Quik* Syrup), 1.22 oz., approx. 2 tbsp.	100
dark, flavored (*Smucker's* Special Recipe), 2 tbsp.	130
fudge (*Hershey's*), 2 tbsp.	100
fudge or regular (*Smucker's Magic Shell*), 2 tbsp.	190
fudge, hot (*Kraft*), 1 tbsp.	70
fudge, hot (*Smucker's*), 2 tbsp.	110
fudge, hot (*Smucker's* Special Recipe), 2 tbsp.	150
fudge, Swiss milk (*Smucker's*), 2 tbsp.	140
milk, with almonds (*Nestlé Candytops*), 1.25 oz.	230
milk, with crisps (*Nestlé Crunch Candytops*), 1.25 oz.	220
nut (*Smucker's Magic Shell*), 2 tbsp.	200

Cinnamon, ground (*Spice Islands*), 1 tsp. ... 6

Clam, meat only:

fresh, mixed species, raw, 4 oz.	84
fresh, mixed species, raw, 9 large or 20 small, 6.3 oz.	133

Clam (cont.)

canned, chopped or minced (*Gorton's*), ½ can	70
canned, chopped or minced, with liquid (*Doxsee*), 6.5 oz.	100
frozen, battered, fried (*Mrs. Paul's*), 2½ oz.	240
frozen, strips (*Gorton's* Microwave Specialty), 3.5 oz.	330

Clam chowder, see "Soup"

Clam dip:

(*Kraft*), 3 tbsp.	50
(*Kraft* Premium), 2 tbsp.	45
Clam juice (*Doxsee*), 3 fl. oz.	4

Clam sauce:

canned, red (*Buitoni*), approx. 5 oz.	190
refrigerated, red (*Contadina Fresh*), 7.5 oz.	120
refrigerated, white (*Contadina Fresh*), 6 oz.	290
Cloves, ground, 1 tsp.	7

Cobbler, frozen, ⅙ pkg. or 4.33 oz.:

apple or strawberry (*Pet-Ritz*)	290
blackberry (*Pet-Ritz*)	250
blueberry (*Pet-Ritz*)	370
cherry (*Pet-Ritz*)	280
peach (*Pet-Ritz*)	260

Cocktail sauce, see "Seafood sauce"

Cocoa mix:

(*Hershey's*), 1 oz. or ⅓ cup	120
(*Swiss Miss* Lite), .76-oz. pkg.	70
chocolate, double rich or milk (*Swiss Miss*), 1-oz. pkt.	110
mix, with mini marshmallows (*Swiss Miss*), 1 oz.	110
mix, sugar free (*Swiss Miss*), .5-oz. pkt.	50
powder (*Nestlé*), 1.5 oz., ½ cup	180

Coconut:

fresh, meat only, 1 piece, 2" x 2" x 2½"	159
fresh, shredded or grated, 1 cup	283
(*Baker's Angel Flake*), ⅓ cup	120
(*Baker's Premium Shred*), ⅓ cup	140
(*Finast* Snowflake), 1 oz.	137
Coconut cream, canned (*Coco Lopez*), 2 tbsp.	120

Cod:

fresh, Atlantic, baked, broiled or microwaved, 4 oz.	119
dried, Atlantic, salted, 1 oz.	81
frozen, fillets (*Booth*), 4 oz.	89
frozen, fillets (*Gordon's Fishmarket Fresh*), 5 oz.	110
frozen, breaded (*Van de Kamp's Light*), 1 piece	250
frozen, breaded, fillets (*Mrs. Paul's Light*), 1 piece	220

Cod entree, frozen:

fillet, au gratin (*Booth*), 9.5 oz.	280
fillet, Florentine (*Booth*), 9.5 oz.	244

Cod entree (cont.)
fillet, with lemon butter and rice (*Booth*), 9.5 oz. 567
Cod liver oil, all flavors (*Hain*), 1 tbsp. 120
Coffee, regular or decaffeinated, prepared:
(*Chock Full O' Nuts*), brewed, 6 fl. oz. 2
freeze-dried, all types (*Taster's Choice*), 6 fl. oz. 4
Coffee, flavored, mix*, 6 fl. oz.:
all varieties (*Hill Bros* Cafe Coffees) 60
all varieties, except Francais, Vienna, or orange cappuccino (*General Foods* International) 50
Francais, Vienna, or orange cappuccino (*General Foods* International) 60
Collards:
fresh, boiled, drained, chopped, ½ cup 17
canned, chopped, seasoned with pork (*Luck's*), 7½ oz. 90
frozen, chopped (*Southern*), 3.5 oz. 30
Cookie:
almond (*Pepperidge Farm* Supreme), 2 pieces 140
almond toast (*Stella D'oro* Mandel), 1 piece 58
animal crackers (*Barnum's Animals*), 5 pieces or ½ oz. 60
anise (*Stella D'oro* Anisette Sponge), 1 piece 51
anise (*Stella D'oro* Anisette Toast), 1 piece 46
apple bar (*Apple Newtons*), ¾-oz. piece 80
apple n' raisin (*Archway*), 1 piece 120
apricot-raspberry (*Pepperidge Farm* Zurich), 1 piece 60
arrowroot (*National*), ¼-oz. piece 20
brownie, chocolate-nut (*Pepperidge Farm*), 2 pieces 110
brownie cream sandwich (*Pepperidge Farm* Capri), 2 pieces 160
brownie nut (*Pepperidge Farm* Beacon Hill), 1 piece 120
butter flavor (*Pepperidge Farm* Chessmen), 2 pieces 90
chocolate (*Nabisco* Middles), ½ oz. 80
chocolate (*Nabisco* Snaps), 4 pieces, ½ oz. 70
chocolate fudge (*Stella D'oro* Swiss), 1 piece 68
chocolate fudge mint (*Keebler* Grasshopper), 2 pieces 70
chocolate chip:
  (*Almost Home* Real), ½-oz. piece 60
  (*Archway*), 1 piece 50
  (*Chewy Chips Ahoy!*), ½-oz. piece 60
  (*Chips Ahoy! Pure*), ½-oz. piece 50
  (*Chips Ahoy! Striped*), ½-oz. piece 90
  (*Keebler Soft Batch/Keebler Chips Deluxe*), 1 piece 80
  (*Nabisco* Snaps), 3 pieces, ½ oz. 70
  (*Pepperidge Farm* Old Fashioned), 3 pieces 150
  chocolate (*Pepperidge Farm* Old Fashioned), 3 pieces ... 160
  chunk (*Pepperidge Farm* Nantucket), 1 piece 120
  chunk, pecan (*Pepperidge Farm* Chesapeake), 1 piece 120
  fudge (*Almost Home*), ½-oz. piece 70

Cookie, chocolate chip **(cont.)**

milk, macadamia (*Pepperidge Farm*), 2 pieces	140
milk, macadamia (*Pepperidge Farm* Sausalito), 1 piece	120
chocolate sandwich:	
(*Pepperidge Farm* Brussels), 2 pieces	110
(*Pepperidge Farm* Lido), 1 piece	90
(*Pepperidge Farm* Milano), 2 pieces	120
coconut (*Pepperidge Farm* Tahiti), 1 piece	90
coffee (*Pepperidge Farm* Cappucdno), 3 pieces	150
creme, chocolate (*Oreo*), ½-oz. piece	50
creme, chocolate (*Oreo Big Stuf*), 1¾-oz. piece	250
creme, chocolate (*Oreo Double Stuf*), ½-oz. piece	70
creme, fudge covered (*Oreo*), ¾-oz. piece	110
mint (*Pepperidge Farm* Brussels Mint), 2 pieces	130
mint or orange (*Pepperidge Farm* Milano), 2 pieces	150
coconut macaroon (*Stella D'oro*), 1 piece	60
date pecan (*Pepperidge Farm* Kitchen Hearth), 2 pieces	110
devil's food (*FFV* Trolley Cakes), 2 pieces, 2 oz.	120
egg biscuit (*Stella D'oro*), 1 piece	43
fig bar (*Fig Newtons*), ½-oz. piece	60
fig bar, vanilla or whole wheat (*FFV*), 1 piece	70
fruit filled, all varieties (*Baker's Own*), ½-oz. piece	70
ginger (*Pepperidge Farm* Gingerman), 2 pieces	70
gingersnaps (*FFV*), 5 pieces, approx. 1oz.	130
gingersnaps (*Nabisco* Old Fashioned), ¼-oz. piece	30
graham crackers:	
(*Keebler/Keebler* Honey Grahams), 4 pieces	70
(*Nabisco/Nabisco Teddy Grahams*), ½ oz.	60
(*Nabisco Cookies 'n Fudge*), ½ oz.	70
all varieties (*Honey Maid*), 2 pieces or ½ oz.	60
chocolate (*Nabisco*), ½-oz. piece	60
cinnamon (*Keebler* Crisp), 4 pieces, approx. ½ oz.	70
fudge covered (*Keebler* Deluxe), 2 pieces	90
hazelnut or lemon nut crunch (*Pepperidge Farm*), 2 pieces	110
marshmallow, chocolate or fudge cake:	
(*Mallomars*), ½-oz. piece	60
(*Nabisco* Puffs), ¾-oz. piece	90
(*Nabisco* Twirls), 1-oz. piece	140
(*Pinwheels*), 1-oz. piece	130
mint sandwich (*FFV*), 2 pieces, approx. 1.1 oz.	160
mint sandwich (*Mystic Mint*), ½-oz. piece	90
molasses (*Archway*), 1 piece	100
molasses (*Pepperidge Farm* Old Fashioned Crisps), 2 pieces	70
oat bran raisin (*Awrey's*), 1 piece	100
oatmeal:	
(*Archway*), 1 piece	110
(*Baker's Bonus*), ½-oz. piece	80

Cookie, oatmeal **(cont.)**

(*Keebler* Old Fashion), 1 piece	80
(*Pepperidge Farm* Old-Fashioned Irish), 3 pieces	140
apple filled (*Archway*), 1 piece	90
date filled, raisin, or raisin bran (*Archway*) 1 piece	100
raisin (*Almost Home*), ½-oz. piece	70
raisin (*Entenmann's*), 2 pieces	80
raisin (*Pepperidge Farm*), 2 pieces	110
raisin (*Pepperidge Farm* Santa Fe), 1 piece	100
peach-apricot bar, vanilla or whole wheat (*FFV*), 1 piece	70
peanut, chocolate filled (*Pepperidge Farm* Nassau), 1 piece	80

peanut butter:

chocolate chip or mint (*Keebler Soft Batch*), 1 piece	80
cream filled (*Pitter Patter*), 1 piece, approx. ½ oz.	90
creme patties (*Nutter Butter*), 2 pieces or ½ oz.	80
sandwich (*FFV*), 2 pieces, approx. 1.1 oz.	170
sandwich (*Nutter Butter*), ½-oz. piece	70
(*Pepperidge Farm* Venice), 2 pieces	120
raisin bran (*Pepperidge Farm* Kitchen Hearth), 2 pieces	110
raisin oatmeal (*Archway*), 1 piece	50
raspberry bar (*Raspberry Newtons*), ¾-oz. piece	80
raspberry filled (*Pepperidge Farm* Chantilly), 1 piece	80

shortbread:

(*FFV* Country), 1 piece	70
(*Lorna Doone*), 3 pieces, ½ oz.	70
(*Pepperidge Farm* Old Fashioned), 2 pieces	150
fudge (*Nabisco Cookies 'n Fudge*), ½-oz. piece	80
fudge striped (*Keebler* Fudge Stripes), 1 piece	50
pecan (*Nabisco*), ½-oz. piece	80
strawberry (*Pepperidge Farm* Fruit Cookies), 3 pieces	150
strawberry bar (*Strawberry Newtons*), ¾-oz. piece	100
sugar (*Bisco* Wafers), 4 pieces or ½ oz.	70
sugar (*Pepperidge Farm* Old Fashioned), 3 pieces	150

vanilla:

(*Nilla* Wafers), ½ oz.	60
(*Pepperidge Farm* Bordeaux), 2 pieces	70
chocolate laced (*Pepperidge Farm* Pirouettes), 2 pieces	70
chocolate-nut coated (*Pepperidge Farm* Geneva), 2 pieces	130
cream filled (*Keebler* French Vanilla Creme), 1 piece	80
creme sandwich (*Nabisco Cookie Break*), ½-oz. piece	50
creme sandwich (*Nabisco Giggles*), ½-oz. piece	60

Cookie, frozen, 1.2 oz., approx. 2 pieces:

chocolate chip, regular or double (*Nestlé* Toll House Ready to Bake)	150
with nuts (*Nestlé* Toll House Ready to Bake)	160
oatmeal raisin (*Nestlé* Toll House Ready to Bake)	130
Cookie, refrigerator, all varieties (*Pillsbury*), 1 piece	70
Coriander, fresh, raw, ¼ cup	1

Coriander seed, 1 tbsp. 5
Corn:
fresh, boiled, kernels from 1 medium ear 83
fresh, boiled, drained, ½ cup 89
canned, on cob, tiny (*Green Giant* Oriental), ½ cup 20
canned, kernel, ½ cup:
  (*Green Giant/Green Giant Niblets*) 80
  golden or white (*Del Monte*) 70
  golden or white (*Stokely*) 90
  with peppers (*Green Giant Mexicorn*) 80
  vacuum pack (*Del Monte*) 90
  cream style (*Green Giant*) 100
  cream style, golden (*Del Monte*) 80
  cream style, white (*Del Monte*) 90
dried (*John Cope's*), 1 oz. dry, 4 oz. prepared 101
frozen:
  on cob (*Birds Eye*), 1 ear 120
  on cob (*Birds Eye Big Ears*), 1 ear 160
  on cob (*Birds Eye Little Ears*), 2 ears 130
  on cob (*Green Giant Niblets*), 1 ear 120
  on cob (*Green Giant Niblets* Supersweet), 1 ear 90
  on cob, baby (*Birds Eye* Deluxe), 2.6 oz. 25
  kernel (*Birds Eye/Birds Eye* Deluxe), 3.3 oz. 80
  kernel (*Green Giant Niblets*), ½ cup 70
  kernel, petite (*Birds Eye* Deluxe), 2.6 oz. 70
  kernel, white (*Green Giant Harvest Fresh*), ½ cup 90
  kernel, white (*Seabrook*), 3.3 oz. 80
  in butter sauce (*Birds Eye* Combinations), 3.3 oz. 90
  in butter sauce (*Green Giant Niblets*), ½ cup 100
  cream style (*Green Giant*), ½ cup 110
  in butter sauce (*The Budget Gourmet* Side Dish), 5.5 oz. .. 190
  white shoepeg, in butter sauce (*Green Giant*), ½ cup 100
  and broccoli (*Green Giant Valley Combination*), ½ cup 45
Corn cake (*Quaker* Grain Cakes), .32-oz. piece 35
Corn chips and similar snacks, 1 oz.:
all varieties (*Doritos* Light) 120
all varieties (*Planters*) 160
all varieties (*Wise*) 160
all varieties, except chili cheese (*Fritos*) 150
all varieties, except light (*Doritos*) 140
cheese flavor:
  (*Cheetos* Puffed Balls or Puffs) 160
  (*Cheez Doodles* Baked Corn Puffs) 150
  (*Cheez Doodles* Fried Corn Puffs) 160
  (*Wise Cheez Waffles*) 140

Corn chips and similar snacks, cheese flavor (**cont.**)

crunchy (*Cheetos*)	150
chili cheese (*Fritos*)	160
(*Dipsy Doodles* Rippled Corn Chips)	160
(*Fritos Crisp 'n Thin*)	160
ranch (*Fritos Wild 'n Mild*)	150
tortilla chips:	
(*Tostitos*)	140
blue (*Bearitos* Organic)	146
blue (*Bearitos* Organic No Salt)	137
nacho (*Tio Sancho*)	70
nacho, sharp (*Tostitos*)	150
taco style (*Hain*)	160
yellow (*Bearitos* Organic)	143
yellow (*Bearitos* Organic No Salt)	148
Corn fritter, frozen (*Mrs. Paul's*), 2 pieces	250
Corn grits:	
dry, white, enriched (*Quaker/Aunt Jemima* Regular or Quick), 3 tbsp.	101
cooked, 1 cup	146
instant, dry, with imitation bacon bits (*Quaker*), 1-oz. pkt.	101
instant, dry, with real cheddar cheese (*Quaker*), 1-oz. pkt.	104
instant, dry, with imitation ham bits (*Quaker*), 1-oz. pkt.	99
Corn soufflé, frozen (*Stouffer's*), ⅓ of 12-oz. pkg.	160
Corn syrup, dark or light (*Karo*), 1 tbsp.	60
Cornbread mix, (*Aunt Jemima* Easy), 1 serving*	196
Cornmeal:	
dry, self-rising, white (*Aunt Jemima*), 1 oz.	98
dry, white or yellow, enriched (*Quaker/Aunt Jemima*), 1 oz.	102
mix, buttermilk, self-rising, white (*Aunt Jemima*), 3 tbsp.	101
mix, white, bolted (*Aunt Jemima*), 1 oz.	99
mix, yellow, bolted (*Aunt Jemima*), 1 oz.	97
Cornstarch (*Argo/Kingsford's*), 1 tbsp.	30
Couscous mix, dry (*Near East*), 1¼ oz.	120
Couscous pilaf mix, dry (*Casbah*), 1 oz.	100
Cowpeas, (see also "Black-eyed peas") boiled, drained, ½ cup	79
Crab, meat only:	
fresh, Alaska King, steamed, meat only, 4 oz.	110
fresh, blue, steamed, meat only, 4 oz.	116
canned, blue, 1 cup, approx. 4.75 oz.	133
canned, Dungeness (*S&W*), 3¼ oz.	81
frozen, snow (*Wakefield*), 3 oz.	60
Crab cakes, deviled, frozen:	
breaded (*Mrs. Paul's*), 3-oz. piece	170
breaded (*Mrs. Paul's* Miniatures), 3½ oz.	250
Crab and shrimp, frozen (*Wakefield*), 3 oz.	60

Crabapple, fresh, whole, with skin, 1 oz. 22
Cracker:
all varieties:
   (*Keebler* Toasteds), 4 pieces, approx. ½ oz. 60
   except peanut butter (*Ritz/Ritz Bits*), ½ oz. 70
bacon flavor (*Nabisco* Thins), 7 pieces or ½ oz. 70
butter flavor:
   (*Escort*), 3 pieces or ½ oz. 70
   (*Keebler Town House*), 4 pieces, approx. ½ oz. 70
   (*Pepperidge Farm* Distinctive), 4 pieces 70
   dairy (*Nabisco American Classic*), 4 pieces, ½ oz. 70
cheese:
   (*Cheese Nips*), 13 pieces or ½ oz. 70
   (*Hain*), 1 oz. 130
   (*Tid-Bits*), 16 pieces, ½ oz. 70
   cheddar (*Better Cheddars*), 10 pieces, ½ oz. 70
   cheddar (*Guppies*), ¼ oz., approx. 12 pieces 40
   cheddar or Parmesan (*Pepperidge Farm* Goldfish), 1 oz. ... 120
   flavor (*Combos*), 1.8 oz. 240
   Swiss (*Nabisco Swiss Cheese*), 7 pieces, ½ oz. 70
   thins (*Pepperidge Farm* Goldfish Thins), 4 pieces 50
crispbread:
   (*Wasa* Breakfast), 1 piece 50
   (*Wasa* Extra Crisp), 1 piece 25
   (*Wasa* Fiber Plus), 1 piece 35
   dark, regular or with caraway (*Finn Crisp*), 2 pieces ... 38
   high fiber (*Ryvita* Crisp Bread), 1 piece 23
   rye, hearty (*Wasa*), 1 piece 45
   rye, light (*Wasa*), 1 piece 25
   rye, original (*Finn Crisp* Hi-Fiber), 1 piece 35
   sesame wheat (*Wasa*), 1 piece 50
   thick (*Kavli Norwegian*), 1 piece 35
   thin (*Kavli Norwegian*), 2 pieces 40
matzo:
   (*Manischewitz* Passover), 1.1-oz. board 129
   American (*Manischewitz*), 1-oz. board 115
   egg (*Manischewitz*), 1.2-oz. board 132
   egg and onion (*Manischewitz*), 1-oz. board 112
   whole wheat with bran (*Manischewitz*), 1-oz. board 110
Melba toast:
   bacon (*Old London* Rounds), ½ oz. 53
   garlic (*Devonsheer* Rounds), ½ oz. 56
   onion or rye (*Old London* Rounds), ½ oz. 52
   plain or honey bran (*Devonsheer*), 1 piece 16
   sesame (*Devonsheer* Rounds), ½ oz. 57
   wheat or white (*Old London*), ½ oz. 51
   whole grain (*Old London*), ½ oz. 52

Cracker (cont.)

multi-grain (*Pepperidge Farm*), 4 pieces	70
oat (*Oat Thins*), 8 pieces, ½ oz.	70
oat bran (*Oat Bran Crisp*), ½ oz.	60
onion (*Hain/Hain* No Salt Added), 1 oz.	130
peanut butter (*Combos*), 1.8 oz.	240
peanut butter sandwich (*Ritz Bits*), 6 pieces, ½ oz.	80
peanut butter and cheese sandwich (*Handi-Snacks*), 1 pkg.	190
plain or pizza (*Pepperidge Farm Goldfish*), 1 oz.	130

rye:

(*Rykrisp*), ½ oz.	40
dark or light (*Ryvita* Crisp Bread), 1 piece	26
seasoned (*Rykrisp*), ½ oz.	45
sesame (*Rykrisp*), ½ oz.	50
saltines, all varieties (*Zesta*), 5 pieces	60
saltines, all varieties, except bits (*Premium*), 5 pieces	60
saltines (*Premium Bits*), 16 pieces	70

sesame:

(*FFV Crisp*), 1 piece	60
(*Hain/Hain* No Salt Added), 1 oz.	140
(*Pepperidge Farm* Distinctive), 4 pieces	80
bread wafer (*Meal Mates*), 3 pieces, ½ oz.	70
golden (*Nabisco American Classic*), 4 pieces, ½ oz.	70

soda or water:

(*Carr's* Table Water—Bite Size), 2 pieces	25
(*Crown Pilot*), ½-oz. piece	70
(*FFV Ocean Crisps*), 1 piece	60
(*Pepperidge Farm* English), 4 pieces	70
(*Royal Lunch*), ½-oz. piece	60
(*Sailor Boy* Pilot), 1 piece	100
soup and oyster (*Dandy/Oysterettes*), ½ oz.	60
sour cream and chive (*Hain/Hain* No Salt Added), 1 oz.	130
vegetable (*Hain/Hain* No Salt Added), 1 oz.	130
vegetable (*Vegetable Thins*), 7 pieces or ½ oz.	70
(*Waverly/Waverly* Low Salt), 4 pieces or ½ oz.	70

wheat:

(*Sociables*), 6 pieces or ½ oz.	70
(*Triscuit/Triscuit Bits*), ½ oz.	60
(*Wheat Thins/Wheat Thins* Low Salt), 8 pieces or ½ oz.	70
cracked (*Nabisco American Classic*), 4 pieces, ½ oz.	70
cracked (*Pepperidge Farm* Distinctive), 3 pieces	100
hearty (*Pepperidge Farm* Distinctive), 4 pieces	100
nutty (*Wheat Thins*), 7 pieces or ½ oz.	80
stone ground (*Wheatsworth*), 4 pieces, ½ oz.	70
toasted, with onion (*Pepperidge Farm* Distinctive), 4 pieces	80
whole (*Carr's*), 2 pieces	70
whole (*Keebler Wheatables*), 12 pieces	70

Cracker, wheat (cont.)
whole grain (*Keebler Harvest Wheats*), 4 pieces 60
zwieback toast (*Nabisco*), 2 pieces, ½ oz. 60
Cracker crumbs and meal:
(*Golden Dipt*), 1 oz. 100
graham cracker, see "Cookie crumbs"
matzo (*Manischewitz Farfel*), 1 cup 180
matzo meal (*Manischewitz*), 1 cup 514
Cranberry, fresh, raw, whole, ½ cup 23
Cranberry juice:
(*Smucker's* Naturally 100%), 8 fl. oz. 130
cocktail (*Ocean Spray*), 6 fl. oz. 110
cocktail (*Sunkist*), 6 fl. oz. 110
cocktail, frozen* (*Welch's*), 6 fl. oz. 100
Cranberry juice cocktail blends, 6 fl. oz.:
with apple, frozen* (*Welch's*) 120
with grape or raspberry (*Welch's*) 110
Cranberry sauce, canned:
whole or jellied (*Ocean Spray*), 2 oz. 90
whole or jellied (*S&W* Old Fashioned), ½ cup 90
blends, all fruit varieties (*Cran.Fruit*) 100
Crayfish, steamed, meat only, 4 oz. 129
Cream:
half and half, 1 tbsp. 20
half and half (*Crowley*), 1 fl. oz. 35
heavy, 1 tbsp., approx. 2 tbsp. whipped 52
light, coffee or table, 1 tbsp. 29
light, whipping, 1 tbsp., approx. 2 tbsp. whipped 44
sour, 1 tbsp. 26
sour (*Friendship*), 1 oz. or 2 tbsp. 55
sour, low fat (*Friendship Lite Delite*), 1 oz. 35
Cream, non-dairy:
all varieties (*Rich's*), ½ oz. 20
(*Crowley*), ½ oz. 16
liquid (*Coffee-mate*), 1 tbsp. 16
powder (*Cremora*), 1 tsp. 10
Cream topping, whipped:
(*Kraft* Real Cream), ¼ cup 30
non-dairy (*Birds Eye Cool Whip*), 1 tbsp. 12
non-dairy (*Birds Eye Cool Whip* Extra Creamy), 1 tbsp. 14
non-dairy (*Kraft* Whipped Topping), ¼ cup 35
Creole sauce, Cajun (*Enrico's* Light), 4 oz. 76
Cress, garden, raw, ½ cup 8
Cress, water, see "Watercress"
Croaker, fresh, raw, Atlantic, meat only, 4 oz. 118
Croissant, 1 piece:
(*Pepperidge Farm* Petite All Butter) 120

Croissant (cont.)
frozen (*Pepperidge Farm* Petite All Butter) 140
frozen, all butter (*Sara Lee*), 1.5-oz. roll 170
frozen, all butter (*Sara Lee* Petite), 1-oz. roll 120
Croissant sandwich, frozen:
chicken and broccoli (*Sara Lee*), 4.5-oz. roll 340
ham and Swiss cheese (*Sara Lee*), 4.25-oz. roll 340
Crookneck or Straightneck squash, fresh:
boiled, drained, 4 oz. 23
canned, yellow, cut (*Allens*), ½ cup 16
frozen, yellow crookneck (*Southern*), 3.5 oz. 21
Croutons, ½ oz.:
all varieties, except cheddar and Romano (*Pepperidge Farm*) 70
Caesar salad (*Brownberry*) 62
cheddar cheese (*Brownberry*) 63
cheddar and Romano cheese (*Pepperidge Farm*) 60
onion and garlic (*Brownberry*) 60
seasoned (*Brownberry*) 59
toasted (*Brownberry*) 56
Cucumber, with peel, raw:
ends trimmed, sliced, ½ cup 7
1 medium, untrimmed, 8¼" long, approx. 10.9 oz. 39
Cucumber dip, creamy (*Kraft* Premium), 2 tbsp. 50
Cumin seed (*Spice Islands*), 1 tsp. 7
Currant, Zante, dried (*Del Monte*), ½ cup 200
Curry powder, 1 tsp. 92
Cuttlefish, mixed species, meat only, raw, 4 oz. 88

D

Food and Measure   **Calories**

Daiquiri mix, instant (*Holland House*), .56 oz. dry 65
Dairy Queen:
sandwiches and chicken:
  chicken breast fillet, 7.1 oz. 608

Dairy Queen, sandwiches and chicken **(cont.)**

chicken breast fillet, with cheese, 7.6 oz. 661
chicken nuggets, all white meat, 3.5-oz. serving 276
chicken nuggets sauce, BBQ, 1 oz. 41
DQ Hounder, 5.3oz. 480
DQ Hounder, with cheese, 5.8 oz. 533
DQ Hounder, with chili, 7.3 oz. 575
fish fillet, 6.2 oz. 430
fish fillet, with cheese, 6.7 oz. 483
hamburger, single, 5.2 oz. 360
hamburger, double, 7.4 oz. 530
hamburger, triple, 10 oz. 710
hamburger with cheese, single, 5.7 oz. 410
hamburger with cheese, double, 8.4 oz. 650
hamburger with cheese, triple, 10 oz. 820
hot dog, plain, 3.5 oz. 280
hot dog, with cheese, 4 oz. 330
hot dog, with chili, 4.5 oz. 320

side dishes:

french fries, regular, 2.5 oz. 200
french fries, large, 4 oz. 320
onion rings, 3 oz. 280

desserts and shakes:

Buster Bar, 5.3 oz. 448
Chipper Sandwich, 4 oz. 318
cone, regular, 5 oz. 240
cone, dipped, chocolate, regular, 5.5 oz. 340
Dilly Bar, 3 oz. 210
DQ Sandwich, 2.1 oz. 140
float, 14 oz. 410
freeze, 14 oz. 500
Fudge Nut Bar, 5 oz. 406
Heath Blizzard, 14.3 oz. 800
malt, regular, 14.7 oz. 760
Mr. Misty, regular, 11.6 oz. 250
Mr. Misty Float, 14.5 oz. 390
Mr. Misty Freeze, 14.5 oz. 500
Mr. Misty Kiss, 3.1 oz. 89
parfait, 10 oz. 430
Peanut Buster Parfait, 10.8 oz. 740
shake, regular, 14.7 oz. 710
sundae, regular, 6.2 oz. 310

Dandelion greens, boiled, drained, chopped, 1 cup 35

Danish pastry, 1 piece:

apple filled (*Awrey's* Round), 4.5 oz. 390
cheese filled (*Awrey's* Round), 4.5 oz. 420

Danish pastry (cont.)

cinnamon-raisin filled (*Awrey's* Square), 3 oz.	290
strawberry filled (*Awrey's* Round), 2.75 oz.	270
frozen, apple (*Sara Lee* Individual), 1.3 oz.	120
frozen, apple or raspberry (*Pepperidge Farm*)	220
frozen, cheese (*Pepperidge Farm*)	240
frozen, cheese (*Sara Lee* Individual), 1.3 oz.	130
frozen, cinnamon-raisin (*Sara Lee* Individual), 1.3 oz.	150
refrigerator, caramel with nuts (*Pillsbury*)	160
refrigerator, cinnamon-raisin or orange, iced (*Pillsbury*)	140
Date, whole (*Dromedary*), 5 pitted	100

Dill seasoning:

(*McCormick/Schilling Parsley Patch* It's a Dilly), 1 tsp.	11
seed, 1 tsp.	6
weed, dried, 1 tsp.	3
Dock, raw, trimmed, chopped, ½ cup	15
Dolphin fish, meat only, raw, 1 oz.	24

Domino's Pizza, 2 slices of large (16″) pie:

cheese	376
deluxe	498
double cheese and pepperoni	545
ham	417
pepperoni	460
sausage and mushroom	430
veggie	498

Donut, 1 piece:

chocolate coated (*Hostess*)	130
chocolate coated (*Tastykake* Choco-Dipped)	181
chocolate coated, mini (*Hostess Donettes*)	60
cinnamon (*Tastykake* Assorted), 1.7 oz.	201
fudge iced (*Tastykake* Premium), 2.5 oz.	350
honey wheat (*Tastykake* Premium), 2.5 oz.	342
honey wheat, mini (*Tastykake*), .4 oz.	65
(*Hostess* Old-Fashioned)	180
glazed (*Hostess* Old-Fashioned)	230
orange glazed (*Tastykake* Premium), 2.5 oz.	357
plain, cinnamon, krunch or powdered sugar (*Hostess*)	110
plain (*Tastykake* Assorted), 1.7 oz.	172
powdered sugar (*Tastykake*, 12/pkg.), 1 oz.	123
powdered sugar (*Tastykake* Assorted), 1.7 oz.	195
powdered sugar, mini (*Hostess Donettes*)	40
frozen, glazed (*Rich's Ever Fresh*), 1.2 oz.	141
frozen, jelly (*Rich's Ever Fresh*), 2.17 oz.	213
Drum, freshwater, raw, meat only, 4 oz.	135

Duck, domesticated:

roasted, ½ duck, 13.5 oz. (1.3 lbs. raw with bone)	1287

Duck (cont.)
roasted, meat with skin, 4 oz. 382
roasted, meat only, 4 oz. 228
Dulcita, frozen:
apple (*Hormel*), 4 oz. 290
cherry (*Hormel*), 4 oz. 300
Dutch brand loaf:
(*Eckrich/Eckrich Smorgas Pac*), 1-oz. slice 70
(*Kahn's*), 1 slice 80
pork and beef, 1-oz. slice 68

E

Food and Measure	Calories

Eclair, chocolate, frozen (*Rich*), 1 piece 210
Eel, mixed species, meat only:
baked, broiled or microwaved, 4 oz. 268
Egg, chicken, fresh:
raw, whole, 1 large, approx. 1.75 oz. 75
raw, white from 1 large egg 17
raw, yolk from 1 large egg 59
poached, whole, 1 large 74
Egg, substitute:
(*Fleischmann's Egg Beaters*), ¼ cup 25
with cheez (*Fleischmann's Egg Beaters*), ½ cup 130
Egg breakfast, frozen:
omelet, cheese sauce and ham (*Swanson Great Starts*), 7 oz. 380
omelet, Spanish (*Swanson Great Starts*), 7¾ oz. 240
scrambled:
with bacon, home fries (*Swanson Great Starts*), 5¼ oz. 360
with home fries (*Swanson Great Starts*), 4⅜ oz. 280
with sausage, hash browns (*Swanson Great Starts*), 6¼ oz. 430
sandwich:
beefsteak and cheese (*Swanson Great Starts* Breakfast on a Muffin),
4.9 oz. 380

Egg breakfast, sandwich **(cont.)**

Canadian bacon and cheese (*Swanson Great Starts* Breakfast on a
Biscuit), 5¼ oz. 420

Canadian bacon and cheese (*Swanson Great Starts* Breakfast on a
Muffin), 4.1 oz. 300

sausage and cheese (*Swanson Great Starts* Breakfast on a Biscuit),
5½ oz. 460

Egg foo yung entree, mix (*La Choy*), 8.8 oz. 164

Egg roll, frozen:

chicken or meat and shrimp (*Chun King*), 3.6 oz. 220

chicken or shrimp and cheese (*Jeno's* Snacks), 3 oz., approx. 6 rolls 190

meat and shrimp (*Jeno's* Snacks), 3 oz., approx. 6 rolls 200

pork (*Chun King* Restaurant Style), 3 oz. 180

shrimp (*Chun King*), 3.6 oz. 200

Egg roll wrapper (*Nasoya*), 1 wrapper 23

Eggnog, nonalcoholic:

canned (*Borden*), ½ cup 160

chilled (*Crowley*), 6 fl. oz. 270

chilled (*Darigold*), 8 fl. oz. 350

chilled (*Darigold* Classic), 8 fl. oz. 390

Eggplant, fresh:

boiled, drained, 4 oz. 32

boiled, drained, cubed, ½ cup 13

Eggplant entree, frozen:

parmigiana (*Celentano*), 8 oz. 280

parmigiana (*Mrs. Paul's*), 4 oz. 240

rollettes (*Celentano*), 11 oz. 320

Elderberry, fresh, ½ cup 53

Enchilada dinner, frozen:

beef (*Banquet*), 12 oz. 500

beef (*Old El Paso* Festive Dinners), 11 oz. 390

beef (*Patio*), 13.25 oz. 520

beef (*Swanson*), 13¾ oz. 480

beef (*Van de Kamp's* Mexican Dinner), ½ pkg. 200

cheese (*Banquet*), 12 oz. 550

cheese (*Old El Paso* Festive Dinners), 1 pkg. 590

cheese (*Patio*), 12.25 oz. 380

cheese (*Van de Kamp's* Mexican Dinners), ½ pkg. 220

chicken (*Old El Paso* Festive Dinners), 11 oz. 460

Enchilada dinner mix:

(*Tio Sancho* Dinner Kit):

sauce mix, 3 oz. 278

1 shell 80

Enchilada entree, frozen:

beef:

(*Hormel*), 1 piece 140

(*Old El Paso*), 1 pkg. 210

Enchilada entree, beef (cont.)

(*Van de Kamp's* Mexican Entrees), 1 pkg.	270
(*Van de Kamp's* Mexican Entrees Family Pack), ¼ pkg.	150
chili gravy and (*Banquet Family Entrees*), 7 oz.	270
shredded (*Van de Kamp's* Mexican Entrees), 1 pkg.	360
sirloin Ranchero (*The Budget Gourmet* Slim Selects), 9 oz.	290

cheese:

(*Hormel*), 1 piece	151
(*Old El Paso*), 1 pkg.	250
(*Stouffer's*), 10⅛-oz. pkg.	590
(*Van de Kamp's* Mexican Entrees), 1 pkg.	300
(*Van de Kamp's* Mexican Entrees Family Pack), ¼ pkg.	200
Ranchero (*Van de Kamp's* Mexican Entrees), ½ pkg.	260

chicken:

(*Old El Paso*), 1 pkg.	220
(*Stouffer's*), 10 oz.	490
(*Van de Kamp's* Mexican Entrees), 1 pkg.	260
with sour cream sauce (*Old El Paso*), 1 pkg.	280
Suiza (*The Budget Gourmet* Slim Selects), 9 oz.	270
Suiza (*Van de Kamp's* Mexican Entrees), ½ pkg.	230

Enchilada sauce (see also "Salsa"):

(*La Victoria*), ½ cup	40
(*Rosarita*), 3 oz.	19
green chili (*Old El Paso*), ¼ cup	18
hot or mild (*Del Monte*), ½ cup	45
hot or mild (*Ortega*), 1 oz.	12
mild (*Old El Paso*), ¼ cup	25

Endive:

1 head, approx. 1.3 lb.	86
trimmed, chopped, ½ cup	4
Endive, French or Belgian, raw, trimmed, 1.9-oz. head	8

Escarole, see "Endive"

F

Food and Measure	Calories

Fajita entree, refrigerated (*Chicken By George*), 5 oz. 170
Falafel, mix* (*Near East*), 3 patties 270
Fast food restaurants, see specific listings
Fat, see specific listings
Fat substitute (*Rokeach Neutral Nyafat*), 1 tbsp. 99
Fennel, fresh (*Frieda* of California), 3.5 oz. 15
Fennel seed (*Spice Islands*), 1 tsp. 8
Fettuccini Alfredo mix (*Hain* Pasta & Sauce), ¼ pkg. 180
Fettuccini entree, frozen:
Alfredo (*Healthy Choice*), 8 oz. 240
Alfredo (*Stouffer's*), ½ of 10-oz. pkg. 270
with meat sauce (*The Budget Gourmet*), 10 oz. 290
primavera (*Green Giant*), 1 pkg. 230
primavera (*Green Giant* Microwave Garden Gourmet), 1 pkg. 260
Figs:
fresh, 1 medium, approx. 1.8 oz. 37
canned, in heavy syrup (*Del Monte*), ½ cup 100
dried, uncooked, 10 figs, approx. 6.6 oz. 477
dried, uncooked, Calimyrna (*Blue Ribbon/Sun-Maid*), ½ cup 250
dried, uncooked, Mission (*Blue Ribbon/Sun-Maid*), ½ cup 210
Filberts, shelled:
dried, unblanced, 1 oz. 191
dry-roasted, 1 oz. 188
oil-roasted, 1 oz. 187
Finnan haddie, see "Haddock, smoked"
Fish, see specific listings
Fish dinner, frozen (see also specific fish listings):
(*Morton*), 9.75 oz. 370
'n' chips (*Swanson*), 10 oz. 500
nuggets (*Swanson*), 9½ oz. 410

Fish entree, frozen (see also specific fish listings):

(*Banquet* Platters), 8.75 oz.	450
buttered, fillets (*Mrs. Paul's*), 2 pieces	160
cakes (*Mrs. Paul's*), 2 pieces, 4 oz.	250
Dijon (*Mrs. Paul's Light*), 8¾ oz.	200
fillet, battered:	
(*Gorton's* Crispy Batter), 2 pieces	300
(*Gorton's* Crispy Batter, Large), 1 piece	320
(*Gorton's* Crunchy), 2 pieces	320
(*Gorton's* Crunchy Microwave), 2 pieces	340
(*Gorton's* Crunchy Microwave, Large), 1 piece	320
(*Gorton's* Potato Crisp), 2 pieces	310
(*Mrs. Paul's*), 2 pieces	430
(*Mrs. Paul's* Crunchy), 2 pieces	280
(*Van de Kamp's*), 1 piece	170
minced (*Mrs. Paul's* Portions), 2 pieces	300
tempura (*Gorton's Light Recipe*), 1 piece	200
fillet, breaded:	
(*Gorton's Light Recipe*), 1 piece	180
(*Mrs. Paul's* Crispy Crunchy), 2 pieces	220
(*Van de Kamp's*), 2 pieces	260
crispy (*Van de Kamp's* Microwave), 1 piece	130
minced (*Mrs. Paul's* Crispy Crunchy Portions), 2 pieces	230
fillet of fish:	
almondine (*Gorton's*), 1 pkg.	340
Divan (*Lean Cuisine*), 12⅜ oz.	260
Florentine (*Lean Cuisine*), 9 oz.	230
in herb butter (*Gorton's*), 1 pkg.	190
Florentine (*Mrs. Paul's Light*), 8 oz.	215
'n' fries (*Swanson* Homestyle Recipe), 6½ oz.	350
Mornay (*Mrs. Paul's Light*), 9 oz.	230
sticks, battered:	
(*Gorton's* Crispy Batter), 4 pieces	260
(*Gorton's* Crunchy), 4 pieces	220
(*Gorton's* Crunchy Microwave), 6 pieces	340
(*Gorton's* Potato Crisp), 4 pieces	260
(*Gorton's* Value Pack), 4 pieces	210
(*Mrs. Paul's* Crunchy), 4 pieces	180
(*Van de Kamp's*), 4 pieces	170
minced (*Mrs. Paul's*), 4 pieces	220
sticks, breaded:	
(*Frionor Bunch O' Crunch*), 4 pieces, 2.7 oz.	210
(*Mrs. Paul's* Crispy Crunchy), 4 pieces	190
(*Van de Kamp's*), 4 pieces	190
crispy (*Van de Kamp's* Microwave), 3 pieces	150
minced (*Mrs. Paul's* Crispy Crunchy), 4 pieces	200
whole wheat (*Booth* Microwave), 2 oz.	150

Fish sticks, see "Fish entrees"

Flatfish, meat only, baked, broiled or microwaved, 4 oz. 133

Flounder, fresh, see "Flatfish"

Flounder entree, frozen:

(*Gorton's Fishmarket Fresh*), 5 oz. 110

(*Seapak*), 4 oz. 90

fillets (*Van de Kamp's Natural*), 4 oz. 80

fillets, Atlantic (*Booth*), 4 oz. 90

fillets, battered (*Mrs. Paul's Crunchy*), 2 pieces 260

fillets, breaded (*Mrs. Paul's Crispy Crunchy*), 2 pieces ... 300

fillets, breaded (*Mrs. Paul's Light*), 1 piece, 4½ oz. 260

fillets, breaded (*Van de Kamp's Light*), 1 piece 240

stuffed (*Gorton's Microwave Entrees*), 1 pkg. 350

Flour (see also specific listings):

all-purpose (*Ballard/Pillsbury Best*), 1 cup 400

all-purpose (*Gold Medal*), 1 cup or 4 oz. 400

bread (*Pillsbury's Best*), 1 cup 400

buckwheat, whole grain, 4 oz. 380

cake (*Swans Down*), ¼ cup 100

carob (St.-John's bread), 4 oz. 204

corn, 4 oz. 417

gluten, 45%, 4 oz. 429

oat flour blend (*Gold Medal*), 1 cup or 4 oz. 390

(*La Pina*), 4 oz. 400

(*Quaker Masa Harina*), ⅓ cup 140

(*Quaker Masa Trigo*), ⅓ cup 150

rye, medium (*Pillsbury's Best*), 1 cup 400

rye and wheat (*Pillsbury's Best* Bohemian Style), 1 cup ... 400

self-rising, (*Ballard/Pillsbury's Best*), 1 cup 380

self-rising, enriched (*Aunt Jemima*), 1 oz. 109

soybean, defatted, 4 oz. 370

soybean, low-fat, 4 oz. 404

whole wheat (*Gold Medal*), 1 cup or 4 oz. 350

whole wheat (*Pillsbury's Best*), 1 cup 400

Frankfurter:

(*Eckrich*, 12 oz. pkg.), 1 link 110

(*Eckrich*, 1 lb. pkg.), 1 link 160

(*Eckrich* Bun Size or Jumbo), 1 link 190

(*JM*), 1.2-oz. link 110

(*JM* German Brand), 2-oz. link 160

(*JM* Jumbo), 2-oz. link 190

(*Kahn's* Bun Size or Jumbo), 1 link 190

(*Kahn's* Wieners), 1 link 140

(*Oscar Mayer* German Brand), 2.7-oz. link 230

(*Oscar Mayer* Wieners), 1.6-oz. link 144

(*Oscar Mayer* Bun-Length Wieners), 2-oz. link 181

bacon and cheddar (*Oscar Mayer* Hot Dogs), 1.6 oz. 143

Frankfurter (cont.)
batter-wrapped, frozen (*Hormel* Corn Dogs), 1 piece 220
batter-wrapped, frozen (*Hormel* Tater Dogs), 1 piece 210
beef:
  (*Boar's Head*), 1 oz. 80
  (*Eckrich* 12 oz.), 1 link 110
  (*Eckrich* 1 lb.), 1 link 150
  (*Eckrich* Bun Size or Jumbo), 1 link 190
  (*Hebrew National*), 1.7-oz. link 149
  (*Hormel* 12 oz.), 1 link 100
  (*Hormel* 1 lb.), 1 link 140
  (*JM*), 1.2-oz. link 100
  (*JM* Jumbo), 2-oz. link 180
  (*Kahn's*), 1 link 140
  (*Kahn's* Bun Size or Jumbo), 1 link 190
  (*Oscar Mayer Bun-Length* Franks), 2-oz. link 186
  with cheddar (*Kahn's* Beef n' Cheddar) 180
  with cheddar (*Oscar Mayer* Franks), 2-oz. link 163
cheese (cheesefurter or cheese smokie):
  (*Eckrich*), 1 link 180
  (*JM* Cheese Franks), 1.6-oz. link 140
  (*Kahn's* Cheese Wiener), 1 link 150
  (*Oscar Mayer* Hot Dogs), 1.6-oz. link 145
  (*Oscar Mayer* Hot Dogs), 2-oz. link 183
with cheese (*JM* German Brand), 2-oz. link 160
chicken, see "Chicken frankfurters"
chili (*Hormel* Frank'n Stuff), 1 link 165
cocktail (*Oscar Mayer* Little Wieners), .3-oz. link 28
hot (*Hillshire Farm* Hot Links), 2 oz. 190
meat (*Hormel* Wieners, 12 oz.), 1 link 110
meat (*Hormel* Wieners, 1 lb.), 1 link 140
Mexicali (*Hormel* Mexicali Dogs), 5 oz. 400
natural casing (*Hillshire Farm* Weiners), 2 oz. 180
pork and beef (*Boar's Head*), 1 oz. 80
smoked:
  (*Hormel Range Brand* Wranglers), 1 link 170
  (*Kahn's* Bun Size Smokey), 1 link 180
  beef (*Hormel* Wranglers), 1 link 170
  beef (*Kahn's* Bun Size Beef Smokey), 1 link 190
  with cheese (*Hormel* Wranglers), 1 link 180
turkey, see "Turkey frankfurters"
Frankfurter wrap (see also "Rolls"), (*Wiener Wrap*), 1 piece 60
French toast, frozen:
  (*Aunt Jemima* Original), 3 oz. 166
  (*Downyflake*), 2 slices 270
  cinnamon swirl (*Aunt Jemima*), 3 oz. 171

French toast (cont.)
raisin (*Aunt Jemima*), 3 oz.	172
sticks (*Farm Rich* Original), 3 oz.	300
sticks, apple cinnamon or blueberry (*Farm Rich*), 3 oz.	310

French toast breakfast, frozen, 6½ oz.:
cinnamon swirl, with sausage (*Swanson Great Starts*)	470
with sausages (*Swanson Great Starts*)	450
Frog's legs, raw, meat only, 4 oz.	84

Frosting, ready-to-use: 1/12 can, except as noted:
Amaretto almond (*Betty Crocker Creamy Deluxe*)	160
butter pecan (*Betty Crocker Creamy Deluxe*)	170
caramel pecan (*Pillsbury Frosting Supreme*)	160

chocolate:
(*Duncan Hines*)	160
(*Pillsbury* Frost It Hot), 1/8 cake	50
double Dutch (*Pillsbury Frosting Supreme*)	140
fudge (*Pillsbury*), 1/8 cake	110
fudge, dark Dutch, or milk (*Duncan Hines*)	160
fudge, milk or mint (*Pillsbury Frosting Supreme*)	150
fudge funfetti (*Pillsbury*)	140
regular, coconut almond, dark Dutch fudge, or milk (*Betty Crocker Creamy Deluxe*)	160
chocolate chip (*Pillsbury Frosting Supreme*)	150
chocolate chip, double (*Betty Crocker Creamy Deluxe*)	170
coconut almond (*Pillsbury Frosting Supreme*)	160
coconut pecan (*Pillsbury Frosting Supreme*)	160
cream cheese (*Pillsbury Frosting Supreme*)	160
decorator, all flavors, except chocolate (*Pillsbury*), 1 tbsp.	70
decorator, chocolate (*Pillsbury*), 1 tbsp.	60
lemon (*Pillsbury Frosting Supreme*)	160
mocha (*Pillsbury Frosting Supreme*)	150
rainbow chip (*Betty Crocker Creamy Deluxe*)	170
rocky road (*Betty Crocker Creamy Deluxe*)	150
sour cream, chocolate or white (*Betty Crocker Creamy Deluxe*)	160
sour cream, vanilla (*Pillsbury Frosting Supreme*)	160
strawberry (*Pillsbury Frosting Supreme*)	160
vanilla (*Duncan Hines*)	160
vanilla (*Pillsbury*), 1/8 cake	120
vanilla (*Pillsbury Frosting Supreme*)	160
vanilla funfetti (*Pillsbury*)	150
white, fluffy (*Pillsbury*)	60
white, fluffy (*Pillsbury* Frost It Hot), 1/8 cake	50
Fructose (*Estee*), 1 tsp.	12

Fruit, see specific listings

Fruit bar, frozen:
all flavors (*Dole Fresh Lites*), 1 bar	25

Fruit bar, frozen **(cont.)**

all flavors, except piña colada (*Dole Fruit & Juice*), 1 bar	70
all flavors (*Dole Sun Tops*), 1 bar	40
berry, wild (*Sunkist* Fruit & Juice Bar), 3 fl. oz.	103
coconut (*Sunkist*), 3 fl. oz.	137
lemonade (*Sunkist*), 3 fl. oz.	68
orange (*Sunkist*), 3 fl. oz.	72
piña colada (*Dole Fruit & Juice*), 1 bar	90
and cream:	
blueberry or peach (*Dole* Fruit & Cream), 1 bar	90
chocolate/banana (*Dole* Fruit & Cream), 1 bar	175
chocolate/strawberry (*Dole* Fruit & Cream), 1 bar	140
orange (*Sunkist*), 3 fl. oz.	84
raspberry or strawberry (*Dole* Fruit & Cream), 1 bar	90
and yogurt, cherry (*Dole* Fruit & Yogurt), 1 bar	80
and yogurt, raspberry or strawberry (*Dole* Fruit & Yogurt), 1 bar	70

Fruit cocktail, canned, with liquid:

(*Del Monte*), ½ cup	80
(*Del Monte Lite*), ½ cup	50
in juice (*Libby Lite*), ½ cup	50
in heavy syrup (*S&W*), ½ cup	90

Fruit juice:

(*Libby's Juicy Juice* Tropical), 6 fl. oz.	100
cocktail (*Welch's* Orchard Harvest Blend Cocktails-In-A-Box), 8.45 fl. oz.	150
cocktail, bottled or frozen* (*Welch's* Orchard Harvest Blend), 6 fl. oz.	110

Fruit, mixed:

canned:

(*Del Monte* Fruit Cup), 5 oz.	100
chunky (*Del Monte*), ½ cup	80
in juice, chunky (*Libby Lite*), ½ cup	50
in juice, chunky (*S&W* Sweetened Clarified), ½ cup	90
tropical or for salad (*Del Monte*), ½ cup	90
dried (*Del Monte*), 2 oz.	130
dried, regular or bits (*Sun-Maid/Sunsweet*), 2 oz.	150
frozen, in syrup (*Birds Eye* Quick Thaw Pouch), 5 oz.	120

Fruit and nut mix (*Planters* Fruit 'n Nut), 1 oz. ... 150

Fruit punch:

canned:

(*Minute Maid*), 8.45-fl.-oz. container	128
(*Minute Maid* Juices to Go), 9.6 fl. oz.	145
(*Minute Maid On The Go*), 10 fl. oz.	152
(*Wyler's*), 6 fl. oz.	84
cocktail (*Hawaiian Punch*), 6 fl. oz.	90
Concord (*Minute Maid*), 8.45 fl. oz. container	131
Concord (*Minute Maid* Juices to Go), 9.6 fl. oz.	148

Fruit punch, canned **(cont.)**

    Concord (*Minute Maid On The Go*), 10 fl. oz. 155

    tropical (*Minute Maid*), 8.45 fl. oz. 130

    tropical (*Minute Maid* Juices to Go), 9.6 fl. oz. 147

  chilled or frozen* (*Minute Maid*), 6 fl. oz. 91

  cocktail (*Welch's* Orchard Fruit Harvest Punch), 10 fl. oz. 180

  cocktail, island fruit (*Hawaiian Punch*), 6 fl. oz. 90

Fruit punch drink:

canned, bottled, or boxed:

  (*Hi-C*), 6 fl. oz. 96

  (*Hi-C* Hula Punch), 6 fl. oz. 87

  (*Mott's*), 9.5-fl. oz. can 161

  mountain berry (*Kool-Aid Koolers*), 8.45-fl. oz. box ... 140

  red (*Hawaiian Punch* Fruit Juicy), 6 fl. oz. 90

  tropical or wild fruit (*Hawaiian Punch*), 6 fl. oz. ... 90

  chilled (*Crowley*), 8 fl. oz. 130

  chilled (*Minute Maid* Light 'N Juicy), 6 fl. oz. 14

  mix, tropical (*Wyler's* Crystals), 8 fl. oz. 85

Fruit punch juice (*Libby's Juicy Juice*), 6 fl. oz. .. 100

Fruit roll, see ''Fruit snack''

Fruit salad, chilled (*Kraft* Pure), ½ cup 80

Fruit snack (see also specific fruit listings):

all flavors (*Fruit Corners/Fruit Roll-Ups* Peel-Outs), 1 roll 50

all flavors, except strawberry, yogurt coated (*Sunkist Fun Fruits*),
.9-oz. pouch 100

assorted (*Flavor Tree* Fruit Circus/Fruit Bears), 1.05 oz. 117

apple, cherry or raspberry, roll (*Flavor Tree*), 1 piece 75

fruit punch or strawberry, roll (*Flavor Tree*), 1 piece 74

grape, roll (*Flavor Tree*), 1 piece 76

strawberry, yogurt coated (*Sunkist Fun Fruits* Creme Supremes),
.9-oz. pouch 114

Fruit spread (see also ''Jams and Preserves''), 1 tsp.:

all flavors (*Polaner* All Fruit Spreadable Fruit) 14

all flavors (*Smucker's* Simply Fruit) 16

all flavors, low sugar (*Smucker's*) 8

Fruit syrup, all flavors (*Smucker's*), 2 tbsp. 100

Fudge topping, see ''Chocolate topping''

G

Food and Measure	Calories

Garbanzos, see "Chickpeas"
Garden salad, canned:
(*Joan of Arc/Read*), ½ cup 70
marinated (*S&W*), ½ cup 60
Garlic, fresh, raw, 1 clove, approx. .1 oz. 4
Garlic bread spread (*Lawry's*), ½ tsp. 47
Garlic and herb dip (*Nasoya Vegi-Dip*), 1 oz. 50
Garlic powder:
(*Spice Islands*), 1 tsp. 5
with parsley (*Lawry's*), 1 tsp. 12
Garlic salt (*Lawry's*), 1 tsp. 4
Garlic seasoning:
(*McCormick/Schilling Season All*), ¼ tsp. 2
(*McCormick/Schilling Parsley Patch*), 1 tsp. 13
Garlic spread, concentrate (*Lawry's*), 1 oz. 15
Gelatin bars, frozen, all flavors (*Jell-O Gelatin Pops*), 1 bar 35
Gelatin dessert mix*:
all flavors (*Jell-O*), ½ cup 80
all flavors (*Royal*), ½ cup 80
Gelatin drink, orange, with *Nutrasweet* (*Knox*), 1 envelope 39
Ginger, root, 1 oz. 20
Ginger, ground (*Spice Islands*), 1 tsp. 6
Ginger, pickled, Japanese, 1 oz. 10
Godfather's Pizza:
original pizza:
  cheese, mini, ¼ of pie 190
  cheese, small, ⅙ of pie 240
  cheese, medium, ⅛ of pie 270
  cheese, large, ¹⁄₁₀ of pie 297
  cheese, large, hot slice, ⅛ of pie 370
  combo, mini, ¼ of pie 240

Godfather's Pizza, original pizza **(cont.)**

combo, small, ⅙ of pie	360
combo, medium, ⅛ of pie	400
combo, large, ⅒ of pie	437
combo, large, hot slice, ⅛ of pie	550

thin crust pizza:

cheese, small, ⅙ of pie	180
cheese, medium, ⅛ of pie	210
cheese, large, ⅒ of pie	228
combo, small, ⅙ of pie	270
combo, medium, ⅛ of pie	310
combo, large, ⅒ of pie	336

stuffed pie pizza:

cheese, small, ⅙ of pie	310
cheese, medium, ⅛ of pie	350
cheese, large, ⅒ of pie	381
combo, small, ⅙ of pie	430
combo, medium, ⅛ of pie	480
combo, large, ⅒ of pie	521

Goose, domestic, roasted:

meat with skin, ½ goose, 2.9 lbs. (2.4 lbs. with bone)	2362
meat with skin, 4 oz.	346
meat only, 4 oz.	270
Goose fat, 1 tbsp.	115

Goose liver, see "Liver" and "Paté"

Gooseberry, fresh, ½ cup	34
Gourmet loaf (*Eckrich*), 1-oz. slice	30

Granola and cereal bars:

all varieties, except oat bran-honey graham (*Nature Valley*), 1 bar	120
with almonds (*Kellogg's Smart Start Rice Krispies*), 1-oz. bar	130
with almonds, chewy (*Sunbelt*), 1 oz.	120
blueberry or strawberry (*Kellogg's Smart Start Nutri-Grain*), 1.4-oz. bar	180
berry or raspberry filled (*Kellogg's Smart Start* Corn Flakes/*Common Sense*), 1.5-oz. bar	170
caramel nut (*Quaker Granola Dipps*), 1-oz. bar	148
chocolate chip (*Quaker Chewy*), 1-oz. bar	128
chocolate chip (*Quaker Granola Dipps*), 1-oz. bar	139
chocolate fudge (*Quaker Granola Dipps*), 1-oz. bar	160
chocolate graham and marshmallow (*Quaker Chewy*), 1-oz. bar	126
with chocolate chips, chewy (*Sunbelt*), 1.75 oz.	220
honey and oats (*Quaker Chewy*), 1-oz. bar	125
nut and raisin, chunky (*Quaker Chewy*), 1-oz. bar	131
oat bran-honey graham (*Nature Valley*), 1 bar	110

peanut butter:

(*Quaker Chewy*), 1-oz. bar	128

Granola and cereal bars, peanut butter **(cont.)**

(*Quaker Granola Dipps*), 1-oz. bar	170
and chocolate chip (*Quaker Chewy*), 1-oz. bar	131
chocolate chip (*Quaker Granola Dipps*), 1-oz. bar	174
chocolate coated (*Hershey's*), 1.2 oz. bar	180
with peanuts, fudge dipped (*Sunbelt*), 1.38 oz. bar	190
raisin bran (*Kellogg's Smart Start*), 1.5-oz. bar	160
raisin and cinnamon (*Quaker Chewy*), 1-oz. bar	128
with raisins, chewy (*Sunbelt*), 1.25 oz. bar	150
with raisins, fudge dipped, chewy (*Sunbelt*), 2.25-oz. bar	200

Grape, seedless or seeded:

fresh:

American type (slipskin), ½ cup	29
American type (slipskin), 10 medium, 1.4 oz.	15
European type (adherent skin), ½ cup	57
European type (adherent skin), 10 medium, 1.75 oz.	36
canned, Thompson seedless, in heavy syrup (*S&W* Premium Thompson), ½ cup	100

Grape drink:

bottled (*Veryfine*), 8 fl. oz.	130
chilled (*Minute Maid* Light 'N Juicy), 6 fl. oz.	13
mix (*Kool-Aid* Presweetened), 8 fl. oz.	80

Grape juice, 6 fl. oz.:

(*Campbell's* Juice Bowl)	110
(*Kraft* Pure 100% Unsweetened), 6 fl. oz.	104
(*Minute Maid*), 8.45 fl. oz.	150
all varieties, except sparkling red (*Welch's*)	120
blend (*Libby's Juicy Juice*), 6 fl. oz.	100
sparkling red (*Welch's*)	128
frozen* (*Sunkist*), 6 fl. oz.	69
frozen*, purple or white (*Welch's*), 6 fl. oz.	100
cocktail, bottled (*Welch's* Orchard), 6 fl. oz.	110
cocktail, boxed (*Welch's* Orchard Cocktails-in-a-Box), 8.45 fl. oz.	150

Grape juice drink:

canned (*Hi-C*), 6 fl. oz.	96
boxed (*Kool-Aid Koolers*), 8.45 fl. oz.	140
boxed (*Tang* Fruit Box), 8.45 fl. oz.	130

Grapefruit:

fresh, pink or red:

California or Arizona, ½ medium, 3¾" diam.	46
California or Arizona, sections, with juice, ½ cup	43
Florida, ½ medium, 3¾" diam.	37
Florida, sections, with juice, ½ cup	34

fresh, white:

California, ½ medium, 3¾" diam.	43
California, sections, with juice, ½ cup	42

Grapefruit (cont.)

Florida, ½ medium, 3¾" diam. 38
Florida, sections, with juice, ½ cup 38

canned or in jars:

chilled (*Kraft* Pure Unsweetened), ½ cup 50
in light syrup (*S&W*), ½ cup 80
in light syrup (*Stokely*), ½ cup 90

Grapefruit juice:

fresh, ½ cup 48

canned, bottled or chilled:

(*Campbells* Juice Bowl), 6 fl. oz. 80
(*Del Monte*), 6 fl. oz. 70
(*Kraft* Pure 100%), 6 fl. oz. 70
(*Minute Maid*), 6 fl. oz. 78
(*Mott's*), 10-fl. oz. bottle 124
(*Ocean Spray*), 6 fl. oz. 70
(*Veryfine* 100%), 8 fl. oz. 101
fresh squeezed (*Sunkist*), 8 fl. oz. 96
regular or pink (*TreeSweet*), 6 fl. oz. 72
frozen* (*Minute Maid*), 6 fl. oz. 83
frozen* (*Sunkist*), 6 fl. oz. 56
cocktail, pink (*Minute Maid* Juices to Go), 9.6 fl. oz. .. 136
cocktail, pink (*Ocean Spray*), 6 fl. oz. 80
cocktail, pink (*Veryfine*), 8 fl. oz. 120

Grapefruit juice drink:

(*Citrus Hill* Plus Calcium), 6 fl. oz. 70

Gravy, see specific listings

Grenadine (*Rose's*), 1 fl. oz. 65

Grouper, baked, broiled, or microwaved, meat only, 4 oz. .. 134

Guacamole, see "Avocado dip"

Guacamole seasoning blend (*Lawry's*), 1 pkg. 60

Guava:

common, 1 medium, approx. 4 oz. 45
strawberry, 1 medium, approx. .2 oz. 4

Guava drink (*Ocean Spray Mauna La'I*), 6 fl. oz. 100

Guava juice (*Welch's* Orchard Tropicals), 6 fl. oz. 100

Guava nectar (*Libby's*), 6 fl. oz. 110

Guava-passion fruit drink (*Ocean Spray Mauna La'I*), 6 fl. oz. 100

Guava-strawberry tropical refresher (*Veryfine*), 8 fl. oz. 120

Guinea hen, fresh, raw:

meat with skin, ½ hen, 12.2 oz. (14.6 oz. with bone) 545
meat only, ½ hen, 9.3 oz. (14.6 oz. with bone and fat) 292

H

Haddock:
fresh, baked, broiled or microwaved, meat only, 4 oz.	127
smoked (finnan haddie), meat only, 4 oz.	132

frozen, fillets:
(*Gorton's Fishmarket Fresh*), 5 oz.	110
(*Seapak*), 4 oz.	90
(*Van de Kamp's* Natural), 4 oz.	90
battered (*Mrs. Paul's* Crunchy), 2 pieces	280
battered (*Van de Kamp's*), 2 pieces	250
breaded (*Mrs. Paul's* Crispy Crunchy), 2 pieces	280
breaded (*Mrs. Paul's* Light), 4¼ oz.	220
breaded (*Van de Kamp's*), 2 pieces	260
breaded (*Van de Kamp's* Light), 1 piece	250
in lemon butter (*Gorton's Microwave Entrees*), 1 pkg.	360

Halibut, meat only:
Atlantic and Pacific, raw, 4 oz.	124
Atlantic and Pacific, baked, broiled or microwaved, 4 oz.	159
Halibut, frozen, battered, fillets (*Van de Kamp's*), 2 pieces	180
Halvah (*Fantastic Foods*), 1.5-oz. bar	232

Ham, fresh (see also "Ham, Cured"):

whole leg:
lean with fat, roasted, 4 oz.	333
lean with fat, 1.5-oz. slice	125
lean with fat, chopped or diced, 1 cup, not packed	411
lean only, roasted, 4 oz.	249
lean only, 1.5-oz. slice	94
lean only, chopped or diced, 1 cup, not packed	309

rump half:
lean with fat, roasted, 4 oz.	311
lean with fat, 1.5-oz. slice, 4⅛"x 2¼"x ¼"	117
lean with fat, chopped or diced, 1 cup, not packed	384

Ham, rump half **(cont.)**

lean only, roasted, 4 oz.	251
lean only, 1.5-oz. slice, 4⅛"x 2¼"x ¼"	94
lean only, chopped or diced, 1 cup, not packed	309
shank half:	
lean with fat, roasted, 4 oz.	344
lean with fat, 1.5-oz. slice, 4⅛"x 2¼"x ¼"	129
lean with fat, chopped or diced, 1 cup, not packed	425
lean only, roasted, 4 oz.	244
lean only, 1.5-oz. slice, 4⅛"x 2¼"x ¼"	91
lean only, chopped or diced, 1 cup, not packed	301

Ham, cured (see also "Ham luncheon meat"):

whole, lean with fat:	
unheated, 1 oz.	70
roasted, 4 oz.	276
roasted, chopped or diced, 1 cup, not packed	341
whole, separable lean only:	
unheated, 1 oz.	42
roasted, 4 oz.	178
roasted, chopped or diced, 1 cup, not packed	219

Ham, cured, boneless (see also "Ham luncheon meat"):

center slice, separable lean with fat, unheated, 1 oz.	57
country style, lean only, raw, 1 oz.	55
regular (approx. 11% fat):	
unheated, 1-oz. slice, 6¼"x 4"x 1/16"	52
unheated, chopped or diced, 1 cup, not packed	255
roasted, 4 oz.	202
roasted, chopped or diced, 1 cup, not packed	249
extra lean (approx. 5% fat):	
unheated, 1-oz. slice, 6¼"x 4"x 1/16"	37
unheated, chopped or diced, 1 cup, not packed	183
roasted, 4 oz.	164
roasted, chopped or diced, 1 cup, not packed	203
steak (*Oscar Mayer* Jubilee), 2-oz. steak	59
whole (*JM*), 3 oz.	140
mini (*JM*), 3 oz.	90
with natural juices (*JM* EZ Cut), 2 oz.	70

Ham, canned:

(*Black Label*, 5 lb. or 3 lb.), 4 oz.	140
(*Black Label* 1½ lb.), 4 oz.	150
(*Hormel Curemaster*), 4 oz.	140
(*EXL*), 4 oz.	120
(*JM* 95% Fat Free), 2 oz.	60
(*Oscar Mayer* Jubilee), 1 oz.	31
chopped (*Hormel*, 8 lb.), 3 oz.	240
chopped (*Hormel*, 12 oz.), 2 oz.	120

Ham, canned (cont.)

chunk (*Hormel*), 6¾ oz.	310
roll (*Hormel*), 4 oz.	170
spiced (*Hormel*), 3 oz.	240

Ham dinner, frozen:

(*Morton*), 10 oz.	290
steak (*Armour Classics*), 10.75 oz.	270
steak, glazed (*Stouffer's Dinner Supreme*), 10.5 oz.	380

Ham entree, frozen:

(*Banquet* Platters), 10 oz.	400
and asparagus bake (*Stouffer's*), 9.5 oz.	510
and cheese casserole (*Pillsbury Microwave Classics*), 1 pkg.	470
scalloped potatoes and (*Swanson* Homestyle Recipe), 9 oz.	340

Ham luncheon meat, cured (see also "Ham, cured, boneless"):

(*Boar's Head* Lower Salt), 1 oz.	28
(*Healthy Deli* Deluxe or Taverne), 1 oz.	31
(*JM* Slice 'n Eat 95% Fat-Free Presliced), 2 slices	60
(*Jones Dairy Farm*), 1 slice	50
(*Kahn's* Low Salt), 1 slice	30
(*Oscar Mayer* Breakfast Ham), 1.5-oz. slice	52
(*Oscar Mayer* Jubilee), 1 oz.	46
(*Swift Premium* Hostess or Sugar Plum), 1 oz.	30
baked (*Oscar Mayer*), .75-oz. slice	21
baked Virginia (*Healthy Deli*), 1 oz.	34
boiled (*Boar's Head* Deluxe), 1 oz.	28
boiled (*Oscar Mayer*), .75-oz. slice	23
Cajun (*Hillshire Farm* Deli Select), 1 oz.	31
chopped (*Eckrich*), 1-oz. slice	45
chopped (*Kahn's*), 1 slice	50
chopped (*Oscar Mayer*), 1-oz. slice	55
honey (*Oscar Mayer*), .75-oz. slice	26
jalapeño (*Healthy Deli*), 1 oz.	25
loaf (*Eckrich*), 1-oz. slice	50
peppered, black, cracked (*Oscar Mayer*), .75-oz. slice	24
smoked (*Eckrich* Slender Sliced), 1 oz.	40
smoked, cooked (*Oscar Mayer*), .75-oz. slice	23
turkey, see "Turkey ham"	

Ham patty:

(*Swift Premium* Brown 'N Serve), 1 piece	130
canned (*Hormel*), 1 piece	180

Ham spread:

deviled (*Hormel*), 1 tbsp.	35
deviled (*Underwood*), ½ can or 2¼ oz.	220
salad (*Oscar Mayer*, 6-oz. Chub), 1 oz.	59

Ham and cheese loaf:

(*Eckrich*), 1-oz. slice	50

Ham and cheese loaf (cont.)
(*Hormel* Perma-Fresh), 2 slices 110
(*Kahn's*), 1 slice 70
(*Oscar Mayer*), 1-oz. slice 76
canned (*Hormel*, 8 lb.), 3 oz. 260
Ham and cheese patty, canned (*Hormel*), 1 piece 190
Ham and cheese spread (*Oscar Mayer*, 8-oz. Chub), 1 oz. 67
Hardee's:
breakfast:
   bacon biscuit, 3.3 oz. 360
   bacon and egg biscuit, 4.4 oz. 410
   bacon, egg and cheese biscuit, 4.8 oz. 460
   Big Country Breakfast, bacon, 7.7 oz. 660
   Big Country Breakfast, country ham, 9 oz. 670
   Big Country Breakfast, ham, 8.9 oz. 620
   Big Country Breakfast, sausage, 9.7 oz. 850
   Biscuit 'N' Gravy, 7.8 oz. 440
   Canadian Rise 'N' Shine biscuit, 5.7 oz. 470
   chicken biscuit, 5.1 oz. 430
   Cinnamon 'N' Raisin biscuit, 2.8 oz. 320
   country ham biscuit, 3.8 oz. 350
   country ham and egg biscuit, 4.9 oz. 400
   ham biscuit, 3.7 oz. 320
   ham and egg biscuit, 4.9 oz. 370
   ham, egg and cheese biscuit, 5.3 oz. 420
   Hash Rounds, 2.8 oz. 230
   pancakes, three, 4.8 oz. 280
   pancakes, three, with bacon strips, 5.3 oz. 350
   pancakes, three, with 1 sausage pattie, 6.2 oz. 430
   Rise 'N' Shine biscuit, 2.9 oz. 320
   sausage biscuit, 4.2 oz. 440
   sausage and egg biscuit, 5.3 oz. 490
   steak biscuit, 5.2 oz. 500
   steak and egg biscuit, 6.3 oz. 550
hamburgers and sandwiches:
   Big Deluxe burger, 7.6 oz. 500
   Big Roast Beef, 4.7 oz. 300
   Big Twin, 6.1 oz. 450
   cheeseburger, 4.3 oz. 320
   cheeseburger, bacon, 7.7 oz. 610
   cheeseburger, quarter pound, 6.4 oz. 500
   Chicken Fillet, 6.1 oz. 370
   chicken sandwich, grilled, 6.8 oz. 310
   Fisherman's Fillet, 7.3 oz. 500
   hamburger, 3.9 oz. 270
   hot dog, all beef, 4.2 oz. 300

Hardee's, hamburger and sandwiches **(cont.)**

Hot Ham 'N' Cheese, 5.3 oz.	330
Mushroom 'N' Swiss burger, 6.6 oz.	490
roast beef, regular, 4 oz.	260
Turkey Club, 7.3 oz.	390
salads and special items:	
Chicken Stix, 9 piece, 5.3 oz.	310
Chicken Stix, 6 piece, 3.5 oz.	210
Crispy Curls, 3 oz.	300
french fries, big, 5.5 oz.	500
french fries, large, 4 oz.	360
french fries, regular, 2.5 oz.	230
salad, chef, 10.4 oz.	240
salad, chicken 'N' pasta, 14.6 oz.	230
salad, garden, 8.5 oz.	210
salad, side, 4 oz.	20
dressings, sauces and condiments:	
barbecue dipping sauce, 1 oz.	30
barbecue sauce, .5-oz. pkt.	14
Big Twin sauce, .5 oz.	50
blue cheese dressing, 2 oz.	210
French dressing, reduced calorie, 2 oz.	130
honey, .5 oz.	45
horseradish, .25-oz. pkt.	25
house dressing, 2 oz.	290
Italian dressing, reduced calorie, 2 oz.	90
sweet mustard dipping sauce, 1 oz.	50
sweet 'n' sour dipping sauce, 1 oz.	40
tartar sauce, .7 oz.	90
Thousand Island dressing, 2 oz.	250
desserts and shakes:	
apple turnover, 3.2 oz.	270
Big Cookie, 1.7 oz.	250
Cool Twist cone:	
cone, chocolate, 4.2 oz.	200
cone, vanilla or vanilla/chocolate, 4.2 oz.	190
sundae, caramel, 6 oz.	330
sundae, hot fudge, 5.9 oz.	320
sundae, strawberry, 5.9 oz.	260
shake, chocolate, 12 oz.	460
shake, strawberry, 12 oz.	440
shake, vanilla, 12 oz.	400
Hazelnuts, see "Filberts"	
Head cheese (*Oscar Mayer*), 1-oz. slice	55
Heart, simmered or braised:	
chicken, broiler-fryer, 1 oz.	52
turkey, 4 oz.	201

Heart (cont.)
veal (calf), 4 oz. 211
Herb and garlic sauce, with lemon juice (*Lawry's*), ¼ cup 36
Herb seasoning and coating mix:
Italian (*McCormick/Schilling* Bag'n Season), 1 pkg. 94
Italian (*Shake 'N Bake*), ¼ pouch 80
Herbs, see specific listings
Herbs, mixed (*Lawry's* Pinch of Herbs), 1 tsp. 9
Herring, meat only:
Atlantic:
  raw, 4 oz. 179
  baked, broiled or microwaved, 4 oz. 230
  kippered, 4 oz. 246
  pickled, 4 oz. 297
canned, see "Sardines"
Pacific, raw, 4 oz. 221
Hickory nuts, dried, shelled, 1 oz. 187
Hollandaise sauce, mix (*McCormick/Schilling*), 1 pkg. 203
Homestyle gravy mix*:
(*French's*), ¼ cup 20
(*Pillsbury*), ¼ cup 15
Hominy, canned:
golden (*Van Camp's*), 1 cup 128
golden or Mexican (*Allens*), ½ cup 80
golden, with red and green peppers (*Van Camp's*), 1 cup 129
white (*Allens*), ½ cup 70
white (*Van Camp's*), 1 cup 138
Hominy grits, see "Corn grits"
Honey (*Golden Blossom Honey*), 1 tbsp. 60
Honey butter (*Honey Butter*), 1 tbsp. or ½ oz. 50
Honey loaf:
(*Eckrich/Eckrich Smorgas Pac*), 1-oz. slice 35
(*Hormel* Perma-Fresh), 2 slices 90
(*Kahn's*), 1 slice 40
(*Oscar Mayer*), 1-oz. slice 35
Honey roll sausage, beef, 1 oz. 52
Honeydew melon:
¹⁄₁₀ medium or 7" x 2" wedge 46
cubed, ½ cup 30
Horseradish, prepared:
regular or cream style (*Kraft*), 1 tbsp. 10
all varieties (*Gold's*), 1 tsp. 4
Horseradish sauce (*Sauceworks*), 1 tbsp. 50
Hot dog, see "Frankfurters"
Hot sauce, see "Pepper sauce" and specific listings
Hummus, mix, dip (*Fantastic Foods*), 2 oz. or ¼ cup 111
Hush puppy, frozen (*SeaPak* Regular), 4 oz. 330

Food and Measure	Calories

Ice (see also "Sherbet" and "Sorbet"):
cherry, Italian (*Good Humor*), 6 fl. oz. 138
daiquiri (*Baskin-Robbins*), 1 regular scoop 140
Ice bars (see also "Fruit bar" and "Gelatin bar"):
all flavors (*Good Humor* Ice Stripes), 1.5-fl.-oz. bar 35
cherry (*Good Humor Calippo*), 4.5-fl.-oz. bar 138
lemon (*Good Humor Calippo*), 4.5-fl.-oz. bar 112
orange (*Good Humor Calippo*), 4.5-fl.-oz. bar 111
Ice cream, ½ cup, except as noted:
almond fudge (*Baskin-Robbins Jamoca*), 1 regular scoop 270
butter almond (*Breyers*) 170
butter almond (*Sealtest*) 160
butter crunch (*Sealtest*) 150
butter pecan (*Breyers*) 180
butter pecan (*Frusen Glädjé*) 280
butter pecan (*Häagen-Dazs*) 290
butter pecan (*Sealtest*) 160
cherry vanilla (*Breyers*) 150
chocolate:
  (*Baskin-Robbins*), 1 regular scoop 270
  (*Baskin-Robbins World Class*), 1 regular scoop 280
  (*Breyers*) 160
  (*Frusen Glädjé*) 240
  (*Häagen-Dazs*) 270
  (*Sealtest*) 140
  Dutch (*Borden Olde Fashioned Recipe*) 130
  swirl (*Borden*) 130
  triple (*Sealtest*) 140
chocolate chip:
  (*Baskin-Robbins*), 1 regular scoop 260
  (*Sealtest*) 150

Ice cream, chocolate chip **(cont.)**

chocolate (*Breyers*)	180
chocolate (*Frusen Glädjé*)	270
chocolate (*Häagen-Dazs*)	290
mint (*Breyers*)	170
vanilla (*Frusen Glädjé*)	280
chocolate raspberry truffle (*Baskin-Robbins International Creams*), 1 regular scoop	310
chocolate, Swiss, almond (*Frusen Glädjé*)	270
coffee (*Breyers*)	140
coffee (*Frusen Glädjé*)	260
coffee (*Häagen-Dazs*)	260
coffee (*Sealtest*)	140
cookies 'n' cream (*Breyers*)	170
heavenly hash (*Sealtest*)	150
honey vanilla (*Häagen-Dazs*)	250
macadamia nut (*Häagen-Dazs*)	330
maple walnut (*Sealtest*)	150
mocha chip (*Frusen Glädjé*)	280
peach, natural (*Breyers*)	140
praline and cream (*Frusen Glädjé*)	280
pralines 'n' cream (*Baskin-Robbins*), 1 regular scoop	280
rocky road (*Baskin-Robbins*), 1 regular scoop	300
rum raisin (*Häagen-Dazs*)	250

strawberry:

(*Baskin-Robbins* Verry Berry), 1 regular scoop	220
(*Borden*)	130
(*Breyers*)	130
(*Frusen Glädjé*)	230
(*Häagen-Dazs*)	250
(*Sealtest*)	130
cream (*Borden Olde Fashioned Recipe*)	130

vanilla:

(*Baskin-Robbins*), 1 regular scoop	240
(*Frusen Glädjé*)	230
(*Häagen-Dazs*)	260
French (*Baskin-Robbins*), 1 regular scoop	280
French (*Sealtest*)	140
natural (*Breyers*)	150
vanilla fudge (*Sealtest*)	140
vanilla Swiss almond (*Frusen Glädjé*)	270
vanilla Swiss almond (*Häagen-Dazs*)	290
vanilla toffee chunk (*Frusen Glädjé*)	270
vanilla twirl (*Breyers*)	160
vanilla-chocolate-strawberry (*Breyers*)	150
vanilla-chocolate-strawberry (*Sealtest*)	130

Ice cream (cont.)

vanilla-chocolate-strawberry (*Sealtest Cubic Scoops*) 140
vanilla-orange (*Sealtest Cubic Scoops*) 130
vanilla-raspberry (*Sealtest Cubic Scoops*) 130
vanilla-raspberry swirl (*Frusen Glädjé*) 230

Ice cream bars:

(*Good Humor* Cool Shark), 3-fl.-oz. bar 68
(*Good Humor* Fat Frog), 3-fl.-oz. bar 154
(*Good Humor* Halo Bar), 2.5-fl.-oz. bar 230
(*Good Humor* Milky Pop), 1.5-fl.-oz. bar 47
(*Heath*), 3-fl.-oz. bar 170
(*Klondike*), 5-fl.-oz. bar 280
(*Klondike* Krispy), 5-fl.-oz. bar 290
assorted (*Good Humor Whammy*), 1.6-fl.-oz. bar 95
almond, toasted (*Good Humor*), 3-fl.-oz. bar 212
chip candy crunch (*Good Humor*), 3-fl.-oz. bar 255
chocolate:
  (*Klondike*), 5-fl.-oz. bar 270
  with dark chocolate coating (*Häagen-Dazs*), 1 bar 390
  fudge cake (*Good Humor*), 6.3-fl.-oz. bar 214
  milk, with almonds, milk chocolate coated (*Nestlé* Premium), 3.7-
  fl.-oz. bar 350
  with milk chocolate coating (*Nestlé Quik*), 3-fl.-oz. bar .. 210
chocolate eclair (*Good Humor*), 3-fl.-oz. bar 188
fudge (*Good Humor*), 2.5-fl.-oz. bar 127
fudge sundae (*Bakers Fudgetastic*), 1 bar 220
fudge sundae, crunchy (*Bakers Fudgetastic*), 1 bar 230
strawberry finger (*Good Humor*), 2.5-fl.-oz. bar 49
vanilla, chocolate coated:
  (*Good Humor*), 3-fl.-oz. bar 198
  caramel peanut center (*Oh Henry!*), 3-fl.-oz. bar 320
  with dark chocolate (*Häagen-Dazs*), 1 bar 390
  with milk chocolate (*Häagen-Dazs*), 1 bar 360
  with chocolate, almonds (*Häagen-Dazs*), 1 bar 370
  with milk chocolate, crisps (*Nestlé Crunch*), 3-fl.-oz. bar .. 180
  with white chocolate (*Nestlé Alpine* Premium), 3.7-fl.-oz. bar 350

Ice cream cones and cups:

(*Little Debbie* Ice Cream Cup), 1 cup 15
sugar (*Baskin-Robbins*), 1 cone 60
waffle (*Baskin-Robbins*), 1 cone 140

Ice cream sandwich, 1 piece:

chocolate chip cookie, chocolate (*Good Humor*), 2.7 fl.oz. 204
chocolate chip cookie, chocolate (*Good Humor*), 4 fl. oz. 246
vanilla (*Good Humor*), 2.5 fl. oz. 165
vanilla (*Good Humor*), 3 fl. oz. 191
vanilla (*Klondike*), 5 fl. oz. 230

Ice cream substitute and imitation, ½ cup, except as noted:

all flavors (*Lite-Lite Tofutti*)	90
cappuccino (*Tofutti* Love Drops)	230
cherry, black (*Sealtest Free*)	90
chocolate (*Sealtest Free*)	100
chocolate (*Simple Pleasures*), 4 oz.	140
chocolate (*Tofutti* Love Drops)	230
chocolate supreme (*Tofutti*)	210
coffee (*Simple Pleasures*), 4 oz.	120
peach (*Simple Pleasures*), 4 oz.	135
peach or strawberry (*Sealtest Free*)	90
rum raisin (*Simple Pleasures*), 4 oz.	130
strawberry (*Simple Pleasures*), 4 oz.	120
vanilla (*Sealtest Free*)	100
vanilla (*Tofutti*)	200
vanilla (*Tofutti* Love Drops)	220
vanilla, chocolate dipped (*Tofutti O's*), 1 piece	40
vanilla-almond bark (*Tofutti*)	230
vanilla-chocolate-strawberry (*Sealtest Free*)	90
vanilla-fudge or vanilla-strawberry (*Sealtest Free*)	100
wildberry (*Tofutti*)	210

Ice milk, ½ cup:

chocolate (*Borden*)	100
chocolate or vanilla (*Breyers* Light)	120
chocolate fudge or praline almond (*Breyers* Light)	130
heavenly hash or toffee fudge twirl (*Breyers* Light)	150
strawberry (*Borden*)	90
strawberry (*Breyers* Light)	110
vanilla raspberry (*Breyers* Light)	130

Icing, cake, see "Frosting"

Italian sausage:

hot (*Hillshire Farm* Links), 2 oz.	180
mild (*Hillshire Farm* Links), 2 oz.	190
smoked, cooked, cured (*Oscar Mayer*), 2.7-oz. link	264

J

Food and Measure	Calories

Jack-in-the-Box:
breakfast:
    Breakfast Jack, 4.4 oz. 307
    crescent, Canadian, 4.7 oz. 452
    crescent, sausage, 5.5 oz. 584
    crescent, supreme, 5.1 oz. 547
    hash browns, 2.2 oz. 116
    pancake platter, 8.1 oz. 612
    scrambled egg platter, 8.8 oz. 662
sandwiches, salads, and entrees:
    bacon cheeseburger, 8.1 oz. 705
    beef fajita pita, 6.2 oz. 333
    cheeseburger, 4 oz. 315
    cheeseburger, double, 5.3 oz. 467
    cheeseburger, ultimate, 10 oz. 942
    chef salad, 14 oz. 295
    chicken fajita pita, 6.7 oz. 292
    chicken fillet, grilled, 7.2 oz. 408
    chicken salad, Mexican, 14.6 oz. 442
    chicken supreme, 8.1 oz. 575
    fish supreme, 8 oz. 554
    hamburger, 3.4 oz. 267
    Jumbo Jack, 7.8 oz. 584
    Jumbo Jack with cheese, 8.5 oz. 677
    Swiss and bacon burger, 6.6 oz. 678
    taco, 2.9 oz. 191
    taco, super, 4.8 oz. 288
    taco salad, 14.2 oz. 503
finger foods:
    chicken strips, 4 pieces, 4.4 oz. 349
    chicken strips, 6 pieces, 6.6 oz. 523

Jack-in-the Box, finger food **(cont.)**

egg rolls, 3 pieces, 6 oz.	405
egg rolls, 5 pieces, 10 oz.	675
shrimp, 10 pieces, 3 oz.	270
shrimp, 15 pieces, 4.4 oz.	404
taquitos, 5 pieces, 5 oz.	363
taquitos, 7 pieces, 7 oz.	508

side dishes, sauces and dressings:

BBQ sauce, 1 oz.	44
bleu cheese dressing, 2.5 oz.	262
buttermilk dressing, 2.5 oz.	362
French dressing, reduced calorie, 2.5 oz.	176
french fries, regular, 3.9 oz.	353
guacamole, .9 oz.	55
mayo-mustard sauce, .7 oz.	124
mayo-onion sauce, .7 oz.	143
onion rings, 3.8 oz.	382
salsa, 1 oz.	8
seafood cocktail sauce, 1 oz.	32
sweet and sour sauce, 1 oz.	40
Thousand Island dressing, 2.5 oz.	312

desserts and shakes:

apple turnover, 4.2 oz.	410
cheesecake, 3.5 oz.	309
shake, chocolate, 11.4 oz.	330
shake, strawberry, 11.6 oz.	320
shake, vanilla, 11.2 oz.	320

Jalapeño bean dip:

(*Wise*), 2 tbsp.	25
medium (*Hain*), 4 tbsp.	70

Jalapeño loaf:

(*Kahn's*), 1 slice	70
(*Oscar Mayer*), 1-oz. slice	72

Jalapeño pepper, see "Pepper, jalapeño"

Jalapeño pepper dip:

(*Kraft/Kraft* Premium), 2 tbsp.	50
nacho (*Price's*), 1 oz.	80

Jams, jellies, and preserves (see also "Fruit spreads"):

all flavors (*Bama*), 2 tsp.	30
all flavors (*Kraft*), 1 tsp.	17
all flavors (*Polaner*), 2 tsp.	35
all flavors (*Smucker's*), 1 tsp.	18
all flavors (*Welch's*), 2 tsp.	35
green or red pepper jelly (*Great Impressions*), 1 tbsp.	50
jalapeño jelly (*Great Impressions*), 1 tbsp.	58

Java plum, fresh, 3 medium, approx. .4 oz. 5

Jelly and peanut butter (*Bama*), 2 tbsp.	150
Jerusalem artichoke, fresh, trimmed, sliced, ½ cup	57
Jicama, see ''Yam bean tuber''	
Jujube, dried, 1 oz.	81

K

Food and Measure	**Calories**

Kale:

fresh, raw, trimmed, 4 oz.	57
fresh, raw, trimmed, chopped, ½ cup	17
fresh, boiled, drained, chopped, ½ cup	21
canned, chopped (*Allens*), ½ cup	25
frozen, chopped (*Frosty Acres*), 3.3 oz.	25
Kale, Scotch, fresh, boiled, drained, chopped, ½ cup	18

Kentucky Fried Chicken:

chicken, original recipe:

breast, center, 4.1 oz.	283
breast, side, 3.2 oz.	267
drumstick, 2 oz.	146
thigh, 3.7 oz.	294
wing, 1.9 oz.	178

chicken, extra crispy:

breast, center, 4.2 oz.	353
breast, side, 3.5 oz.	354
drumstick, 2.1 oz.	173
thigh, 4 oz.	371
wing, 2 oz.	218
chicken, Kentucky nuggets, .6-oz. piece	46

Kentucky nuggets sauces:

barbecue, 1 oz.	35
honey, .5 oz.	49
mustard, 1 oz.	36
sweet and sour, 1 oz.	58

side dishes:

buttermilk biscuit, 2.3 oz.	232

Kentucky Fried Chicken, side dishes **(cont.)**
Chicken Littles sandwich, 1.7 oz. 169
cole slaw, 3.2 oz. 119
corn-on-the-cob, 5 oz. 176
french fries, regular, 2.7 oz. 244
mashed potatoes and gravy, 3.5 oz. 71
Ketchup, see "Catsup"
Kidneys:
beef, simmered, 4 oz. 163
lamb, braised, 4 oz. 155
pork, braised, 4 oz. 171
veal, braised, 4 oz. 185
Kielbasa (see also "Polish sausage"):
(*Hillshire Farm* Bun Size), 2 oz. 180
(*Hillshire Farm* Polska Flavorseal or Links), 2 oz. 190
(*Hormel* Kolbase), 3 oz. 220
(*Eckrich Lean Supreme* Polska), 1 oz. 72
(*Oscar Mayer International Sausages*), 1 oz. 83
beef or mild (*Hillshire Farm* Polska Flavorseal), 2 oz. ... 190
skinless (*Eckrich* Polska), 1 link 180
skinless (*Hormel*), ½ link 180
Kiwifruit, 1 medium, approx. 3.1 oz. 46
Knockwurst:
(*Hillshire Farm* Links), 2 oz. 180
beef (*Hebrew National*), 3-oz. link 263
Kohlrabi, fresh, boiled, drained, sliced, ½ cup 24
Kumquat, 1 medium, approx. .7 oz. 12

L

Food and Measure   **Calories**

Lamb, domestic, choice grade:
cubed for stew or kabob (leg and shoulder):
braised or stewed, 4 oz. 253
broiled, 4 oz. 211

Lamb (cont.)

foreshank, braised or stewed:

   lean with fat, 4 oz. 276

   lean with fat, 1 slice, approx. 1 oz. 69

   lean only, 4 oz. 212

   lean only, 1 slice, approx. 1 oz. 53

ground, broiled, 4 oz. 321

ground, broiled, 1 cup, approx. 4.1 oz. 328

leg, whole, roasted:

   lean with fat, 4 oz. 293

   lean with fat, 1 slice, approx. 1 oz. 73

   lean only, 4 oz. 217

   lean only, 1 slice, approx. 1 oz. 54

leg, shank half, roasted:

   lean with fat, 4 oz. 255

   lean with fat, 1 slice, approx. 1 oz. 64

   lean only, 4 oz. 204

   lean only, 1 slice, approx. 1 oz. 51

leg, sirloin half, roasted:

   lean with fat, 4 oz. 331

   lean with fat, 1 slice, approx. 1 oz. 83

   lean only, 4 oz. 231

   lean only, 1 slice, approx. 1 oz. 58

loin:

   lean with fat, broiled, 4 oz. 358

   lean with fat, broiled. 2.25 oz. (4.2 oz. raw chop with bone) 201

   lean with fat, roasted, 4 oz. 350

   lean only, broiled, 4 oz. 245

   lean only, broiled, 1.6 oz (4.2 oz. raw chop with bone and fat) ... 100

   lean only, roasted, 4 oz. 229

rib:

   lean with fat, broiled, 4 oz. 409

   lean with fat, roasted, 4 oz. 407

   lean only, broiled, 4 oz. 266

   lean only, roasted, 4 oz. 263

shoulder, whole:

   lean with fat, braised or stewed, 4 oz. 390

   lean with fat, broiled, 4 oz. 315

   lean with fat, roasted, 4 oz. 313

   lean only, braised or stewed, 4 oz. 321

   lean only, broiled, 4 oz. 238

   lean only, roasted, 4 oz. 231

shoulder, arm:

   lean with fat, braised or stewed, 4 oz. 392

   lean with fat, broiled, 4 oz. 319

   lean with fat, roasted, 4 oz. 316

Lamb, shoulder, arm **(cont.)**
    lean only, braised or stewed, 4 oz. 316
    lean only, broiled, 4 oz. 227
    lean only, roasted, 4 oz. 218
  shoulder, blade:
    lean with fat, braised or stewed, 4 oz. 391
    lean with fat, broiled, 4 oz. 315
    lean with fat, roasted, 4 oz. 319
    lean only, braised or stewed, 4 oz. 327
    lean only, broiled, 4 oz. 239
    lean only, roasted, 4 oz. 237
Lamb's-quarters, boiled, drained, 4 oz. 36
Lard, pork, 1 tbsp. 115
Lasagna dinner, frozen (*Banquet Extra Helping*), 16.5 oz. . 645
Lasagna entree, frozen:
(*Celentano*), 8 oz. 370
(*Green Giant* Entrees), 12 oz. 490
(*Stouffer's*), 10½ oz. 360
(*Tyson Gourmet Selection*), 11.5 oz. 380
cheese (*The Budget Gourmet* Three Cheese), 10 oz. 400
fiesta (*Stouffer's*), 10¼ oz. 430
with meat sauce (*Banquet Family Entrees*), 7 oz. 270
with meat sauce (*The Budget Gourmet* Slim Selects), 10 oz. . 290
with meat sauce (*Healthy Choice*), 9 oz. 260
with meat sauce (*Swanson* Homestyle Recipe), 10½ oz. 400
primavera (*Celentano*), 11 oz. 330
sausage, Italian (*The Budget Gourmet*), 10 oz. 420
seafood (*Mrs. Paul's* Light), 9½ oz. 290
vegetable (*Stouffer's*), 10½ oz. 420
zucchini (*Lean Cuisine*), 11 oz. 260
Lasagna entree, packaged:
Italian style (*Hormel Top Shelf*), 1 serving 360
vegetable (*Hormel Top Shelf*), 10.6 oz. 275
Leeks, fresh, boiled, drained, 1 medium, approx. 4.4 oz. .. 38
Lemon, peeled, 1 medium, 2⅛" diam. 17
Lemon extract (*Virginia Dare*), 1 tsp. 22
Lemon juice:
fresh, 1 tbsp. 4
frozen (*Sunkist*), 1 fl. oz. 7
reconstituted, natural strength (*ReaLemon* 100%), 1 fl. oz. . 6
Lemon pepper:
seasoning (*Lawry's*), 1 tsp. 6
sodium free (*McCormick/Schilling Parsley Patch*), 1 tsp. .. 13
Lemon-lime drink (*Veryfine*), 8 fl. oz. 120
Lemonade:
(*Minute Maid* Light 'n Juicy), 6 fl. oz. 8

Lemonade (cont.)

(*Sunkist*), 8 fl. oz.	141
(*Veryfine*), 8 fl. oz.	120
frozen* (*Sunkist*), 8 fl. oz.	92
frozen*, all varieties (*Minute Maid*), 6 fl. oz.	77
Lentil pilaf mix (*Casbah*), 1 oz. dry or ½ cup cooked	115
Lentil pilaf mix (Casbah*), 1 oz. dry or ½ cup cooked	100
Lettuce:	
bibb, Boston or butterhead, 5"-diam. head	21
cos or romaine, shredded, 1 cup	8
iceberg, trimmed, 6"-diam. head	70
loose leaf, shredded, 1 cup	10
Lime, 1 medium, 2" diam., approx. 2.8 oz.	20
Lime juice:	
fresh, 1 tbsp.	4
reconstituted, natural strength (*ReaLime*), 1 fl. oz.	6
Limemade, frozen* (*Minute Maid*), 6 fl. oz.	71
Ling, raw, meat only, 4 oz.	100
Lingcod, raw, meat only, 4 oz.	96
Linguine entree, frozen:	
with clam sauce (*Lean Cuisine*), 9⅝ oz.	270
with scallops and clams (*The Budget Gourmet* Slim Selects), 9.5 oz.	280
with shrimp (*The Budget Gourmet*), 10 oz.	330
with shrimp (*Healthy Choice*), 9.5 oz.	230
Linguini entree, packaged, with clam sauce (*Hormel Top Shelf*),	
1 serving	330
Liquor, pure distilled (bourbon, gin, vodka, rye, etc.):	
80 proof, 1 fl. oz.	65
90 proof, 1 fl. oz.	74
100 proof, 1 fl. oz.	83
Liver:	
beef, braised, 4 oz.	183
beef, pan-fried, 4 oz.	246
chicken, broiler-fryer, simmered, 4 oz.	180
chicken, broiler-fryer, chopped or diced, 1 cup	219
duck, domesticated, raw, 1 oz.	39
goose, domesticated, raw, 1 oz.	38
lamb, braised, 4 oz.	249
pork, braised, 4 oz.	187
turkey, simmered, 4 oz.	192
veal (calf), braised, 4 oz.	187
veal (calf), pan-fried, 4 oz.	278
Liver cheese (*Oscar Mayer),* 1.34-oz. slice	116
Liver loaf (*Hormel* Perma-Fresh), 2 slices	160
Liver sausage, see "Braunschweiger"	
Liverwurst:	
(*Hickory Farms*), 1 oz.	97

Liverwurst (cont.)
(*Jones Dairy Farm* Chub), 1 oz. 80
(*Jones Dairy Farm* Slices), 1 slice 75
Liverwurst spread:
canned (*Hormel*), ½ oz. 35
canned (*Underwood*), ½ can or 2.25 oz. 190
Lobster, northern:
boiled, poached or steamed, meat only, 4 oz. 111
boiled, poached or steamed, 1 cup, approx. 5.1 oz. 142
Lobster entree, frozen, Newburg (*Stouffer's*), 6½ oz. 380
Loganberry, fresh, trimmed, 1 cup 89
Loquat, 1 medium, approx. .6 oz. 5
Lotus:
root, boiled, drained, 4 oz. 75
seed, dried, 1 oz., 47 small or 36 large 94
Luncheon meat (see also specific listings):
(*Oscar Mayer*), 1-oz. slice 98
canned (*Spam,* 12 oz.), 2 oz. serving 170
canned, with cheese chunks or smoke flavor (*Spam*), 2 oz. .. 170
canned, deviled (*Spam*), 1 tbsp. 35
spiced (*Hormel* Perma-Fresh), 2 slices 118
spiced, (*Kahn's* Luncheon Loaf), 1 slice 80
Luxury loaf (*Oscar Mayer*), 1-oz. slice 38
Lychee nut:
1 medium, approx. .6 oz. 6
dried, shelled, 1 oz. 79

Food and Measure	Calories

Macadamia nuts, oil roasted, 1 oz. 204
Macaroni (see also ''Pasta''):
dry (*Creamette*), 2 oz. 210
dry (*Ronzoni*), 2 oz. 210
cooked, elbow, 1 cup 197
cooked, small shells, 1 cup 162

Macaroni and beef or cheese, see "Macaroni and cheese mix" and "Macaroni entree"

Macaroni and cheese mix*:

(*Golden Grain*), 1 serving	310
(*Kraft* Dinner/Family Size Dinner), ¾ cup	290
shells (*Velveeta* Dinner), ¾ cup	260
spirals (*Kraft* Dinner), ¾ cup	330

Macaroni entree, canned:

and beef, in tomato sauce (*Franco-American* Hearty Pasta), 7½ oz.	200
and cheese (*Franco-American*), 7⅜ oz.	170
and cheese (*Hormel Micro-Cup*), 7.5-oz. container	189
shells and cheddar (*Lipton Hearty Ones*), 11 oz.	367

Macaroni entree, frozen:

and beef, with tomatoes (*Stouffer's*), 5.75 oz.	170
and cheese:	
(*Banquet* Casserole), 8 oz.	350
(*Banquet Family Entree*), 8 oz.	290
(*Freezer Queen Family Side Dish*), 4 oz.	110
(*Green Giant* One Serving), 7.5 oz.	230
(*Stouffer's*), ½ of 12-oz. pkg.	250
(*Stouffer's*), ¼ of 20-oz. pkg.	210
(*Swanson* Homestyle Recipe Entrees), 10 oz.	400
pie (*Swanson* Pot Pie), 7 oz.	220

Mace, ground, 1 tsp. 8

Mackerel, meat only:

fresh, Atlantic, baked, broiled, or microwaved, 4 oz.	297
fresh, king, raw, 4 oz.	120
fresh, Pacific and Jack, raw, meat only, 4 oz.	178
fresh, Spanish, baked, broiled, or microwaved, 4 oz.	179
canned, Atlantic, with liquid, 8 oz.	415
canned, Jack, drained, 4 oz.	177

Mahi mahi, see "Dolphinfish"

Malted milk, dry powder:

chocolate flavor, ¾ oz. or 2–3 heaping tsp.	83
natural flavor, ¾ oz. or 2–3 heaping tsp.	86

Mandarin orange, see "Tangerine"

Mango, fresh:

1 medium, approx. 10.6 oz.	135
peeled and seeded, sliced, ½ cup	54

Mango nectar, canned (*Libby's*), 6 fl. oz. 110

Manhattan cocktail mix, liquid (*Holland House*), 1 fl. oz. 28

Manicotti entree, frozen:

(*Buitoni* Single Serving), 9-oz. pgk.	470
(*Celentano*), 8 oz.	300
cheese filled (*Le Menu*), 8½ oz.	410
cheese, with meat sauce (*The Budget Gourmet*), 10 oz.	450

Maple sugar, 1 oz.	99
Maple syrup (see also "Pancake Syrup"), 1 tbsp.	50
Margarine, salted or unsalted, 1 tbsp., except as noted:	
(*Mazola*)	100
(*Parkay* Regular, Soft or Squeeze)	100
blend (*Country Morning* Stick), 1 tsp.	35
blend (*Country Morning* Tub), 1 tsp.	30
safflower (*Hain*)	100
spread (*Kraft* "Touch of Butter" Bowl)	50
spread (*Kraft* "Touch of Butter" Stick)	60
spread (*Parkay* 50% Vegetable Oil)	60
with sweet cream (*Land O'Lakes* Stick), 1 tsp.	30
with sweet cream (*Land O'Lakes* Tub), 1 tsp.	25
whipped (*Parkay* Cup or Stick)	60
Margarita mix:	
bottled (*Holland House*), 1 fl. oz.	27
instant (*Holland House*), .5 oz.	57
strawberry, bottled (*Holland House*), 1 fl. oz.	31
strawberry, instant (*Holland House*), .56 oz.	66
Marjoram, dried, 1 tsp.	4
Marmalade, orange (*Smucker's*), 1 tsp.	18
Marshmallow creme (*Kraft*), 1 oz.	90
Mayonnaise, 1 tbsp.:	
(*Hain* Real or Eggless, No Salt Added)	110
(*Hellmann's/Best Foods*)	100
cholesterol-free (*Hellmann's*)	50
imitation (*Nucoa Heart Beat*)	40
tofu (*Nasoya Naoynaise*)	40
McDonald's:	
breakfast:	
apple bran muffin, 3 oz.	190
apple danish, 4.1 oz.	390
biscuit, plain, with spread, 2.6 oz.	260
biscuit, with bacon, egg and cheese, 5.5 oz.	440
biscuit, with sausage, 4.3 oz.	440
biscuit, with sausage and egg, 6.3 oz.	520
cheese danish, iced, 3.9 oz.	390
cinnamon-raisin danish, 3.9 oz.	440
Egg McMuffin, 4.9 oz.	290
eggs, scrambled, 3.5 oz.	140
English muffin, with butter, 2.1 oz.	170
hash brown potatoes, 1.9 oz.	130
hotcakes with butter and syrup, 6.2 oz.	410
raspberry danish, 4.1 oz.	410
sausage, pork, 1.7 oz.	180
Sausage McMuffin, 4.1 oz.	370

McDonald's, breakfast **(cont.)**

Sausage McMuffin with egg, 5.9 oz.	440

sandwiches and chicken:

Big Mac, 7.6 oz.	560
cheeseburger, 4.1 oz.	310
Chicken McNuggets, 4 oz.	290
Filet-O-Fish, 5 oz.	440
hamburger, 3.6 oz.	260
McChicken, 6.7 oz.	490
McD.L.T., 8.3 oz.	580
Quarter Pounder, 5.9 oz.	410
Quarter Pounder with cheese, 6.8 oz.	520

Chicken McNuggets sauces:

barbecue, 1 oz.	50
honey, 1.5 oz.	45
hot mustard, 1 oz.	70
sweet & sour, 1 oz.	60
french fries, medium, 3.4 oz.	320

salads, 1 serving:

chef salad, 10 oz.	230
chunky chicken salad, 8.8 oz.	140
garden salad, 7.5 oz.	110
side salad, 4.1 oz.	60

salad dressings:

blue cheese, ⅕ pkt.	70
French, red, reduced calorie, ¼ pkt.	40
peppercorn, ⅕ pkg.	80
Thousand Island, ⅕ pkg.	78
vinaigrette, lite, ¼ pkg.	15

desserts and shakes:

apple pie, 2.9 oz.	260
cookies, chocolaty chip, 2.3 oz.	330
milk shake, lowfat, chocolate, or strawberry, 10.3 oz.	320
milk shake, lowfat, vanilla, 10.3 oz.	290

yogurt, lowfat, frozen:

cone, vanilla, 3 oz.	100
sundae, caramel, 6.1 oz.	270
sundae, hot fudge, 6 oz.	240
sundae, strawberry, 6 oz.	210

Meat, see specific listings

Meat, potted, canned (*Hormel* Food Product), 1 tbsp.	30

Meat loaf dinner, frozen:

(*Armour Classics*), 11.25 oz.	360
(*Banquet*), 11 oz.	440
(*Swanson*), 10¾ oz.	430
homestyle (*Stouffer's Dinner Supreme*), 12⅛ oz.	410

Meat loaf entree, frozen:
(*Banquet Cookin' Bag*), 4 oz. 200
tomato sauce and (*Freezer Queen Family Suppers*), 7 oz. 230
Meat loaf entree mix*, homestyle (*Lipton Microeasy*), ¼ pkg. 390
Meat loaf seasoning (*Lawry's* Seasoning Blends), 1 pkg. 355
Meat tenderizer, seasoned or unseasoned (*Tone's*), 1 tsp. 7
Meatball dinner, Swedish, frozen (*Armour Classics*), 11.25 oz. 330
Meatball entree, frozen:
Italian style, with noodles, peppers (*The Budget Gourmet*), 10 oz. ... 310
Swedish (*Swanson* Home style Recipe), 8½ oz. 350
Swedish, in gravy with parsley noodles (*Stouffer's*), 11 oz. 480
Meatball entree, mix, Italian (*Hunt's Minute Gourmet*), 7.6 oz. 331
Meatball stew, canned (*Dinty Moore*), 8 oz. 240
Melon balls, cantaloupe and honeydew, frozen, ½ cup 28
Mesquite sauce, with lime juice (*Lawry's*), ¼ cup 24
Mexican bean dip (*Hain*), 4 tbsp. 60
Mexican dinner, frozen (see also specific listings):
(*Swanson Hungry-Man*), 20¼ oz. 820
(*Van de Kamp's* Mexican Entrees), ½ pkg. 220
fiesta (*Patio*), 12.25 oz. 470
style (*Banquet*), 12 oz. 490
style (*Patio*), 13.25 oz. 540
combination (*Banquet*), 12 oz. 520
combination (*Swanson*), 14¼ oz. 520
Milk, cow, fluid:
buttermilk (*Crowley*), 1 cup 110
buttermilk, lowfat, 1½% (*Borden* Golden Churn), 1 cup 120
lowfat, 1% (*Borden*), 1 cup 100
lowfat, 1% (*Knudsen* Nice 'n Light), 1 cup 130
lowfat, 2% (*Borden* Hi-Protein), 1 cup 140
skim (*Borden*), 1 cup 90
skim (*Borden Skim-Line*), 1 cup 100
skim (*Knudsen*), 1 cup 80
whole (*Borden/Borden* Hi-Calcium), 1 cup 150
whole (*Crowley*), 1 cup 150
Milk, canned:
condensed, sweetened (*Borden/Eagle*), ⅓ cup 320
evaporated (*Pet*), ½ cup 170
evaporated, skim (*Pet 99*), ½ cup 100
Milk, chocolate, see ''Chocolate milk''
Milk, dry:
buttermilk, sweet cream, 1 oz. 110
nonfat, instant, 1 oz. 101
nonfat, regular, 1 oz. 103
whole, 1 oz. 141
Milk, goat's, whole, 1 cup 168

Milk, sheep's, whole, 1 cup	264
Millet, cooked, 1 cup	287
Mincemeat, see "Pie fillings"	
Miso, 1 oz.	58
Molasses, gold or green (*Grandma's*), 1 tbsp.	70
Monkfish, fresh, meat only, raw, 4 oz.	88
Mortadella, beef and pork, 1-oz. slice	88
Muffins (see also "Toaster muffins and pastries"):	
apple or corn (*Awrey's*), 2.5-oz. piece	220
apple cinnamon or banana walnut, mini (*Hostess*), 5 pieces, 1 pkg.	160
blueberry (*Awrey's*), 2.5-oz. piece	210
blueberry, mini (*Hostess*), 5 pieces, 1 pkg.	150
cranberry (*Awrey's*), 1.5-oz. piece	120
English:	
(*Pepperidge Farm*), 1 piece	140
(*Thomas'*), 1 piece	130
(*Wonder*), 1 piece	130
all varieties (*Oatmeal Goodness*), 1 piece	140
cinnamon raisin (*Pepperidge Farm*), 1 piece	150
multi-grain (*Hi Fiber*), 1 piece	120
oat bran (*Thomas'*), 1 piece	116
raisin (*Thomas'*), 1 piece	153
sourdough (*Pepperidge Farm*), 1 piece	135
wheat, honey (*Thomas'*), 1 piece	129
oat bran, plain, or pineapple raisin (*Awrey's*), 2.75-oz. piece	180
oat bran (*Hostess*), 1 piece, approx. 1.5 oz.	170
raisin-bran (*Awrey's*), 2.5-oz. piece	190
sourdough (*Wonder*), 1 piece	130
Muffins, frozen, 1 piece:	
apple cinnamon spice (*Sara Lee*), 2.5 oz.	220
banana nut (*Pepperidge Farm Old Fashioned*)	170
blueberry (*Pepperidge Farm* Old Fashioned)	170
blueberry (*Sara Lee*), 2.5 oz.	200
cinnamon swirl (*Pepperidge Farm* Old Fashioned)	190
corn (*Pepperidge Farm* Old Fashioned)	180
corn, golden (*Sara Lee*), 2.5 oz.	250
oat bran or raisin bran (*Sara Lee*), 2.5 oz.	220
oat bran with apple (*Pepperidge Farm* Old Fashioned)	190
raisin bran (*Pepperidge Farm* Old Fashioned)	170
Muffins, refrigerated (*Roman Meal*), 2.2-oz. piece	212
Mulberry, fresh, 10 berries, approx. .5 oz.	61
Mullet, striped, baked, broiled, or microwaved, meat only, 4 oz.	170
Mushroom:	
fresh, raw, trimmed, 1 medium, approx. .7 oz.	5
fresh, boiled, drained, pieces, 1 cup	21
canned (*B in B*), ¼ cup	12

Mushroom (cont.)
canned, in butter sauce (*Green Giant*), ½ cup 30
canned, whole, pieces and stems (*Green Giant*), ½ cup 25
shiitake, fresh, cooked, 4 mushrooms or ½ cup pieces 40
shiitake, dried, 4 mushrooms, approx. .5 oz. 44
Mushroom gravy:
canned (*Franco-American*), 2 oz. 25
mix* (*French's*), ¼ cup 20
Mussels, blue, fresh, meat only, steamed, 4 oz. 195
Mustard, prepared:
(*Kraft* Pure), 1 tbsp. 10
Dijon (*Grey Poupon*), 1 tbsp. 18
horseradish (*Kraft*), 1 tbsp. 14

N

Food and Measure	Calories

Nachos, mix:
(*Tio Sancho* Microwave Snacks):
  cheese sauce, 3.5 oz. 247
  chips, 4 oz. 567
Nacho seasoning (*Lawry's* Seasoning Blends), 1 pkg. 141
Natto, 1 oz. 60
Nectarine, fresh:
1 medium, 2½" diam., approx. 5.3 oz. 67
pitted, sliced, ½ cup 34
New England Brand sausage:
(*Eckrich*), 1-oz. slice 35
(*Oscar Mayer*), .8-oz. slice 31
New Zealand spinach, boiled, drained, chopped, 1 cup 22
Newberg sauce, with sherry, canned (*Snow's*), ⅓ cup 120
Noodle, egg:
dry (*Goodman's* Country Style), 2 oz. 220
cooked, 1 cup 212

Noodle, Chinese:
cellophane or long rice, dehydrated, 2 oz. 199
chow mein, 1 cup 237
Noodle, Japanese:
soba, cooked, 1 cup, approx. .4 oz. 13
somen, cooked, 1 cup 230
Noodle and chicken dinner, frozen:
(*Banquet*), 10 oz. 350
(*Banquet Family Favorites*), 10 oz. 340
(*Swanson*), 10½ oz. 260
Noodle dishes, canned:
and beef, in sauce (*Heinz*), 7½ oz. 170
and chicken (*Hormel/Dinty Moore Micro-Cup*), 7.5-oz. container 180
with franks (*Van Camp's Noodle Weenee*), 1 cup 245
and tuna (*Heinz*), 7½ oz. 170
Noodle dishes, mix*, ½ cup, except as noted:
Alfredo (*Lipton* Noodles and Sauce) 220
Alfredo (*Mueller's Chef's Series*) 190
beef (*Lipton* Noodles and Sauce) 180
butter (*Lipton* Noodles and Sauce) 200
butter and herb (*Lipton* Noodles and Sauce) 190
carbonara Alfredo (*Lipton* Noodles and Sauce) 210
cheese (*Kraft* Dinner), ¾ cup 340
cheese (*Lipton* Noodles and Sauce) 190
chicken (*Kraft* Dinner), ¾ cup 240
chicken broccoli (*Lipton* Noodles and Sauce) 200
chicken flavor (*Lipton* Noodles and Sauce) 180
chicken flavor (*Mueller's Chef's Series*) 160
chicken mushroom (*Noodle Roni*), 1 serving 300
fettuccini or garlic butter (*Noodle Roni*), 1 serving 300
garlic and butter (*Mueller's Chef's Series*) 170
herb butter (*Noodle Roni*), 1 serving 160
Parmesan (*Lipton* Noodles and Sauce) 210
Parmesano or Romanoff (*Noodle Roni*), 1 serving 240
pesto (*Noodle Roni*), 1 serving 220
sour cream and chives or Stroganoff (*Lipton* Noodles and Sauce) ... 200
sour cream and chives or Stroganoff (*Mueller's Chef's Series*) 190
Stroganoff (*Noodle Roni*), 1 serving 350
Noodle entree, frozen:
and beef with gravy (*Banquet Family Entree*), 8 oz. 200
and julienne beef with sauce (*Banquet Family Entrees*), 7 oz. 170
Romanoff (*Stouffer's*), ⅓ of 12-oz. pkg. 170
Nut topping (*Planters*), 1 oz. 180
Nutmeg, ground, 1 tsp. 12
Nuts, see specific listings
Nuts, mixed, 1 oz., except as noted:
dry-roasted (*Planters*) 160

Nuts, mixed (cont.)
dry-roasted (*Planters* Unsalted) 170
oil-roasted (*Flavor House*) 180

O

Food and Measure	Calories

Oats (see also ''Cereal''):
whole grain, 1 oz. 110
rolled or oatmeal, cooked, 1 cup 145
Oat bran:
raw, 1 oz. 70
cooked, ½ cup 44
Ocean perch, meat only:
fresh, Atlantic, baked, broiled, or microwaved, 4 oz. 137
frozen (*Booth*), 4 oz. 100
frozen (*Gorton's Fishmarket Fresh*), 5 oz. 140
frozen, fillets (*Van de Kamp's* Natural), 4 oz. 110
frozen, breaded, fillets (*Mrs. Paul's* Crispy Crunchy), 2 pieces 310
frozen, breaded, fillets (*Van de Kamp's* Light), 1 piece 260
Octopus, fresh, raw, 4 oz. 93
Oil:
corn, cottonseed, safflower, sesame, or soybean, 1 tbsp. 120
olive or peanut, 1 tbsp. 119
Okra:
fresh, boiled, drained, 8 pods, 3″ × ⅝″ 27
fresh, boiled, drained, sliced, ½ cup 19
frozen, cut (*Southern*), 3.5 oz. 25
frozen, whole, baby (*Frosty Acres*), 3.3 oz. 30
Old-fashioned drink mix, liquid (*Holland House*), 1 fl. oz. 33
Old-fashioned loaf (*Oscar Mayer*), 1-oz. slice 64
Olive, pickled, canned or bottled:
all types, pitted or regular, all sizes (*S&W*), 1 oz. 46
green, with pits, 10 small, approx. 1.2 oz. 33
green, with pits, 10 large, approx. 1.6 oz. 45

Olive (cont.)

green, with pits, 10 giant, approx. 2.75 oz.	76
green, pitted, 1 oz.	33
ripe, Manzanillo or Mission, pitted:	
all sizes (*Lindsay*), 1 oz.	32
(*Lindsay*), 10 small	37
(*Lindsay*), 10 medium	44
(*Lindsay*), 10 large	50
(*Lindsay*), 10 extra large	63
ripe, mixed varieties, pitted (*Vlasic*), 1 oz.	37
ripe, mixed varieties, sliced or chopped (*Lindsay*), 1 oz.	29
ripe, salt-cured, oil-coated, Greek style, 10 medium	65
ripe, Sevillano and Ascolano, pitted, (*Lindsay*)	23

Olive loaf:

(*Boar's Head*), 1 oz.	60
(*Eckrich*), 1-oz. slice	80
(*Hormel* Perma-Fresh), 2 slices	110
(*Oscar Mayer*), 1-oz. slice	62

Olive oil, see "Oil"

Onion, mature:

fresh, raw, chopped, 1 tbsp.	4
fresh, boiled, drained, chopped, ½ cup	47
canned, sweet (*Heinz*), 1 oz.	40
canned, whole, small (*S&W*), ½ cup	35
frozen (*Ore-Ida*), 2 oz.	20
frozen, whole, with cream sauce (*Birds Eye* Combinations), 5 oz.	140
frozen, rings (*Ore-Ida* Onion Ringers), 2 oz.	140
frozen, rings, crispy (*Farm Rich* Onion O's), 5 rings	190
frozen, rings, crispy (*Mrs. Paul's*), 2½ oz.	180
Onion, cocktail, lightly spiced (*Vlasic*), 1 oz.	4
Onion, dried, minced, with green onion (*Lawry's*), 1 tsp.	7
Onion, green (scallion), fresh, whole, chopped, ½ cup	16
Onion, Welsh, trimmed, 1 oz.	10

Onion dip:

bean (*Hain*), 4 tbsp.	70
creamy or French (*Kraft1* Premium), *1 oz.*	45
French (*Bison*), 1 oz.	60
French or green (*Kraft*), 2 tbsp.	60
Onion flavored snacks (*Funyuns*), 1 oz.	140

Onion gravy:

canned (*Heinz*), 2 oz.	25
mix* (*McCormick/Schilling*), ¼ cup	22
Onion powder (*Spice Islands*), 1 tsp.	8

Orange, fresh:

California, navel, 1 medium, 2⅞" diam.	65
California, navel, sections, ½ cup	38
California, Valencia, 1 medium, 2⅝" diam.	59

Orange (cont.)
California, Valencia, sections, ½ cup 44
Florida, 1 medium, 2¹¹⁄₁₆″ diam. 69
Florida, sections, ½ cup 42
Orange, canned, Mandarin, see "Tangerine"
Orange drink:
(*Crowley*), 8 fl. oz. 130
(*Veryfine*), 8 fl. oz. 130
mix* (*Kool-Aid* Pre-sweetened), 8 fl. oz. 80
Orange extract (*Virginia Dare*), 1 tsp. 22
Orange flavor breakfast drink:
chilled or frozen* (*Bright & Early*), 6 fl. oz. 90
mix (*Tang*), 6 fl. oz.* 90
Orange juice:
fresh, ½ cup 56
canned, bottled or packaged:
  (*Campbell's* Juice Bowl), 6 fl. oz. 90
  (*Del Monte* Unsweetened), 6 fl. oz. 80
  (*Minute Maid*), 8.45 fl. oz. 129
  (*Ocean Spray*), 6 fl. oz. 90
  (*TreeSweet*), 6 fl. oz. 78
  (*Veryfine* 100%), 8 fl. oz. 121
  blend (*Minute Maid* Juices to Go), 9.6 fl. oz. 149
  blend (*Minute Maid On The Go*), 10 fl. oz. 155
  blend (*Veryfine*), 8 fl. oz. 120
chilled:
  (*Citrus Hill* Plus Calcium or Select), 6 fl. oz. 90
  (*Sunkist*), 6 fl. oz. 84
  fresh squeezed (*Sunkist*), 6 fl. oz. 77
  or frozen (*Minute Maid*), 6 fl. oz. 91
  or frozen, calcium fortified (*Minute Maid*), 6 fl. oz. 93
frozen* (*Sunkist*), 8 fl. oz. 112
frozen* (*TreeSweet*), 6 fl. oz. 84
cocktail (*Welch's* Orchard), 10 fl. oz. 150
Orange juice drink:
(*Citrus Hill* Lite Premium), 6 fl. oz. 60
(*Kool-Aid* Koolers), 8.45 fl. oz. 110
(*Minute Maid* Light 'n Juicy), 6 fl. oz. 16
(*Tang* Fruit Box), 8.45 fl. oz. box 130
Orange sauce, Mandarin (*La Choy*), 1 tbsp. 24
Orange-banana juice (*Smucker's* Naturally 100%), 8 fl. oz. 120
Orange-grapefruit juice, chilled (*Kraft* Pure 100%), 6 fl. oz. 80
Orange-pineapple juice, chilled (*Kraft* Pure 100%), 6 fl. oz. 80
Oregano (*Spice Islands*), 1 tsp. 6
Oysters, meat only:
fresh, Eastern, raw or steamed, 6 medium (70 per quart raw) 58
fresh, Pacific, raw, 1 medium, approx. 1.75 oz. or 20 per quart 41

Oysters (cont.)
canned (*Bumble Bee*), 1 cup 218
canned, whole (*S&W* Fancy), 2 oz. 95
Oyster plant, see "Salsify"

P

Food and Measure	Calories

P&B loaf:
(*Kahn's*), 1 slice 40
(*JM*), 1-oz. slice 70
Pancake, frozen:
(*Aunt Jemima* Original Microwave), 3.5 oz. 211
(*Pillsbury* Original Microwave), 3 pieces 240
blueberry (*Aunt Jemima*), 3:5 oz. 220
blueberry (*Downyflake*), 2 pieces 170
blueberry (*Pillsbury* Microwave), 3 pieces 250
buttermilk (*Aunt Jemina* Microwave), 3.5 oz. 210
buttermilk (*Aunt Jemima* Lite Microwave), 3 pieces 140
buttermilk (*Pillsbury* Microwave), 3 pieces 260
wheat, harvest (*Pillsbury* Microwave), 3 pieces 240
Pancake batter, frozen:
(*Aunt Jemima* Original), 3.6 oz. 183
blueberry (*Aunt Jemima*), 3.6 oz. 204
buttermilk (*Aunt Jemima*), 3.6 oz. 180
Pancake breakfast, frozen:
and blueberries in sauce (*Swanson Great Starts*), 7 oz. ... 410
and sausages (*Swanson Great Starts*), 6 oz. 470
and strawberries in sauce (*Swanson Great Starts*), 7 oz. .. 430
Pancake and waffle mix*, 3 pieces, 4″ each:
(*Aunt Jemima* Complete) 231
(*Aunt Jemima* Original) 116
(*Hungry Jack* Panshakes) 250

Pancake and waffle mix (cont.)
blueberry (*Hungry Jack*) 320
buckwheat (*Aunt Jemina*) 142
buttermilk (*Aunt Jemima*) 122
buttermilk (*Aunt Jemima* Complete) 231
buttermilk (*Hungry Jack* Complete) 180
whole wheat (*Aunt Jemima*) 161
Pancake syrup (see also "Maple syrup"):
(*Aunt Jemima* ButterLite), 1 fl. oz. 50
(*Aunt Jemima* Lite), 1 fl. oz. 54
(*Aunt Jemima* Original), 1 fl. oz. 109
(*Vermont Maid*), 1 tbsp. 50
Pancreas:
beef, braised, 4 oz. 307
pork, braised, 4 oz. 248
veal, braised, 4 oz. 290
Papaya, fresh, peeled and seeded, cubed, ½ cup 27
Papaya nectar (*Libby's*), 6 fl. oz. 110
Papaya punch (*Veryfine*), 8 fl. oz. 120
Paprika, 1 tsp. 6
Parsley:
fresh, raw, 10 sprigs, approx. .4 oz. 3
fresh, chopped, ½ cup 10
dried, flakes, 1 tsp. 1
Parsley seasoning (*McCormick/Schilling Parsley Patch*), 1 tsp. 6
Parsnips:
fresh, boiled, drained, 1 medium, 9″ × 2¼″ diam. 130
fresh, boiled, drained, sliced, ½ cup 63
Passion fruit, purple, 1 medium, approx. 1.2 oz. 18
Passion fruit juice cocktail (*Welch's* Orchard Tropicals), 6 fl. oz. ... 100
Passion fruit-orange tropical refresher (*Veryfine*), 8 fl. oz. 110
Pasta (spaghetti, vermicelli, linguine, etc.), plain:
dry, uncooked (*Creamette*), 2 oz. 210
dry, cooked, 1 cup 197
dry, cooked, protein fortified, 1 cup 229
dry, spinach, cooked, 1 cup 183
dry, whole wheat, cooked, 1 cup 174
fresh-refrigerated, with egg, cooked, 4 oz. 149
fresh-refrigerated, spinach, with egg, cooked, 4 oz. 147
Pasta dinner, frozen (see also specific pasta listings):
Dijon (*Green Giant* Microwave Garden Gourmet), 1 pkg. 300
shells, stuffed, 3-cheese (*Le Menu* Light Style), 10 oz. 280
Pasta dishes, canned (see also specific pasta listings):
garden medley (*Lipton Hearty Ones*), 11 oz. 323
Italiano (*Lipton Hearty Ones*), 11 oz. 328

Pasta dishes, canned **(cont.)**

rings, in sauce (*Buitoni*), 7.5 oz.	150
rings or twists and meatballs, in sauce (*Buitoni*), 7.5 oz.	210
twists, in pizza sauce (*Franco-America* Hearty Pasta), 7.5 oz.	220
twists, in sauce (*Buitoni*), 7.5 oz.	150

Pasta dishes, frozen (see also ''Pasta entree'' and specific listings):

Alfredo, with broccoli (*The Budget Gourmet* Side Dish), 5.5 oz.	200
cheddar, creamy (*Green Giant Pasta Accents*), ½ cup	100
Dijon (*Green Giant* Garden Gourmet), 1 pkg.	260
garden herb (*Green Giant Pasta Accents*), ½ cup	80
garlic seasoning (*Green Giant Pasta Accents*), ½ cup	110
Florentine (*Green Giant* Garden Gourmet), 1 pkg.	230
marinara (*Green Giant* One Serving), 5.5 oz.	180
Parmesan, with sweet peas (*Green Giant* One Serving), 5.5 oz.	170
sour cream primavera (*Green Giant Pasta Accents*), ½ cup	110

Pasta dishes, mix*, ½ cup:

Alfredo (*McCormick/Schilling Pasta Prima*)	253
bacon vinaigrette or ranch (*Country Recipe* Pasta Salad)	140
broccoli, cheddar with fusilli (*Lipton* Pasta & Sauce)	200
broccoli, creamy (*Lipton* Pasta Salad)	200
buttermilk or cucumber, creamy or homestyle (*Mueller's* Salad Bar)	250
carbonara Alfredo (*Lipton* Pasta & Sauce)	140
cheese supreme (*Lipton* Pasta & Sauce)	139
chicken broccoli (*Lipton* Pasta & Sauce)	129
Dijon, creamy (*Country Recipe* Pasta Salad)	190
garlic or mushroom, creamy (*Lipton* Pasta & Sauce)	210
herb and garlic (*McCormick/Schilling Pasta Prima*)	163
herb tomato (*Lipton* Pasta & Sauce)	180
Italian, creamy (*Country Recipe* Pasta Salad)	160
Italian, creamy (*Mueller's* Salad Bar)	290
Italian, robust (*Lipton* Pasta Salad)	160
Italian, zesty (*Mueller's* Salad Bar)	140
mushroom and chicken flavors (*Lipton* Pasta & Sauce)	124
Oriental with fusilli (*Lipton* Pasta & Sauce)	130
pasta salad (*McCormick/Schilling* Pasta Prima)	195
pesto (*McCormick/Schilling Pasta Prima*)	193

Pasta entree, frozen (see also specific pasta listings):

baked, and cheese (*Celentano*), 6 oz.	290
carbonara (*Stouffer's*), 9¾-oz. pkg.	620
casino (*Stouffer's*), 9¼-oz. pkg.	300
Mexicali (*Stouffer's*), 10-oz. pkg.	490
Oriental (*Stouffer's*), 9⅞-oz. pkg.	300
primavera (*Stouffer's*), 10⅝-oz. pkg.	540
shells, and beef (*The Budget Gourmet*), 10 oz.	340
shells, cheese, with tomato sauce (*Stouffer's*), 9¼ oz.	330
shells, stuffed (*Buitoni* Single Serving), 9 oz.	460
shells, stuffed (*Celentano*), 8 oz.	330

Pasta sauce (see also "Tomato sauce" and specific listings):

all varieties (*Hunt's*), 4 oz.	70
all varieties (*Enrico's*), 4 oz.	60
all varieties (*Prego Al Fresco*), 4 oz.	100
all varieties, except sausage and green pepper (*Prego* Extra Chunky), 4 oz.	110
(*Pastorelli Italian Chef*), 4 oz.	81
(*Prego* No Salt Added), 4 oz.	100
marinara (*Prego*), 4 oz.	100
meat flavored (*Prego*), 4 oz.	150
plain or mushroom (*Prego*), 4 oz.	140
sausage and green pepper (*Prego* Extra Chunky), 4 oz.	170
mix (*Lawry's* Rich & Thick), 1 pkg.	147
mix (*McCormick/Schilling*), 1 pkg.	26
mix, with imported mushrooms (*Lawry's*), 1 pkg.	143

Pastrami:

(*Hillshire Farm* Deli Select), 1 oz.	31
(*Oscar Mayer*), .6-oz. slice	16
round (*Boar's Head*), 1 oz.	40
round (*Healthy Deli*), 1 oz.	34
turkey, see "Turkey pastrami"	

Pastry pockets, refrigerated (*Pillsbury*), 1.6-oz. piece	230

Pate, canned:

chicken liver, 1 oz.	57
goose liver, smoked, 1 oz.	131

Pea pods, Chinese, see "Peas, edible-podded"

Peaches:

fresh, 1 medium, 2½" diam., approx. 4 per lb.	37
fresh, peeled, slices, ½ cup	37

canned, ½ cup, halves or slices, except as noted:

(*Motts* Peach Fruit Pak), 3.75 oz.	75
cling (*Del Monte*)	80
cling, diced (*Del Monte* Fruit Cup), 5 oz.	110
cling, spiced, with pits (*Del Monte*), 3½ oz.	80
freestone (*Del Monte*)	90
freestone or cling, in heavy syrup (*S&W*)	100
dried, uncooked (*Sun-Maid/Sunsweet*), 2 oz.	140

Peach butter (*Smucker's*), 1 tsp.	15
Peach drink, canned (*Hi-C*), 6 fl. oz.	101

Peach juice:

(*Smucker's* Naturally 100%), 8 fl. oz.	120
orchard blend (*Dole Pure & Light*), 6 fl. oz.	90
Peach nectar, canned (*Libby's*), 6 fl. oz.	100

Peanuts, 1 oz. shelled, except as noted:

in shell, unroasted, 1 oz.	470
(*Beer Nuts*)	180
butter toffee (*Flavor House*)	150

Peanuts (cont.)

dry-roasted (*Frito-Lay's*), 1⅛ oz.	190
dry-roasted (*Planters* Unsalted)	170
dry-roasted, regular or Spanish (*Planters*)	160
French-burnt (*Brach's*)	130
honey roasted (*Eagle Honey Roast*)	170
honey roasted (*Planters*)	170
honey-roasted, dry-roasted (*Planters*)	160
oil-roasted (*Flavor House*)	170
oil-roasted (*Planters/Planters* Cocktail or Redskin)	170
Peanut butter, 2 tbsp.:	
(*Bama* Smooth or Chunky)	200
(*JIF* Smooth or Chunky)	190
(*Peter Pan* Crunchy or Extra Crunchy)	190
(*Skippy* Creamy or Super Chunk)	190
(*Smucker's* Natural Salted or Unsalted)	200
salt free (*Peter Pan* Creamy)	195
jelly and, see "Jelly and peanut butter"	
Peanut butter flavor baking chips (*Reese's*), ¼ cup, 1.5 oz.	230
Peanut butter topping, caramel (*Smucker's*), 2 tbsp.	150
Pear:	
fresh, Bartlett, 1 medium, 2½″ × 3½″	98
fresh, with skin, slices, ½ cup	49
canned, Bartlett, ½ cup:	
halves or slices (*Del Monte*)	80
halves or slices (*Del Monte Lite*)	50
in juice, halves or slices (*Libby Lite*)	60
in heavy syrup, halves (*S&W*)	100
dried, uncooked, halves, ½ cup	236
Pear nectar, canned, ½ cup	75
Peas, crowder, canned, fresh (*Allens*), ½ cup	80
Peas, edible-podded:	
fresh, raw, ½ cup	30
fresh, boiled, drained, ½ cup	34
frozen, Chinese (*Chun King*), 1.5 oz.	20
Peas, green or sweet:	
fresh, raw, podded, ½ cup	58
fresh, boiled, drained, ½ cup	67
canned, ½ cup:	
(*Del Monte/Del Monte* No Salt Added)	60
early, June, or sweet (*Green Giant*)	50
seasoned (*Del Monte*)	60
sweet, mini (*Green Giant*)	60
sweet, with tiny pearl onions (*S&W*)	60
frozen, ½ cup, except as noted:	
(*Birds Eye*), 3.3 oz.	80

Peas, green or sweet, frozen **(cont.)**

early, June (*Green Giant Harvest Fresh*) 60
sweet (*Green Giant/Green Giant Harvest Fresh*) 50
tender tiny (*Birds Eye* Deluxe), 3.3 oz. 60
in butter sauce, early (*Green Giant* One Serving), 4.5 oz. ... 90
in butter sauce, early or sweet (*LeSueur*) 70
in butter sauce, sweet (*Green Giant*) 80

Peas, green, combinations, frozen, ½ cup except as noted:

and carrots, see "Peas and carrots"
and cauliflower in cream sauce (*The Budget Gourmet* Side Dish),
5.75 oz. 170
mini, with pea pods and water chestnuts, in butter sauce (*Le Sueur*) 80
with onions and carrots, in butter sauce (*Le Sueur*) 80
and pearl onions (*Birds Eye* Combinations), 3.3 oz. 70
and pearl onions, with cheese sauce (*Birds Eye* Cheese Sauce
Combinations), 5 oz. 140
and potatoes, with cream sauce (*Birds Eye* Combinations), 5 oz. 190
sugar snap, with carrots and water chestnuts (*Birds Eye* Farm Fresh),
3.2 oz. 50
and water chestnuts Oriental (*The Budget Gourmet* Side Dish), 5 oz. 120

Peas, purple hull:

canned, fresh (*Allens*), ½ cup 100
frozen (*Frosty Acres*), 3.3 oz. 130

Peas and carrots:

canned (*Del Monte*), ½ cup 50
canned (*Stokely*), ½ cup 50
frozen (*Frosty Acres*), 3.3 oz. 60
frozen (*Southern*), 3.5 oz. 64

Pecans, 1 oz. shelled, except as noted:

in shell, dried, 4 oz. 401
halves, pieces or chips (*Planters*) 190
dry-roasted 187
oil-roasted 195

Pecan topping, in syrup (*Smucker's*), 2 tbsp. 130

Pepper, ground:

black, 1 tsp. 5
red or cayenne, 1 tsp. 6
white, 1 tsp. 7
seasoned (*Lawry's*), 1 tsp. 9

Pepper, bell, see "Pepper, sweet"

Pepper, chili, hot, canned or in jars:

green, whole or diced (*Del Monte*), ½ cup 20
green, whole (*Old El Paso*), 1 chili 8
green, all varieties (*Ortega*), 1 oz. 10

Pepper, condiment (see also specific pepper listings):

cherry style, mild (*Vlasic*), 1 oz. 8

Pepper, condiment **(cont.)**

hot, whole or diced (*Ortega*), 1 oz.	8
pepperonicini or hot rings (*Vlasic*), 1 oz.	4
rings, hot (*Vlasic*), 1 oz.	4

Pepper, jalapeño:

whole (*Old El Paso*), 2 peppers	14
whole or sliced (*Del Monte*), ½ cup	30
hot (*Vlasic*), 1 oz.	10
marinated (*La Victoria*), 1 tbsp.	4
nacho (*La Victoria*), 1 tbsp.	2

Pepper, sweet, green or red:

fresh, raw, 1 medium, 3¾″ × 3″	20
fresh, raw, chopped, ½ cup	13
fresh, boiled, drained, chopped, ½ cup	19
frozen, green (*Seabrook*), 1 oz.	6
frozen, red (*Seabrook*), 1 oz.	8

Pepper, stuffed, entree, frozen:

green, with beef in tomato sauce (*Stouffer's*), 7¾ oz.	200
sweet red (*Celentano*), 13 oz.	350
Pepper sauce, hot (*Tabasco*), ¼ tsp.	<1

Peppered loaf:

(*Eckrich*), 1-oz. slice	35
(*Kahn's*), 1 slice	40
(*Oscar Mayer*), 1-oz. slice	43

Pepperoni:

(*Hickory Farms*), 1 oz.	140
(*Hormel* Regular or Chunk, Rosa or Rosa Grande), 1 oz.	140
(*Hormel* Perma-Fresh), 2 slices	80
(*JM*), 8 slices, approx. .5 oz.	70
bits (*Hormel*), 1 tbsp.	35

Perch (see also "Ocean perch"), meat only:

fresh, mixed species, baked, broiled or microwaved, 4 oz.	133
frozen (*Booth*), 4 oz.	100
frozen, fillets, battered (*Van de Kamp's*), 2 pieces	260
frozen, fillets, breaded (*Mrs. Paul's* Light), 4¼ oz.	270

Persimmon, fresh:

Japanese, 1 medium, 2½″ diam.	118
Japanese, dried, 1 medium, approx. 1.3 oz.	93
native, 1 medium, approx. 1.1 oz.	32

Pesto sauce:

mix (*French's* Pasta Toss), 2 tsp.	20
refrigerated (*Contadina Fresh*), 2⅓ oz.	350
Pheasant, fresh, raw, meat with skin, 1 oz.	51

Picante sauce:

(*Gebhardt*), 1 tbsp.	4
(*Old El Paso*), 2 tbsp.	10

Picante sauce (cont.)
(*Wise*), 2 tbsp. 12
mild (*Azteca*), 1 tbsp. 4
Pickle, 1 oz., except as noted:
bread and butter, chunks (*Vlasic* Old Fashion) 25
bread and butter, slices (*Claussen* Bread 'n Butter) 20
bread and butter, slices (*Mrs. Fanning's*), 2 slices, ⅔ oz. 16
bread and butter, sweet (*Vlasic* Butter Chips) 30
bread and butter, sweet (*Vlasic* Butter Stix) 18
dill:
  whole (*Heinz* Genuine/Processed) 2
  halves (*Heinz* Deli Style) 4
  spears (*Claussen*) 4
  hamburger chips, half salt (*Vlasic*) 2
  hamburger slices (*Heinz*) 2
  kosher, all varieties (*Heinz/Heinz* Old-Fashioned) 4
  kosher, all varieties (*Vlasic*) 4
  without garlic (*Claussen*) 6
  zesty, spears or crunchy (*Vlasic*) 4
kosher, whole (*Claussen*) 3
kosher, slices (*Claussen*) 3
mixed, garden, hot and spicy (*Vlasic*) 4
sweet:
  (*Claussen*) 51
  (*Heinz/Heinz* Gherkins) 35
  (*Heinz* Cucumber Stix) 25
  gherkins, midget (*Heinz*) 35
  half salt (*Vlasic* Sweet Butter Chips) 30
  mixed (*Heinz*) 40
  salad cubes (*Heinz*) 30
  slices (*Heinz*) 35
  slices (*Heinz* Cucumber Slices) 20
Pickle, relish, see "Relish"
Pickle loaf:
(*Eckrich/Eckrich Smorgas Pac*), 1-oz. slice 80
(*Hormel* Perma-Fresh), 2 slices 102
(*Kahn's*), 1 slice 80
(*Kahn's* Family Pack), 1 slice 70
beef (*Kahn's* Family Pack), 1 slice 60
Pickle and pimiento loaf (*Oscar Mayer*), 1-oz. slice 63
Picnic loaf (*Oscar Mayer*), 1-oz. slice 62
Pie, frozen:
apple (*Banquet* Family Size), ⅙ pie, 3⅓ oz. 250
apple or peach (*Mrs. Smith's Pie In Minutes*), ⅛ of 8″ pie 210
banana cream (*Banquet*), ⅙ pie, 2⅓ oz. 180
banana cream (*Pet-Ritz*), ⅙ pie, 2⅓ oz. 170

Pie, frozen (cont.)

blackberry (*Banquet* Family Size), ⅙ pie, 3⅓ oz.	270
blueberry (*Banquet* Family Size), ⅙ pie, 3⅓ oz.	270
blueberry or cherry (*Mrs. Smith's Pie in Minutes*), ⅛ of 8" pie	220
cherry (*Banquet* Family Size), ⅙ pie, 3⅓ oz.	250
chocolate or coconut cream (*Banquet*), ⅙ pie, 2⅓ oz.	190
chocolate or coconut cream (*Pet-Ritz*), ⅙ pie, 2⅓ oz.	190
lemon cream (*Banquet*), ⅙ pie, 2⅓ oz.	170
lemon cream (*Pet-Ritz*), ⅙ pie, 2⅓ oz.	190
lemon meringue (*Mrs. Smith's*), ⅛ of 8" pie	210
mincemeat (*Banquet* Family Size), ⅙ pie, 3⅓ oz.	260
neopolitan cream (*Pet-Ritz*), ⅙ pie, 2⅓ oz.	180
peach (*Banquet* Family Size), ⅙ pie, 3⅓ oz.	245
pecan (*Mrs. Smith's Pies in Minutes*), ⅛ of 8" pie	330
pumpkin (*Banquet* Family Size), ⅙ pie, 3⅓ oz.	200
pumpkin (*Mrs. Smith's Pie in Minutes*), ⅛ of 8" pie	190
strawberry cream (*Banquet*), ⅙ pie, 2⅓ oz.	170
strawberry cream (*Pet-Ritz*), ⅙ pie, 2⅓ oz.	170

Pie, snack:

apple (*Drake's*), 1 pie, approx. 2 oz.	210
apple (*Hostess*), 1 pie	390
apple (*Tastykake*), 4-oz. pie	345
apple, French (*Tastykake*), 4.2-oz. pie	399
blackberry (*Hostess*), 1 pie	380
blueberry or cherry (*Hostess*), 1 pie	410
blueberry (*Tastykake*), 4-oz. pie	359
blueberry apple (*Drake's*), 1 pie, approx. 2 oz.	210
cherry (*Tastykake*), 4-oz. pie	368
cherry apple (*Drake's*), 1 pie, approx. 2 oz.	220
chocolate pudding (*Hostess*), 1 pie	490
coconut cream (*Tastykake*), 4-oz. pie	432
lemon (*Drake's*), 1 pie, approx. 2 oz.	210
lemon (*Tastykake*), 4-oz. pie	361
peach (*Hostess*), 1 pie	380
peach (*Tastykake*), 4-oz. pie	343
pineapple (*Tastykake*), 4-oz. pie	362
pumpkin (*Tastykake*), 4-oz. pie	356
strawberry (*Hostess*), 1 pie	340
(*Tastykake* Tasty Klair), 4-oz. pie	436
vanilla pudding (*Hostess*), 1 pie	470
vanilla pudding (*Tastykake*), 4.2-oz. pie	437

Pie, snack, frozen

apple, country (*Sara Lee*), 2.75-oz. pie	230
Boston cream (*Pepperidge Farm* Hyannis), 1 ramikin	230
fudge brownie (*Sara Lee*), 2.1-oz. pie	280
Mississippi mud (*Pepperidge Farm*), 1 ramikin	310
pecan, southern (*Sara Lee*), 2.1-oz. pie	260

Pie crust shell, frozen or refrigerated:	
(*Mrs. Smith's*, 8"), ⅛ shell	80
(*Mrs. Smith's* 9⅝"), ⅛ shell	120
(*Pet-Ritz*, 9⅝"), ⅙ shell, 1.25 oz.	170
(*Pillsbury* All Ready), ⅛ of 2 crust pie	240
deep dish (*Pet-Ritz*), ⅙ shell, 1 oz.	130
graham cracker (*Pet-Ritz*), ⅙ shell, .83 oz.	110
Pie crust shell mix* (*Flako*), 1 serving	247
Pie filling, canned, 4 oz., except as noted:	
apple, regular, deluxe or turnover (*Lucky Leaf/Musselman's*)	120
apricot (*Lucky Leaf/Musselman's*)	150
blackberry or boysenberry (*Lucky Leaf/Musselman's*)	120
black raspberry (*Lucky Leaf/Musselman's*)	190
blueberry (*Lucky Leaf/Musselman's* Plus)	145
cherry (*Lucky Leaf/Musselman's*)	120
gooseberry (*Lucky Leaf/Musselman's*)	180
lemon (*Lucky Leaf/Musselman's*)	200
mincemeat:	
(*Lucky Leaf/Musselman's*)	190
with brandy (*S&W* Old Fashioned)	234
condensed (*Borden None Such*), ¼ pkg.	220
ready-to-use (*Borden None Such*), ⅓ cup	200
ready-to-use, with brandy and rum (*Borden None Such*), ⅓ cup	220
peach (*Lucky Leaf/Musselman's*)	150
pineapple (*Lucky Leaf/Musselman's*)	110
pumpkin (*Lucky Leaf/Musselman's*)	170
raisin (*Lucky Leaf/Musselman's*)	130
strawberry or strawberry rhubarb (*Lucky Leaf/Musselman's*)	120
vanilla creme (*Lucky Leaf/Musselman's*)	150
Pie filling mix, see "Pudding mix"	
Pigeon peas:	
boiled, drained, ½ cup	86
mature, dry, cooked, ½ cup	102
Pignolias, see "Pine nuts"	
Pig's feet, pickled (*Penrose*), 1 piece, approx. 6 oz.	220
Pig's knuckles, pickled (*Penrose*), 1 piece, approx. 6 oz.	290
Pike, meat only:	
northern, baked, broiled or microwaved, 4 oz.	128
walleye, raw, 4 oz.	104
Pimiento spread (*Price's*), 1 oz.	80
Pimientos, all varieties, drained (*Dromedary*), 1 oz.	10
Piña colada mix:	
bottled (*Holland House*), 1 fl. oz.	33
instant (*Holland House*), .56 oz.	82
Pine nuts, dried, shelled:	
pignolia, 1 oz.	146
pignolia, 1 tbsp.	51

Pine nuts (cont.)

pinyon, 1 oz.	161
pinyon, 10 kernels	6

Pineapple:

fresh, diced, ½ cup	39
fresh, sliced, 3½″ diam. × ¾″ slice, approx. 3 oz.	42
canned, ½ cup, except as noted:	
(*Mott's* Pineapple Fruit Pak), 3.75 oz.	86
in juice, all cuts (*Dole*)	70
in juice, crushed (*Empress*)	70
in juice, spears (*Del Monte*), 2 spears	50
in syrup, all cuts (*Del Monte*)	90
in syrup, all cuts (*Dole*)	95
in heavy syrup, slices (*S&W* 100% Hawaiian), 2 slices	90

Pineapple juice:

canned (*Del Monte*), 6 fl. oz.	100
canned (*Dole*), 6 fl. oz.	103
chilled or frozen* (*Minute Maid*), 6 fl. oz.	99
Pineapple nectar (*Libby's*), 6 fl. oz.	110

Pineapple topping:

(*Kraft*), 1 tbsp.	50
(*Smucker's*), 2 tbsp.	130
Pineapple-banana juice cocktail (*Welch's* Orchard), 6 fl. oz.	100

Pineapple-grapefruit juice:

(*Dole*), 6 fl. oz.	90
with pink grapefruit (*Dole*), 6 fl. oz.	101
Pineapple-grapefruit juice drink, canned:	
pink or regular (*Del Monte*), 6 fl. oz.	90

Pineapple-orange juice, 6 fl. oz.:

(*Dole*)	100
chilled or frozen (*Minute Maid*)	91
Pineapple-orange juice drink (*Del Monte*), 6 fl. oz.	90
Pineapple-orange-banana juice (*Dole*), 6 fl. oz.	90

Pistachio nuts:

dried, 1 oz., approx. 47 kernels	164
dry-roasted, 1 oz.	172
dry-roasted (*Planters*), 1 oz.	170

Pizza, frozen:

bacon (*Totino's* Temptin' Toppings), ¼ pie	220
Canadian bacon (*Jeno's* Crisp 'n Tasty), ½ pie	250
Canadian bacon (*Tombstone*), ¼ pie	340
Canadian bacon (*Totino's* Party Pizza), ½ pie	310
(*Celentano* 9-Slice Pizza), 2.7 oz.	150
(*Celentano* Thick Crust), 4.3 oz.	290
(*Celeste* Suprema), ¼ pie	381

Pizza (cont.)

(*Celeste* Supreme Pizza For One), 1 pie	678

cheese:

(*Celeste*), ¼ pie	317
(*Celeste* Pizza For One), 1 pie	497
(*Jeno's* Crisp 'n Tasty), ½ pie	270
(*Pillsbury* Microwave), ½ pie	240
(*Stouffer's*), ½ of 8½-oz. pkg.	320
(*Stouffer's* Extra Cheese), ½ of 9¼-oz. pkg.	370
(*Tombstone*), ¼ pie	330
(*Totino's My Classic* Deluxe), ⅙ pie	210
(*Totino's* Party Pizza), ½ pie	340
(*Totino's* Temptin' Toppings), ¼ pie	210
double cheese, and hamburger (*Tombstone* Double Top), ¼ pie	530
double cheese, and sausage (*Tombstone* Double Top), ¼ pie	510
and hamburger (*Tombstone* Italian Thin Crust), ¼ pie	320
and pepperoni (*Tombstone*), ¼ pie	380
and sausage (*Tombstone*), ¼ pie	350
three-cheese (*Totino's* Pan Pizza), ⅙ pie	290
two-cheese (*Tombstone* Thin Crust), ¼ pie	330
combination (*Jeno's* 4-Pack), 1 pie	180
combination (*Pillsbury* Microwave), ½ pie	310
combination (*Totino's My Classic* Deluxe), ⅙ pie	270
combination (*Totino's* Party Pizza), ½ pie	380
combination (*Totino's* Slices), 1 slice	200
deluxe (*Celeste*), ¼ pie	378
deluxe (*Celeste* Pizza For One), 1 pie	582
deluxe (*Stouffer's*), ½ of 10-oz. pkg.	370
hamburger (*Jeno's* Crisp 'n Tasty), ½ pie	290
hamburger (*Totino's* Party Pizza), ½ pie	370
hamburger (*Totino's* Temptin' Toppings), ¼ pie	210
Mexican style (*Totino's* Temptin' Toppings), ¼ pie	220

pepperoni:

(*Celeste*), ¼ pie	368
(*Celeste* Pizza For One), 1 pie	546
(*Jeno's* Crisp 'n Tasty), ½ pie	280
(*Pillsbury* Microwave), ½ pie	300
(*Stouffer's*), ½ of 8¾-oz. pkg.	350
(*Tombstone* Real Deluxe), ¼ pie	380
(*Totino's My Classic* Deluxe), ⅙ pie	260
(*Totino's* Pan Pizza), ⅙ pie	330
(*Totino's* Party Pizza), ½ pie	370
(*Totino's* Slices), 1 slice	190
(*Totino's* Temptin' Toppings), ¼ pie	220
double cheese (*Tombstone* Double Top), ½ pie	560

Pizza (cont.)

pepperoni or sausage (*Jeno's* Snacks), 4 pies or ⅓ pkg.	140

sausage:

(*Celeste*), ¼ pie	376
(*Celeste* Pizza For One), 1 pie	571
(*Jeno's* Crisp 'n Tasty), ½ pie	300
(*Pillsbury* Microwave), ½ pie	280
(*Stouffer's*), ½ of 9⅜-oz. pkg.	360
(*Tombstone* Deluxe), ¼ pie	350
(*Tombstone* Deluxe Microwave), 8.7-oz. pkg.	520
(*Totino's* Pan Pizza), ⅙ pie	320
(*Totino's* Party Pizza), ½ pie	390
(*Totino's* Slices), 1 slice	200
(*Totino's* Temptin' Toppings), ¼ pie	210
smoked, with pepperoni seasoning (*Tombstone*), ¼ pie	350
sausage and mushroom (*Celeste* Pizza For One), 1 pie	592

sausage and pepperoni:

(*Jeno's* Crisp'n Tasty), ½ pie	300
(*Stouffer's*), ½ of 9⅜-oz. pkg.	380
(*Tombstone* Double Top), ¼ pie	540
(*Tombstone* Microwave), 8-oz. pkg.	560
(*Totino's* Small Microwave), 4.2 oz.	310
(*Totino's* Pan Pizza), ⅙ pie	340
(*Totino's* Temptin' Toppings), ¼ pie	230
(*Tombstone* Thin Crust Supreme), ¼ pie	340
vegetable (*Celeste*), ¼ pie	310
vegetable (*Celeste* Pizza For One), 1 pie	490
vegetable (*Totino's* Party Pizza), ½ pie	300
vegetable (*Totino's* Temptin' Toppings), ¼ pie	180

Pizza, French bread, frozen:

Canadian-style bacon (*Stouffer's*), ½ pkg.	360
cheese (*Banquet Zap*), 4.5 oz.	310
cheese (*Pillsbury* Microwave), 1 piece	370
cheese (*Stouffer's*), 5.2-oz. piece	340
cheese, double (*Stouffer's*), 6-oz. piece	410
deluxe (*Banquet Zap*), 4.5 oz.	330
deluxe (*Stouffer's*), ½ pkg.	430
hamburger (*Stouffer's*), ½ pkg.	410
pepperoni (*Banquet Zap*), 4.5 oz.	350
pepperoni (*Pillsbury* Microwave), 1 piece	430
pepperoni (*Stouffer's*), ½ pkg.	410
pepperoni and mushroom (*Stouffer's*), ½ pkg.	430
sausage (*Pappalo's*), 1 piece	410
sausage (*Pillsbury* Microwave), 1 piece	410
sausage (*Stouffer's*), ½ pkg.	420
sausage and mushrooms (*Stouffer's*), ½ pkg.	410

Pizza, French bread (cont.)
sausage and pepperoni (*Pillsbury* Microwave), 1 piece 450
sausage and pepperoni (*Stouffer's*), ½ pkg. 450
vegetable deluxe (*Stouffer's*), ½ pkg. 420
Pizza crust (*Pillsbury* All Ready), ⅛ of crust 90
Pizza Hut, 2 slices of medium pie:
hand-tossed, cheese, 7.8 oz. 518
hand-tossed, pepperoni, 6.9 oz. 500
hand-tossed, supreme, 8.4 oz. 540
hand-tossed, super supreme, 8.6 oz. 463
pan pizza, cheese, 7.2 oz. 492
pan pizza, pepperoni, 7.4 oz. 540
pan pizza, supreme, 9 oz. 589
pan pizza, super supreme, 9.1 oz. 563
Personal Pan Pizza, pepperoni, 9 oz. 675
Personal Pan Pizza, supreme, 9.3 oz. 647
Thin 'n Crispy, cheese, 5.2 oz. 398
Thin 'n Crispy, pepperoni, 5.1 oz. 413
Thin 'n Crispy, supreme, 7.1 oz. 459
Thin 'n Crispy, super supreme, 7.2 oz. 463
Pizza rolls, frozen, 3 oz. (approximately 6 rolls):
cheese, hamburger or pepperoni and cheese (*Jeno's*) 240
pepperoni and cheese or sausage and pepperoni (*Jeno's*) 230
sausage and cheese (*Jeno's* Microwave) 250
Pizza sauce:
(*Contadina* Pizza Squeeze), ¼ cup 30
canned (*Contadina* Quick & Easy), ¼ cup 30
canned (*Enrico's* Homemade Style All Natural), 4 oz. 60
canned, with Italian cheese (*Contadina*), ¼ cup 30
canned, with pepperoni (*Contadina*), ¼ cup 40
Plantain, fresh:
raw, 1 medium, approx. 9.7 oz. 218
cooked, sliced, ½ cup 89
Plum:
fresh, Japanese or hybrid, 1 medium, 2⅛" diam., approx. 2.5 oz. . . 36
canned, purple, in light syrup (*Stokely*), ½ cup 100
canned, purple, in heavy syrup (*Stokely*), ½ cup 130
canned, purple, in extra heavy syrup (*S&W* Fancy), ½ cup 135
Plum sauce, tangy (*La Choy*), 1 oz. 45
Poi, ½ cup 134
Polenta mix* (*Fantastic Polenta*), ½ cup 106
Polish sausage (see also "Kielbasa"):
(*Hillshire Farm* Links), 2 oz. 190
(*Hormel*), 2 links 170
(*Oscar Mayer International Sausages*), 2.7-oz. link 229
hot (*OHSE*), 1 oz. 70

Pollack, meat only:

fresh, Atlantic, raw, 4 oz.	104
fresh, walleye, baked, broiled, or microwaved, 4 oz.	128
frozen, fillets, breaded (*Mrs. Paul's Light*), 4¼ oz.	240
Pomegranate, fresh, 1 medium, 3⅜" diam. × 3¾"	104
Pompano, Florida, meat only, baked, broiled, or microwaved, 4 oz.	239

Popcorn, popped (see also "Candy"):

(*Bachman*), ½ oz.	80
(*Bachman* Light), ½ oz.	50
(*Bearitos* Organic Lite), 1 oz.	132
(*Frito-Lay's*), ½ oz.	70
(*Orville Redenbacher* Natural), 3 cups	80
(*Orville Redenbacher* Natural Salt Free), 3 cups	90
regular or butter flavor (*Jiffy Pop* Pan Popcorn), 4 cups	130
butter flavor (*Orville Redenbacher*), 3 cups	80
butter flavor (*Orville Redenbacher* Salt Free), 3 cups	80
caramel (*Orville Redenbacher*), 2.5 cups	240
cheese and cheese flavor:	
(*Bachman*), ½ oz.	90
(*Bearitos* Organic), 1 oz.	137
cheddar, white (*Cape Cod*), ½ oz.	80
cheddar, white (*Smartfood*), ½ oz.	80
cheddar, white (*Wise*), ½ oz.	70
honey caramel (*Keebler* Pop Deluxe), 1 oz.	120
microwave:	
cheddar cheese flavor (*Jolly Time*), 3 cups	180
natural or butter flavor (*Jiffy Pop*), 4 cups	140
natural or butter flavor (*Jolly Time*), 3 cups	150
natural or butter flavor (*Planters*), 3 cups	140
natural or butter flavor (*Pop Weaver's*), 4 cups	140
frozen, original or butter flavor (*Pillsbury*), 3 cups	210
white or yellow, air-popped (*Pops-Rite*), 1-oz. kernels	100
white or yellow, oil-popped (*Pops-Rite*), 1-oz. kernels	220

Poppy seeds, 1 tsp. 15

Porgy, see "Scup"

Pork, fresh (see also "Ham" and "Pork, boneless"):

back rib, raw (*JM* Gourmet), 5½ oz.	220
loin, whole, lean with fat:	
braised, 4 oz.	417
broiled, 4 oz.	392
broiled, 2.9 oz. (3.7 oz. raw chop with bone)	284
roasted, 4 oz.	362
loin, whole, lean only:	
braised, 4 oz.	310
broiled, 4 oz.	291

Pork, loin, whole, lean only **(cont.)**
    broiled, 2.3 oz. (3.7 oz. raw chop with bone and fat) 169
    roasted, 4 oz. 272
loin, blade, lean with fat:
    braised, 4 oz. 465
    broiled, 4 oz. 446
    broiled, 2.1 oz. (3.7 oz. raw chop with bone) 303
    roasted, 4 oz. 413
loin blade, lean only:
    braised, 4 oz. 355
    broiled, 4 oz. 340
    broiled, 2.1 oz. (3.7 oz. raw chop with bone and fat) 177
    roasted, 4 oz. 316
loin, center, lean with fat:
    braised, 4 oz. 401
    broiled, 4 oz. 358
    broiled, 3.1 oz. (3.7 oz. raw chop with bone) 275
    roasted, 4 oz. 346
loin, center, lean only:
    braised, 4 oz. 308
    broiled, 4 oz. 262
    broiled, 2.5 oz. (3.7 oz. raw chop with bone and fat) 166
    roasted, 4 oz. 272
loin, center rib, lean with fat:
    braised, 4 oz. 416
    broiled, 4 oz. 389
    broiled, 2.7 oz. (3.7 oz. raw chop with bone) 264
    roasted, 4 oz. 361
loin, center rib, lean only:
    braised, 4 oz. 314
    broiled, 4 oz. 293
    broiled, 2.2 oz. (3.7 oz. raw chop with bone and fat) 162
    roasted, 4 oz. 278
loin, sirloin, lean with fat:
    braised, 4 oz. 399
    broiled, 4 oz. 375
    broiled, 3 oz. (3.7 oz. with chop with bone) 278
    roasted, 4 oz. 330
loin, sirloin, lean only:
    braised, 4 oz. 296
    broiled, 4 oz. 276
    broiled, 2.4 oz. (3.7 oz. raw chop with bone and fat) 165
    roasted, 4 oz. 268
loin, top, lean with fat:
    braised, 4 oz. 432

Pork, loin, top, lean with fat **(cont.)**

broiled, 4 oz.	408
broiled, 3 oz. (3.7 oz. raw chop with bone)	295
roasted, 4 oz.	374

loin, top, lean only:

braised, 4 oz.	314
broiled, 4 oz.	293
broiled, 2.3 oz. (3.7 oz. raw chop with bone and fat)	165
roasted, 4 oz.	278

shoulder, whole:

separable lean with fat, roasted, 4 oz.	370
separable lean only, roasted, 4 oz.	277
roasted, chopped or diced, 1 cup not packed	341

shoulder, arm (picnic):

lean with fat, braised, 4 oz.	391
lean with fat, roasted, 4 oz.	375
lean only, braised, 4 oz.	281
lean only, roasted, 4 oz.	259

shoulder, Boston blade, lean with fat:

braised, 4 oz.	421
broiled, 4 oz.	397
broiled, 6.5 oz. (7.4 oz. raw steak w/bone)	647

shoulder, Boston blade, lean only:

braised, 4 oz.	333
broiled, 4 oz.	311
broiled, 5.2 oz. (7.4 oz. raw steak with bone and fat)	413
roasted, 4 oz.	290

spareribs, lean with fat:

raw, 1 oz.	81
raw (*JM* Gourmet), 4½ oz.	250
braised, 6.3 oz. (1 lb. raw with bone)	703
tenderloin, lean only, roasted, 4 oz.	188
tenderloin, lean only, roasted, 12.6 oz. (1 lb. raw)	596

Pork, boneless:

chop (*JM* America's Cut), 6-oz. chop	330
ground (*JM*) 3 oz.	190
loin, whole or half, center cut (*JM*), 3 oz.	190
tenderloin (*JM*), 3 oz.	120
canned (*Hormel*), 3 oz.	200

Pork entree, canned, chow mein (*La Choy* Bi-Pack), ¾ cup | 80

Pork entree, frozen or refrigerated:

barbequed:

back ribs (*John Morrell Pork Classics*), 4¾ oz.	240
chops, center cut (*John Morrell Pork Classics*), 4½ oz.	230
loin, thin sliced (*John Morrell Pork Classics*), 5 slices, 3 oz.	150
spareribs (*John Morrell Pork Classics*), 4½ oz.	250
tenderloin (*John Morrell Pork Classics*), 3 oz.	130

Pork entree, frozen or refrigerated **(cont.)**
steaks, braised (*Hormel*), 3 oz. 220
sweet and sour (*Chun King*), 13 oz. 400
Pork entree mix*, Cajun (*Hunt's Minute Gourmet*), 7.9 oz. 500
Pork gravy, canned:
(*Franco-American*), 2 oz. 40
(*Heinz*), 2 oz. 30
with chunky pork (*Hormel Great Beginnings*), 5 oz. 140
Pork luncheon meat:
(*Eckrich* Slender Sliced), 1 oz. 45
canned (*Hormel*), 3 oz. 240
Pork skins, fried (*Baken-Ets*), 1 oz. 160
Pot roast, see ''Beef dinner, frozen''
Potato (see also ''Potato, mix'' and ''Potato dishes''):
baked in skin, 1 medium, 4¾″ × 2⅓″ diam. 220
baked in skin, pulp only, ½ cup, approx. 2.2 oz. 57
baked in skin, skin only, 2 oz. 112
boiled in skin, pulp only, 1 round, 2½″ diam. 119
microwaved in skin, 1 medium, 4¾″ × 2⅓″ diam. 212
canned:
  all cuts, white (*Allens*), ½ cup 45
  whole or sliced (*Del Monte*), ½ cup 45
  scalloped, and ham (*Hormel Micro-Cup*), 7.5-oz. container 260
frozen, 3 oz., except as noted:
  whole, small (*Ore-Ida*) 70
  fried or French-fried:
    (*Heinz* Deep Fries) 160
    (*Ore-Ida Country Style Dinner Fries*) 110
    (*Ore-Ida Crispers!*) 230
    (*Ore-Ida Crispy Crowns*) 160
    (*Ore-Ida Golden Fries*) 120
    (*Ore-Ida Lites*) 90
    cottage cut (*Ore-Ida*) 120
    crinkle cut (*Ore-Ida Golden Crinkles*) 120
    crinkle cut (*Ore-Ida Pixie Crinkles*) 140
    crinkle cut (*Quick 'n Crispy*), 4 oz. 370
    crinkle cut, microwave (*Ore-Ida*), 3.5 oz. 180
    shoestring (*Heinz* Deep Fries) 200
    shoestring (*Ore-Ida*) 140
    shoestring (*Quick 'n Crispy*), 4 oz. 390
    shoestring (*Seabrook*) 140
    skinny (*MicroMagic*) 350
    sticks (*MicroMagic* Tater Sticks), 4 oz. 390
    thin cuts (*Quick 'n Crispy*), 4 oz. 370
    wedges (*Ore-Ida Home Style Potato Wedges*) 100
    wedges (*Quick 'n Crispy*), 4 oz. 280
    with onions (*Ore-Ida Crispy Crowns*) 170

Potato, frozen **(cont.)**

hash browns (*Ore-Ida Golden Patties*), 2.5 oz.	140
hash browns (*Ore-Ida Southern Style*)	70
hash browns, with cheddar (*Ore-Ida Cheddar Browns*)	90
hash browns, microwave (*Ore-Ida*), 2 oz.	130
O'Brien (*Ore-Ida*)	60
puffs, all varieties, except microwave (*Ore-Ida Tater Tots*)	140
puffs, microwave (*Ore-Ida Tater Tots*), 4 oz.	200

Potato, mix*, ½ cup, except as noted:

au gratin (*Idahoan*)	130
au gratin, tangy or cheddar and bacon casserole (*French's*)	130
cheddar, spicy or hash brown (*Idahoan*)	140
herb and butter (*Idahoan*)	150
mashed (*Country Store* Flakes), ⅓ cup flakes	70
mashed (*French's Idaho*)	130
mashed (*French's Idaho* Spuds)	140
mashed (*Hungry Jack* Flakes)	140
mashed, microwave (*Idahoan Instamash*), ¼ pkg. or ½ cup	70
scalloped, cheese or crispy top with onion mix (*French's*)	140
scalloped, creamy Italian (*French's*)	120
sour cream and chive (*French's*)	150
sour cream and chive (*Idahoan*)	130
Stroganoff, creamy (*French's*)	130
western (*Idahoan*)	120

Potato, sweet, see "Sweet potato"

Potato chips and crisps, 1 oz.:

(*Bachman* Plain, Ridge/Ruffled or Unsalted)	160
(*Bachman* Kettle Cooked)	140
(*Cape Cod/Cape Cod* No Salt Added)	150
(*Cottage Fries* No Salt Added)	160
(*Lay's/Lay's* Unsalted)	150
(*Ruffles*)	150
(*Wise* Plain or Rippled)	150
(*Wise New York Deli*)	160
(*Wise Ridgies* regular or Super Crispy)	150
all flavored varieties (*Bachman*)	150
all varieties (*Pringles* Light)	150
all varieties (*Pringles* Regular/*Pringles Idaho* Rippled)	170
barbecue (*Wise/Wise Ridgies*)	150
Cajun (*Ruffles Cajun Spice*)	150
cheddar and sour cream (*Ruffles*)	150
hot or onion garlic flavor (*Wise*)	160
ranch (*Ruffles*)	160
salt and vinegar flavor (*Lay's*)	150
skins, all varieties (*Tato Skins*)	150
sour cream and onion flavor (*Lay's*)	160
sour cream and onion flavor (*Ruffles*)	150

Potato dishes, frozen:
au gratin (*Green Giant* One Serving), 5.5 oz. 200
au gratin (*Stouffer's*), ⅓ of 11½ oz. pkg. 110
and broccoli, in cheese sauce (*Green Giant* One Serving), 5.5 oz. . . . 130
cheddared (*The Budget Gourmet* Side Dish), 5.5 oz. 230
cheddared, and broccoli (*The Budget Gourmet*), 5 oz. 130
new, in sour cream sauce (*The Budget Gourmet* Side Dish), 5 oz. . . . 120
scalloped (*Stouffer's*), ⅓ of 11½-oz. pkg. 90
stuffed:
   baked with cheese flavored topping (*Green Giant*), 5 oz. 200
   baked with sour cream and chives (*Green Giant*), 5 oz. 230
   with cheddar cheese (*Oh Boy!*), 6 oz. 142
   with real bacon (*Oh Boy!*), 6 oz. 116
   with sour cream and chives (*Oh Boy!*), 6 oz. 129
three cheese (*The Budget Gourmet* Side Dish), 5.75 oz. 230
Potato flour, 1 cup 628
Potato pancake mix* (*French's* Idaho), 3 cakes, 3″ each 90
Potato salad, canned:
German (*Joan of Arc/Read*), ½ cup 120
homestyle (*Joan of Arc/Read*), ½ cup 340
Potato sticks, canned, shoestring (*Allens*), 1 oz. 140
Poultry, see specific listings
Poultry salad spread, chicken and turkey, 1 tbsp. 26
Preserves, see ''Jams, jellies and preserves''
Pretzels, 1 oz., except as noted:
all varieties (*Bachman*) 110
all varieties (*Mr. Salty*) 110
all varieties (*Rold Gold*) 110
cheddar flavor (*Combos*), 1.8 oz. 240
Prickly pear, 1 medium, approx. 4.8 oz. 42
Prosciutto, boneless (*Hormel*), 1 oz. 90
Prunes, dried:
uncooked:
   with pits (*Del Monte/Del Monte* Moist Pak), 2 oz. 120
   with pits (*Sunsweet*), 2 oz. 120
   pitted (*Del Monte*), 2 oz. 140
   pitted (*Sunsweet*), 2 oz. 140
cooked, with pits, unsweetened, ½ cup 113
cooked, pitted, unsweetened, 4 oz. 121
Prune juice, canned or bottled, 6 fl. oz.:
(*Mott's/Motts* Country Style) 130
(*S&W* Unsweetened) 120
(*Sunsweet*) 130
Pudding, ready-to-serve:
banana or butterscotch (*Del Monte* Pudding Cup), 5 oz. 180
butterscotch (*Crowley*), 4.5 oz. 150
butterscotch (*White House*), 3.5 oz. 113

Pudding, ready-to-serve (cont.)

butterscotch or vanilla flavored, frozen (*Rich's*), 3 oz.	130

chocolate:

(*Crowley*), 4.5 oz.	190
(*Hunt's Snack Pack*), 4.25 oz.	160
(*Hunt's Snack Pack* Lite), 4 oz.	100
(*Swiss Miss*), 4 oz.	180
(*White House*), 3.5 oz.	120
frozen (*Rich's*), 3 oz.	140
chocolate or fudge (*Del Monte* Pudding Cup), 5 oz.	190
lemon (*White House*), 3.5 oz.	152
rice (*Crowley*), 4.5 oz.	125
rice (*White House*), 3.5 oz.	111

tapioca:

(*Crowley*), 4.5 oz.	135
(*Del Monte* Pudding Cup), 5 oz.	180
(*Hunt's Snack Pack*), 4.25 oz.	160
(*Swiss Miss*), 4 oz.	150
(*White House*), 3.5 oz.	131

vanilla:

(*Crowley*), 4.5 oz.	140
(*Del Monte* Pudding Cup), 5 oz.	180
(*Hunt's Snack Pack*), 4.25 oz.	170
(*Swiss Miss*), 4 oz.	160
(White House), 3.5 oz.	111

Pudding, mix*, ½ cup:

banana cream or butterscotch (*Jell-O* Instant)	160
banana cream or butterscotch (*Royal*)	160
banana cream or butterscotch (*Royal* Instant)	180
butter almond, toasted (*Royal* Instant)	170
butter pecan (*Jell-O* Instant)	170
butterscotch (*Jell-O*)	170

chocolate:

(*Royal/Royal* Dark 'n Sweet)	180
(*Royal* Instant/*Royal* Dark 'n Sweet Instant)	190
chocolate chip or mint (*Royal* Instant)	190
regular, fudge, or milk (*Jell-O*)	160
regular, fudge, or milk (*Jell-O* Instant)	180
coconut cream (*Jell-O* Instant)	180
coconut, toasted (*Royal* Instant)	170
custard or flan with caramel sauce (*Royal*)	150
custard, egg, golden (*Jell-O Americana*)	160
flan (*Jell-O*)	150
lemon (*Jell-O* Instant)	170
lemon (*Royal* Instant)	180
lemon or key lime (*Royal*)	160
pistachio (*Jell-O* Instant)	170

Pudding, mix (cont.)
pistachio (*Royal* Instant) 170
rennet custard, all flavors (*Junket*) 120
rice (*Jell-O Americana*) 170
tapioca, vanilla (*Jell-O Americana*) 160
vanilla (*Jell-O/Jell-O* French Instant) 160
vanilla (*Jell-O* French/*Jell-O* Instant) 170
vanilla (*Royal*) 160
vanilla (*Royal* Instant) 180
Pudding bars, frozen, all flavors: (*Jell-O Pudding Pops*), 1 bar 80
Puff pastry, frozen:
sheets (*Pepperidge Farm*), ¼ sheet 260
shells, mini (*Pepperidge Farm*), 1 shell 50
Pumpkin:
fresh, boiled, drained, 4 oz. 23
fresh, boiled, drained, mashed, ½ cup 24
canned (*Del Monte*), ½ cup 35
canned (*Stokely*), ½ cup 40
Pumpkin flower, boiled, drained, ½ cup 10
Pumpkin pie, see "Pie"
Pumpkin pie spice, 1 tsp. 6
Pumpkin seeds:
roasted, whole, in shell, 1 oz., approx. 85 seeds 127
dried, 1 oz., approx. 142 kernels 154
Purslane:
raw, trimmed, ½ cup 4
boiled, drained, ½ cup 10

Q

Food and Measure	Calories

Quail:
raw, meat with skin, 1 quail, 3.8 oz. (4.3 oz. with bone) 210
raw, breast, meat only, 1 oz. 38
Quince, fresh, whole, 1 medium, approx. 5.3 oz. 53

R

Food and Measure	Calories

Rabbit, meat only:
domesticated, roasted, 4 oz. 175
domesticated, stewed, 4 oz. 234
domesticated, stewed, diced, 1 cup 288
wild, stewed, 4 oz. 196
Radish:
sliced, ½ cup 10
10 medium, ¾"–1" diam., approx. 1.8 oz. 7
Radish, Oriental:
raw, sliced, ½ cup 8
raw, 1 medium, 7" × 2¼" diam., approx. 15.1 oz. 62
boiled, drained, sliced, ½ cup 13
dried, 1 oz. 77
Radish, white icicle, raw, 1 medium, approx. .6 oz. 2
Raisins:
golden (*Del Monte*), 3 oz. 260
natural (*Del Monte*), 3 oz. 250
seedless (*Sun-Maid*), ½ cup 290
seedless, regular and golden (*Dole*), ½ cup 260
Thompson seedless (*Cinderella*), ½ cup 250
Raspberry:
fresh, trimmed, ½ cup 31
frozen, in light syrup, red (*Birds Eye* Quick Thaw Pouch), 5 oz. 100
Raspberry juice:
blend (*Dole Pure & Light* Country Raspberry), 6 fl. oz. 87
red (*Smucker's* Naturally 100%), 8 fl. oz. 120
cocktail (*Welch's* Orchard), 10-fl. oz. bottle 160
Ravioli, canned or in jars, 7.5 oz., except as noted:
beef, in meat sauce (*Franco-American* Hearty Pasta) 280
beef, in meat sauce (*Franco-American* RavioliOs) 250

Ravioli (cont.)
beef in tomato sauce (*Hormel Micro-Cup*) 247
cheese, in sauce (*Buitoni*) 190
cheese in tomato sauce (*Chef Boyardee*) 200
meat, in sauce (*Buitoni*) 180
Ravioli, frozen:
(*Celentano*), 6.5 oz. 380
cheese (*Buitoni* 1 lb. pkg.), ¼ pkg. or 4 oz. 360
mini (*Celentano*), 4 oz. 250
Ravioli entree, frozen (*The Budget Gourmet* Slim Selects), 10 oz. 260
Red snapper, see "Snapper"
Redfish, see "Ocean perch"
Refried beans, see "Beans, refried"
Relish:
hamburger or piccalilli (*Heinz*), 1 oz. 30
hot dog, India or sweet (*Heinz*), 1 oz. 35
hot dog (*Vlasic*), 1 oz. 40
pickle (*Claussen*), 1 tbsp. 14
sweet, 1 tbsp. 21
sweet (*Vlasic*), 1 oz. 30
Rhubarb:
raw, trimmed, diced, ½ cup 13
frozen, cooked, sweetened, ½ cup 139
Rib sauce (*Dip n'Joy* Saucy Rib), 1 oz. 60
Rice, ⅓ cup, except as noted:
basmati, cooked (*Fantastic Foods*) 103
basmati, white, long grain cooked (*Texmati*) 82
brown, long grain, cooked (*Mahatma/River*) 110
brown, long grain, cooked (*Uncle Ben's* Whole Grain), ⅔ cup 130
brown, long grain, precooked (*Uncle Ben's*) 90
white, long grain, cooked (*Carolina/Mahatma/River/Water Maid*) 100
white, long grain, cooked (*Uncle Ben's Converted*), ⅔ cup 120
white, long grain, instant cooked:
   (*Carolina/Mahatma* Enriched) 110
   (*Success* Boil-in-Bag Enriched) 100
   (*Uncle Ben's* Boil-In-Bag) 90
   (*Uncle Ben's* Rice In An Instant), ⅔ cup 120
white, precooked (*Minute*), ⅔ cup 120
Rice, wild, see "Wild rice"
Rice bran, crude, 1 oz. 90
Rice cake:
plain (*Quaker/Quaker* Unsalted), .32-oz. piece 35
plain, mini (*Hain/Hain* Unsalted), ½ oz. 50
barley and oats (*Mother's*), .32-oz. piece 34
buckwheat (*Mother's* Unsalted), .32-oz. piece 35
corn or sesame (*Quaker/Mother's*), .32-oz. piece 35

Rice cake (cont.)
multigrain (*Quaker/Mother's*), .32-oz. piece	34
rye (*Quaker*), .32-oz. piece	34

Rice dishes, canned:
fried (*La Choy*), ¾ cup	190
Spanish (*Old El Paso*), ½ cup	70
Spanish (*Van Camp's*), 1 cup	150

Rice, dishes, frozen (see also specific listings):
and broccoli, in cheese sauce (*Green Giant* One Serving), 4.5 oz.	180
and broccoli, in cheese-flavored sauce (*Green Giant Rice Originals*), ½ cup	120
country style (*Birds Eye* International), 3.3 oz.	90
French or Spanish style (*Birds Eye* International), 3.3 oz.	110
fried, with chicken (*Chun King*), 8 oz.	260
fried, with pork (*Chun King*), 8 oz.	270
Italian blend white rice and spinach in cheese sauce (*Green Giant Rice Originals*), ½ cup	140
medley (*Green Giant Rice Originals*), ½ cup	100
peas and mushrooms, with sauce (*Green Giant* One Serving), 5.5 oz.	130
pilaf (*Green Giant Rice Originals*), ½ cup	110
Oriental, and vegetables (*The Budget Gourmet* Side Dish), 5.75 oz. ..	210
white and wild rice (*Green Giant Rice Originals*), ½ cup	130
wild, sherry (*Green Giant* Microwave Garden Gourmet), 1 pkg.	210

Rice dishes, mix*, ½ cup:
Alfredo, without butter (*Country Inn*)	140
almondine (*Hain* 3-Grain Side Dish)	130
asparagus au gratin, without butter (*Country Inn*)	130
asparagus with hollandaise sauce (*Lipton* Rice and Sauce)	170
au gratin, herbed, without butter (*Country Inn*)	140
beef flavor (*Lipton* Rice and Sauce)	150
beef or chicken flavor (*Golden Grain/Rice-A-Roni*)	170
broccoli au gratin, without butter (*Country Inn*)	130
broccoli au gratin or zesty cheddar (*Golden Grain/Rice-A-Roni Savory Classics*)	180
brown and wild, regular or mushroom (*Uncle Ben's*)	130
Cajun (*Lipton* Rice and Sauce)	150
cauliflower au gratin, without butter (*Country Inn*)	130
chicken and chicken flavor:	
(*Lipton* Rice and Sauce)	150
and broccoli, without butter (*Suzi Wan*)	120
creamy, and mushroom, without butter (*Country Inn*)	140
homestyle, and vegetable, without butter (*Country Inn*)	140
and mushroom (*Golden Grain/Rice-A-Roni*)	180
royale, without butter (*Country Inn*)	120
and vegetables (*Golden Grain/Rice-A-Roni*)	150
Florentine, without butter (*Country Inn*)	140

Rice dishes, mix **(cont.)**
Florentine, chicken (*Golden Grain/Rice-A-Roni Savory Classics*) 130
green bean almondine (*Golden Grain/Rice-A-Roni Savory Classics*) .. 210
herb and butter (*Golden Grain/Rice-A-Roni*) 140
herb and butter (*Lipton* Rice and Sauce) 150
long grain and wild:
   (*Minute*) 150
   (*Uncle Ben's Original*) 120
   chicken stock sauce (*Uncle Ben's*) 160
   mushrooms and herbs or original (*Lipton* Rice and Sauce) 150
Mexican (*Old El Paso*) 140
mushroom (*Lipton* Rice and Sauce) 150
Oriental (*Hain* 3-Grain Goodness) 120
Parmesan and herbs (*Golden Grain/Rice-A-Roni Savory Classics*) ... 170
pilaf:
   (*Golden Grain/Rice-A-Roni*) 190
   (*Lipton* Rice and Sauce) 170
   brown rice, with miso (*Quick Pilaf*) 145
   garden (*Golden Grain/Rice-A-Roni Savory Classics*) 140
   Spanish, brown rice (*Quick Pilaf*) 136
   vegetable, without butter (*Country Inn*) 120
risotto (*Golden Grain/Rice-A-Roni*) 200
risotto, chicken and cheese, without butter (*Country Inn*) 120
Spanish (*Golden Grain/Rice-A-Roni*) 150
Spanish (*Lipton* Rice and Sauce) 140
Stroganoff (*Golden Grain/Rice-A-Roni*) 190
sweet and sour, without butter (*Suzi Wan*) 130
teriyaki, without butter (*Suzi Wan*) 120
three-flavor, without butter (*Suzi Wan*) 120
vegetable medley, without butter (*Country Inn*) 140
with vegetables, broccoli, and cheddar (*Lipton* Rice and Sauce) ... 180
vegetable, spring, and cheese (*Golden Grain/Rice-A-Roni*) 170
yellow (*Golden Grain/Rice-A-Roni*) 250
Rice seasoning, Mexican (*Lawry's* Seasoning Blends), 1 pkg. 94
Rockfish, baked, broiled or microwaved, meat only, 4 oz. 137
Roe (see also "Caviar"), mixed species, 1 tbsp. 22
Roll (see also "Biscuits," "Croissants," etc.) 1 piece, except as
noted:
brown and serve:
   (*Pepperidge Farm* Hearth) 50
   all varieties (*Wonder*) 80
   club (*Pepperidge Farm*) 100
   French (*Pepperidge Farm,* 3 per pkg.), ½ roll 120
   French (*Pepperidge Farm,* 2 per pkg.), ½ roll 180
cinnamon, homestyle (*Awrey's*) 240
crescent, butter (*Pepperidge Farm*) 110

Roll (cont.)

Dijon (*Pepperidge Farm*)	230
dinner (*Arnold* 24 Dinner Party)	51
dinner (*Pepperidge Farm*)	60
dinner (*Pepperidge Farm* Old Fashioned)	50
dinner (*Wonder*)	80
egg (*Levy's* Old Country Deli), 1 oz.	146
egg, sandwich (*Arnold* Dutch)	123
finger, with poppy seeds (*Pepperidge Farm*)	50
finger, with sesame seeds (*Pepperidge Farm*)	60
frankfurter (*Arnold*)	100
frankfurter (*Arnold* New England Style)	108
frankfurter (*Pepperidge Farm* Side or Top Sliced)	140
frankfurter, Dijon (*Pepperidge Farm*)	160
French style (*Pepperidge Farm*, 4 per pkg.), ½ piece	120
hamburger (*Arnold*)	115
hamburger (*Wonder*)	120
hamburger (*Pepperidge Farm*)	130
hoagie (*Wonder*)	400
hoagie, soft (*Pepperidge Farm*)	210
kaiser (*Arnold* Francisco)	184
onion (*Levy's* Old Country Deli), 1 oz.	153
pan (*Wonder*)	80
Parker House (*Pepperidge Farm*)	60
party (*Pepperidge Farm*)	30
sandwich, onion and poppy seed (*Pepperidge Farm*)	150
sandwich, sesame seed (*Pepperidge Farm*)	140
soft (*Pepperidge Farm* Family)	100
sourdough French style (*Pepperidge Farm*)	100

Roll, refrigerated, 1 piece, except as noted:

butterflake (*Pillsbury*)	140
cinnamon (*Pillsbury Best* Quick)	210
cinnamon, iced (*Hungry Jack*), 2 pieces	290
cinnamon, iced (*Pillsbury*)	110
crescent (*Pillsbury*)	100

Roll, sweet, frozen:

cinnamon, all butter (*Sara Lee*), 2-oz. piece	230
cinnamon, all butter, icing packet (*Sara Lee*), .5-oz. packet	60
cinnamon bun (*Rich's Ever Fresh*), 2.5-oz. piece	293
honey bun, mini (*Rich's Ever Fresh*), 1.36-oz. piece	133
Rosemary, dried, 1 tsp.	4

Rotini entree, frozen:

cheddar (*Green Giant* Microwave Garden Gourmet), 1 pkg.	230
Roughy, orange, meat only, raw, 4 oz.	144

Roy Rogers:

breakfast, 1 serving:

crescent roll	287

Roy Rogers, breakfast **(cont.)**

crescent sandwich	408
crescent sandwich, with bacon	446
crescent sandwich, with ham	456
crescent sandwich, with sausage	564
egg and biscuit platter	557
egg and biscuit platter, with bacon	607
egg and biscuit platter, with ham	605
egg and biscuit platter, with sausage	713
pancake platter, with syrup and butter	386
pancake platter, with syrup, butter and bacon	436
pancake platter, with syrup, butter and ham	434
pancake platter, with syrup, butter and sausage	542

chicken fried:

breast	412
breast and wing	604
leg (drumstick)	140
thigh	296
thigh and leg	436
wing	192

sandwiches, 1 serving:

bacon cheeseburger	552
bar burger	573
cheeseburger	525
cheeseburger, small	275
hamburger	472
hamburger, small	222
*Express*burger	561
Express bacon cheeseburger	641
Express cheeseburger	613
fish sandwich	514
roast beef sandwich, regular	350
roast beef sandwich, large	373
roast beef sandwich, with cheese	403
roast beef sandwich, with cheese, large	427

side dishes:

biscuit	231
coleslaw	110
French fries, 4 oz.	320
French fries, small, 3 oz.	238
French fries, large, 5.5 oz.	440

desserts and shakes:

shake, chocolate	358
shake, strawberry	315
shake, vanilla	306
sundae, caramel, 5.2 oz.	293
sundae, hot fudge, 5.4 oz.	337

Roy Rogers, desserts and shakes **(cont.)**

sundae, strawberry, 5 oz.	216
Vitari, 1 oz.	30

Rutabaga:

fresh, boiled, drained, cubed, ½ cup	29
canned (*Allens*), ½ cup	20
Rye cake (*Quaker* Grain Cakes), .32-oz. cake	35

S

Food and Measure	Calories

Sablefish:

raw, meat only, 4 oz.	221
smoked, 4 oz.	291
Saffron, 1 tsp.	2
Sage, ground (*Spice Islands*), 1 tsp.	4

Salad dressing, bottled, 1 tbsp., except as noted:

bacon and buttermilk (*Kraft*)	80
bacon and tomato (*Kraft*)	70
blue cheese (*Roka*)	60
blue cheese, chunky (*Kraft*)	60
blue cheese, chunky (*Wish-Bone*)	75
buttermilk (*Hain* Old Fashioned)	70
buttermilk, creamy (*Kraft*)	80
Caesar (*Lawry's* Classic), ½ oz.	65
Caesar (*Wish-Bone*)	77
Caesar, creamy (*Hain/Hain* Low Salt)	60
Caesar, golden (*Kraft*)	70
Chinese vinegar with sesame and ginger (*Lawry's* Classic), ½ oz.	73
coleslaw or creamy cucumber (*Kraft*)	70
creamy (*Rancher's Choice*)	90
cucumber dill (*Hain*)	80
Dijon vinaigrette (*Hain*)	50
Dijon vinaigrette (*Wish-Bone* Classic)	60

Salad dressing (cont.)

French:

(*Catalina*)	70
(*Kraft*)	60
(*Kraft* Miracle)	70
(*Wish-Bone* Deluxe)	60
creamy (*Hain*)	60
garlic (*Wish-Bone*)	55
sweet 'n spicy (*Wish-Bone*)	63
garlic, creamy (*Kraft*)	50
garlic, French (*Wish-Bone*)	55
garlic and sour cream (*Hain*)	70
herb, savory (*Hain* No Salt Added)	90
honey and sesame (*Hain*)	60

Italian:

(*Kraft* Presto or Zesty)	70
(*Wish-Bone*)	46
(*Wish-Bone* Robusto)	47
blended (*Wish-Bone*)	37
with blue cheese (*Lawry's* Classic), ½ oz.	93
with cheese (*Wish-Bone*)	89
creamy (*Wish-Bone*)	56
creamy, with real sour cream (*Kraft*)	50
herbal (*Wish-Bone* Classic)	70
with Parmesan cheese (*Lawry's* Classic), ½ oz.	78
traditional or creamy (*Hain*)	80
mayonnaise type (*Miracle Whip*)	70
mayonnaise type (*Spin Blend*)	60
oil and vinegar (*Kraft*)	70
olive oil, Italian (*Wish-Bone* Classic)	34
olive oil vinaigrette (*Wish-Bone*)	28
onion and chive, creamy (*Kraft*)	70
(*Ott's Famous*)	40
poppyseed (*Hain* Rancher's)	60
ranch (*Wish-Bone*)	78
red wine, with cabernet (*Lawry's* Classic), ½ oz.	69
red wine vinaigrette (*Wish-Bone*)	51
Russian (*Wish-Bone*)	46
Russian, regular or creamy (*Kraft*)	60
San Francisco, with Romano cheese (*Lawry's* Classic), ½ oz.	68
Thousand Island (*Hain*)	50
Thousand Island (*Wish-Bone*)	63
Thousand Island, regular or bacon (*Kraft*)	60
vinegar, red wine and oil (*Kraft*)	60
vintage, with sherry (*Lawry's* Classic), ½ oz.	55
white wine, with chardonnay (*Lawry's* Classic), ½ oz.	77

Salad dressing mix:

dry, bacon (*Lawry's*), 1 pkg. 65
dry, Caesar (*Lawry's*), 1 pkg. 75
dry, Italian (*Lawry's*), 1 pkg. 45
dry, Italian with cheese (*Lawry's*), 1 pkg. 74
prepared, all varieties, except buttermilk and mild Italian (*Good Seasons*), 1 tbsp. 80
prepared, buttermilk (*Good Seasons* Farm Style) 60
prepared, mild Italian (*Good Seasons*), 1 tbsp. 90
Salad seasoning (*McCormick/Schilling* Salad Supreme), 1 tsp. 11

Salami:

beef (*Boar's Head*), 1 oz. 60
beef (*Hebrew National* Original Deli Style), 1 oz. 80
beef (*Hormel* Perma-Fresh), 2 slices 50
beer (*Eckrich*), 1-oz. slice 70
beer (*Oscar Mayer* Salami for Beer), .8-oz. slice 55
beer, beef (*Oscar Mayer* Salami for Beer), .8-oz. slice 66
cooked (*Kahn's*), 1 slice 60

cotto:

  (*Eckrich*), 1-oz. slice 70
  (*Hormel* Chub), 1 oz. 100
  (*Hormel* Perma-Fresh), 2 slices 105
  (*Kahn's* Family Pack), 1 slice 45
  (*Oscar Mayer*), .8-oz. slice 54
  beef (*Eckrich*), 1.3 oz. 100
  beef (*Oscar Mayer*), .8-oz. slice 46

Genoa:

  (*Hickory Farms*), 1 oz. 110
  (*Hormel/Hormel* Gran Valore), 1 oz. 110
  (*Hormel DiLusso*), 1 oz. 100
  (*Hormel* San Remo Brand), 1 oz. 118
  (*Oscar Mayer*), .3-oz. slice 34

hard:

  (*Hickory Farms*), 1 oz. 120
  (*Hormel*), 1 oz. 110
  (*Hormel* National Brand), 1 oz. 120
  (*Hormel* Perma-Fresh), 2 slices 80
  (*Oscar Mayer*), .3 oz-slice 34

(*Hormel* Party), 1 oz. 90
piccolo (*Hormel* Stick), 1 oz. 120
turkey, see "Turkey salami"

Salisbury steak, see "Beef dinner" and "Beef entree"

Salmon:

fresh, meat only, 4 oz.:

  Atlantic, raw 161
  chinook, raw 204

Salmon, fresh, meat only **(cont.)**

chinook, smoked	133
chum, raw	136
coho, boiled, poached, or steamed	210
pink, raw	132
red sockeye, raw	191
red sockeye, baked, broiled, or microwaved	245

canned, ½ cup:

chum, keta (*Bumble Bee*)	153
pink (*Del Monte*)	160
pink, Alaska (*Deming's*)	140
red (*Del Monte*)	180
red, blueback (*Rubenstein's*)	170
red sockeye (*Bumble Bee*)	188
red sockeye, Alaska (*Deming's*)	170
red sockeye, blueback (*S&W Fancy*)	190
frozen, steaks, without seasoning mix (*SeaPak*), 8-oz. pkg.	270

Salsa (see also "Chili sauce," "Taco sauce," etc.):

burrito (*Del Monte*), ¼ cup	20
green chile, hot (*Ortega*), 1 oz.	10
green chile, mild or medium (*Ortega*), 1 oz.	8
mild or hot, regular (*Enrico's* Chunky Style), 2 tbsp.	8
ranchera (*Ortega*), 1 oz.	12
roja, mild (*Del Monte*), ¼ cup	20
taco, hot or mild (*Ortega*), 1 oz.	10
Texas (*Hot Cha Cha*), 1 oz.	6
thick'n chunky (*Old El Paso*), 2 tbsp.	6

Salsify, fresh, boiled, drained, sliced, ½ cup | 46

Salt:

1 tbsp.	0
seasoned (*Lawry's*), 1 tsp.	4

Salt, imitation, seasoned (*Lawry's Salt-Free*), 1 tsp. | 3

Salt pork, raw, 1 oz. | 212

Sandwich spread (see also specific listings):

(*Best Foods/Hellmann's*), 1 tbsp.	50
(*Kraft*), 1 tbsp.	50
meat (*Oscar Mayer* Chub), 1 oz.	67

Sapodilla, fresh, 1 medium, 2½" × 3" diam., approx. 7.5 oz. | 140

Sardines, canned:

Atlantic, in oil, 2 medium, 3" × 1" × ½", approx. .8 oz.	50
Norwegian Brisling, in oil (*S&W*), 1.5 oz.	130
Pacific, in tomato sauce, 1 medium, approx. 1.3 oz.	68
in tomato sauce (*Del Monte*), ½ cup	360

Sauces, see specific listings

Sauerkraut, canned or in jars, ½ cup:

(*Claussen*)	17

Sauerkraut (cont.)
(*Del Monte*) 25
shredded (*Allens*) 21
Sauerkraut juice (*S&W*), 5 fl. oz. 14
Sausage (see also specific listings):
beef (*Jones Dairy Farm* Golden Brown), 1 link 75
brown and serve:
   (*Jones Dairy Farm* Light), 1 oz. 60
   (*Swift Premium* Original Brown 'N Serve), 1 link 130
   (*Swift Premium* Original Brown 'N Serve), 1 patty 120
   beef (*Swift Premium* Brown 'N Serve), 1 link 120
   maple flavored (*Swift Premium* Brown 'N Serve), 1 link 120
   microwave (*Swift Premium* Brown 'N Serve), 1 link 120
   uncooked (*Hormel*), 2 links 180
German (*Hickory Farms*), 1 oz. 100
Italian, see "Italian sausage"
Polish, see "Kielbasa" and "Polish Sausage"
pork:
   (*Hormel Little Sizzlers*), 2 links 103
   (*Hormel* Midget Links), 2 links 143
   (*Jones Dairy Farm*), 1 link 140
   (*Oscar Mayer Little Friers*), 1 link, cooked 82
   hot (*JM*), cooked, 1 patty, approx. .5 oz. 70
   mild (*Jones Dairy Farm* Golden Brown), 1 link 100
   patty (*Jones Dairy Farm*), 1 patty 155
   patty (*Jones Dairy Farm* Golden Brown), 1 patty 155
   spicy (*Jones Dairy Farm*), 1 link 100
smoked:
   (*Eckrich* Lean Supreme), 1 oz. 70
   (*Eckrich* Skinless), 1 link 180
   (*Hillshire Farm* Bun Size), 2 oz. 180
   (*Hillshire Farm* Flavorseal or Links), 2 oz. 190
   (*Hormel* Smokies), 2 links 160
   (*Oscar Mayer* Little Smokies), .3-oz link 28
   (*Oscar Mayer* Smokie Links), 1.5-oz. link 124
   beef (*Eckrich*), 1 oz. 100
   beef (*Eckrich Smok-Y-Links*), 2 links 160
   beef (*Hillshire Farm* Bun Size or Flavorseal), 2 oz. 180
   beef (*Oscar Mayer* Smokies), 1.5-oz. link 123
   cheese (*Eckrich Smok-Y-Links*), 2 links 160
   cheese (*Hormel* Smokie Cheezers), 2 links 168
   cheese (*Oscar Mayer* Smokies), 1.5-oz. link 127
   ham or maple flavored (*Eckrich Smok-Y-Links*), 2 links 150
   hot (*Hillshire Farms* Flavorseal), 2 oz. 180
Swedish, see "Swedish sausage"
Vienna, see "Vienna sausage"

Sausage, canned, hot or mild (*Hormel*), 1 patty 150
"Sausage," vegetarian, frozen (*Morningstar Farms* Breakfast Links),
3 links, 2.4 oz. 190
Sausage breakfast biscuit, frozen (*Swanson Great Starts* Breakfast
On a Biscuit), 4¾ oz. 410
Savory, ground, 1 tsp. 4
Scallop, meat only:
fresh, mixed species, raw, 2 large or 5 small, approx. 1.1 oz. 26
frozen, fried (*Mrs. Paul's*), 3 oz. 200
Scallop and shrimp dinner, Mariner, frozen (*The Budget Gourmet*),
11.5 oz. 320
Scrapple (*Jones Dairy Farm*), 1 slice 65
Scrod entree, baked, frozen (*Gorton's Microwave Entrees*), 1 pkg. 320
Sea bass, meat only, baked, broiled, or microwaved, 4 oz. 141
Seafood cocktail sauce, (*Del Monte*), ¼ cup 70
Seafood and crabmeat salad (*Longacre* Saladfest), 1 oz. 45
Seafood dinner, with herbs, frozen (*Armour Classics Lite*), 10 oz. ... 190
Seafood entree, frozen:
casserole (*Pillsbury Microwave Classic*), 1 pkg. 420
combination platter, breaded (*Mrs. Paul's*), 9 oz. 600
creole with rice (*Swanson* Homestyle Recipe), 9 oz. 240
Newberg (*The Budget Gourmet*), 10 oz. 350
Newburg (*Healthy Choice*), 8 oz. 200
Seasonings, see specific listings
Sea trout, mixed species, raw, meat only, 4 oz. 116
Seaweed:
agar, dried, 1 oz. 87
Irish moss, raw, 1 oz. 14
kelp, raw, 1 oz. 12
spirulina, dried, 1 oz. 82
wakame, raw, 1 oz. 13
Semolina, whole grain, 1 cup 602
Sesame butter (see also "Tahini mix"):
paste, from whole sesame seeds, 1 tbsp. 95
tahini, from raw, stone-ground kernels, 1 tbsp. 86
tahini, from roasted and toasted kernels, 1 tbsp. 89
Sesame chips (*Flavor Tree*), ¼ cup 163
Sesame nut mix, dry roasted (*Planters*), 1 oz. 160
Sesame seasoning (*McCormick/Schilling Parsley Patch*), 1 tsp. 15
Sesame seed (*Spice Islands*), tsp. 9
Sesame sticks (*Flavor Tree*), ¼ cup 133
Shad, fresh, American, raw, meat only, 4 oz. 224
Shallot:
raw, trimmed, 1 oz. 20
raw, chopped, 1 tbsp. 7
freeze-dried, 1 tbsp. 3

Shark, mixed species, meat only, raw, 4 oz. 148
Sheepshead, meat only, baked, broiled, or microwaved, 4 oz. 143
Sherbet (see also "Sorbet" and "Ice"):
orange (*Borden*), ½ cup 110
orange (*Darigold*), ½ cup 120
rainbow (*Baskin-Robbins*), 1 regular scoop 160
Shortening:
lard and vegetable oil, 1 tbsp. 115
hydrogenated soybean and cottonseed or palm, 1 tbsp. 113
vegetable, regular or butter flavor (*Crisco*), 1 tbsp. 110
Shrimp, mixed species, meat only:
fresh, raw, 1 oz. or 4 large 30
fresh, boiled, poached, or steamed, 4 oz. 112
fresh, boiled, poached, or steamed, 4 large, approx. .8 oz. 22
canned (*Louisiana Brand*), 2 oz. 58
canned, medium, deveined (*S&W*), 1 oz. 65
frozen:
    battered, plain or crabmeat stuffed (*SeaPak*), 4 oz. 260
    breaded, fried (*Mrs. Paul's*), 3 oz. 200
    breaded, butterfly (*SeaPak*), 4 oz. 150
    butterfly (*Gorton's* Specialty), 4 oz. 160
    crisps (*Gorton's* Specialty), 4 oz. 280
    crunchy, whole (*Gorton's* Microwave Specialty), 5 oz. 380
Shrimp dinner, frozen:
Creole (*Healthy Choice*), 11.25 oz. 210
marinara (*Healthy Choice*), 10.5 oz. 220
Shrimp entree, chow mein, canned (*La Choy* Bi-Pack), ¾ cup 50
Shrimp entree, frozen:
Cajun style (*Mrs. Paul's* Light), 9 oz. 230
and chicken Cantonese, with noodles (*Lean Cuisine*), 10⅛ oz. ... 270
and clams with linguini (*Mrs. Paul's* Light), 10 oz. 240
with garlic butter and vegetable rice (*Booth*), 10 oz. 400
with lobster sauce (*La Choy Fresh & Lite*), 10 oz. 240
New Orleans, with wild rice (*Booth*), 10 oz. 230
primavera (*Mrs. Paul's* Light), 9½ oz. 180
primavera, with fettuccini (*Booth*), 10 oz. 200
scampi (*Gorton's* Microwave Entrees), 1 pkg. 470
Shrimp salad (*Longacre* Saladfest), 1 oz. 45
Shrimp and seafood salad (*Longacre* Saladfest), 1 oz. 42
Sloppy Joe seasoning:
(*Lawry's* Seasoning Blends), 1 pkg. 126
mix (*McCormick/Schilling*), 1 serving 18
Smelt, rainbow, meat only, baked, broiled or microwaved, 4 oz. 141
Snack mix (see also specific listings):
(*Eagle*), 1 oz. 140
all varieties, except traditional (*Ralston Chex*), 1 oz. 130

Snack mix (cont.)

regular or no salt (*Flavor Tree* Party Mix), ¼ cup	163
traditional (*Ralston Chex*), 1 oz.	120

Snails sea, see "Whelk"

Snapper, mixed species, meat only, baked, broiled or microwaved,

4 oz.	145

Snow peas, see "Peas, edible-podded"

Soft drinks, 12 fl. oz., except as noted:

all varieties (*Schweppes* Royal)	70
cherry, black (*Shasta*)	162
cherry cola (*Coca-Cola*)	152
cherry cola (*Pepsi* Wild Cherry)	163
cherry cola (*Shasta*)	140
chocolate (*Yoo-Hoo*), 9 fl. oz.	140
citrus mist (*Shasta*)	170
club soda or seltzer, all flavors (*Schweppes*)	0
cola:	
(*Coca-Cola* Classic)	144
(*Coca-Cola* Regular/Caffeine-free)	154
(*Jolt*)	170
(*Pepsi* Regular/Caffeine-free)	160
(*Shasta*)	147
(*Shasta* Free)	151
cream (*A&W*)	168
cream (*Shasta* Creme)	154
ginger ale (*Canada Dry*), 8 fl. oz.	90
ginger ale (*Canada Dry* Golden), 8 fl. oz.	100
ginger ale, regular or raspberry (*Schweppes*)	130
ginger beer (*Schweppes*)	140
grape (*Canada Dry* Concord), 8 fl. oz.	130
grape (*Schweppes*)	190
grape (*Shasta*)	177
grapefruit (*Schweppes*)	160
grapefruit (*Wink*), 8 fl. oz.	120
half and half (*Canada Dry*), 8 fl. oz.	110
lemon, bitter (*Schweppes*)	164
lemon sour (*Schweppes*)	158
lemon-lime (*Schweppes*)	144
lemon-lime or mandarin lime (*Spree*)	154
lemon tangerine (*Spree*)	165
(*Mountain Dew*)	179
orange (*Minute Maid*)	174
orange (*Shasta*)	177
orange, Mandarin (*Slice*)	193
orange, sparkling (*Schweppes*)	176
pop, red (*Shasta*)	158

Soft drinks (cont.)

root beer (*A&W*)	180
root beer (*Ramblin'*)	176
root beer (*Shasta*)	154
(*7Up*)	144
(*7Up* Cherry)	148
(*Sprite*)	142
strawberry (*Shasta*)	147
tonic (*Canada Dry*), 8 fl. oz.	90
tonic (*Schweppes*)	128

Sole, fresh, see "Flatfish"

Sole, frozen:

(*Gorton's Fishmarket Fresh*), 5 oz.	110
Atlantic (*Booth*), 4 oz.	90
breaded, (*Mrs. Paul's* Light), 4¼ oz.	260
breaded, fillets (*Van de Kamp's* Light), 1 fillet	240

Sole dinner, au gratin, frozen (*Healthy Choice*), 11 oz. ... 270

Sole entree, frozen:

in lemon butter (*Gorton's Microwave Entrees*), 1 pkg.	380
with lemon butter sauce (*Healthy Choice*), 8.25 oz.	230
in wine sauce (*Gorton's Microwave Entrees*), 1 pkg.	180

Sorbet (see also "Sherbet" and "Ice"):

key lime or orange and vanilla ice cream (*Häagen Dazs*), ½ cup	200
orange, mandarin (*Dole*), 4 oz.	110
peach or pineapple (*Dole*), 4 oz.	120
raspberry or strawberry (*Dole*), 4 oz.	110
raspberry, red (*Baskin-Robbins*), 1 regular scoop	140
raspberry and vanilla ice cream (*Häagen Dazs*), ½ cup	180

Sorghum, whole-grain, 1 oz. ... 96

Soup, canned, ready-to-serve:

bean (*Grandma Brown's*), 1 cup	190
bean with ham (*Campbell's* Chunky Old Fashioned), 9⅝ oz.	250
bean with ham (*Hormel Micro-Cup* Hearty Soups), 1 container	191
beef:	
(*Progresso*), 9½ oz.	160
barley (*Progresso*), 9½ oz.	150
broth (*College Inn*), 1 cup	18
broth (*Swanson*), 7¼ oz.	18
chunky (*Campbell's* Chunky), 9½ oz.	170
hearty (*Campbell's* Home Cookin'), 10¾ oz.	140
minestone (*Progresso*), 9½ oz.	170
noodle (*Progresso*), 9½ oz.	160
Stroganoff style (*Campbell's* Chunky), 10¾ oz.	320
vegetable (*Hormel Micro-Cup* Hearty Soups), 1 container	71
vegetable (*Lipton Hearty Ones*), 11-oz. container	229
vegetable (*Progresso*), 9½ oz.	150

Soup, canned, ready-to-serve **(cont.)**

borscht (*Gold's*), 8 oz. 100
borscht (*Rokeach*), 1 cup 96
borscht, with beets (*Manischewitz*), 1 cup 80
chickarina (*Progresso*), 9½ oz. 110

chicken:

(*Progresso* Home Style), 9½ oz. 90
barley (*Progresso*), 9¼ oz. 120
broth (*College Inn*), 1 cup 35
broth (*Hain*), 8¾-fl. oz. 70
broth (*Swanson*), 7¼ oz. 30
chunky (*Campbell's* Chunky Old Fashioned), 9½ oz. 150
cream of, with mushrooms (*Progresso*), 9½ oz. 180
creamy mushroom (*Campbell's* Chunky), 9⅜ oz. 290
hearty (*Progresso*), 9½ oz. 140
noodle (*Campbell's* Chunky), 9½ oz. 180
noodle (*Hain*), 9½ oz. 120
noodle (*Hormel Micro-Cup* Hearty Soups), 1 container ... 108
noodle (*Lipton Hearty Ones* Homestyle), 11-oz. container 227
noodle (*Progresso*), 9½ oz. 130
nuggets with vegetable, noodles (*Campbell's* Chunky), 9½ oz. ... 190
with rice (*Campbell's* Chunky), 9½ oz. 140
rice (*Progresso*), 9½ oz. 120
vegetable (*Campbell's* Chunky), 9½ oz. 170
vegetable, country (*Campbell's* Home Cookin'), 9½ oz. .. 110
vegetable and rice (*Hormel Micro-Cup* Hearty Soups), 1 container 114
chili beef (*Campbell's* Chunky), 9¾ oz. 260

clam chowder:

Manhattan (*Campbell's* Chunky), 9½ oz. 150
Manhattan (*Progresso*) 9½ oz. 120
New England (*Campbell's* Chunky), 9½ oz. 250
New England (*Hain*), 9¼ oz. 180
New England (*Hormel Micro-Cup* Hearty Soups), 1 container ... 118
New England (*Progresso*), 9¼ oz. 220
corn chowder (*Progresso*), 9¼ oz. 270
escarole in chicken broth (*Progresso*), 9¼ oz. 30
fisherman's chowder (*Campbell's* Chunky), 9½ oz. 230
ham and bean (*Progresso*), 9½ oz. 180
ham and butterbean (*Campbell's* Chunky), 10¾ oz. can 280
lentil (*Progresso*), 9½ oz. 170
lentil, hearty (*Campbell's* Home Cookin'), 9½ oz. 150
lentil, vegetarian (*Hain*), 9½ oz. 160
lentil with sausage (*Progresso*), 9½ oz. 180
macaroni and bean (*Progresso*), 9½ oz. 170

minestrone:

(*Campbell's* Chunky), 9½ oz. 170

Soup, canned, ready-to-serve, minestrone **(cont.)**

    (*Campbell's* Home Cookin' Old World), 9½ oz. 130
    (*Hain*), 9½ oz. 170
    (*Hormel Micro-Cup* Hearty Soups), 1 container 104
    (*Lipton Hearty Ones*), 11-oz. container 189
    (*Progresso*), 9½ oz. 160
    extra zesty (*Progresso*), 9½ oz. 180
mushroom, cream of (*Progresso*), 9¼ oz. 140
mushroom, creamy (*Campbell's* Chunky), 9⅜ oz. 240
mushroom barley (*Hain*), 9½ oz. 100

pea, split:

    (*Grandma Brown's*), 1 cup 208
    (*Hain*), 9½ oz. 170
    green (*Progresso*), 9½ oz. 180
    with ham (*Campbell's* Chunky), 9½ oz. 210
    with ham (*Campbell's* Home Cookin'), 9½ oz. 190
    with ham (*Progresso*), 9½ oz. 170
sirloin burger (*Campbell's* Chunky), 10¾ oz. can 230
steak, pepper (*Campbell's* Chunky), 9½ oz. 160
steak and potato (*Campbell's* Chunky), 9½ oz. 170

tomato:

    beef with rotini (*Progresso*), 9½ oz. 170
    garden (*Campbell's* Home Cookin'), 9½ oz. 130
    with tortellini (*Progresso*), 9¼ oz. 140
    with vegetables (*Progresso*), 9½ oz. 110
tortellini (*Progresso*), 9½ oz. 80
turkey rice (*Hain*), 9½ oz. 100
turkey vegetable (*Campbell's* Chunky), 9⅜ oz. 150

vegetable:

    (*Campbell's* Chunky), 9½ oz. 140
    (*Progresso*), 9½ oz. 100
    beef (*Campbell's* Chunky Old Fashioned), 9½ oz. 160
    beef (*Campbell's* Home Cookin' Old Fashioned), 9½ oz. ... 140
    chicken (*Hain*), 9½ oz. 120
    country (*Hormel Micro-Cup* Hearty Soups), 1 container 89
    Mediterranean (*Campbell's* Chunky), 9½ oz. 160
    pasta, Italian (*Hain*), 9½ oz. 160
    vegetarian (*Hain*), 9½ oz. 140

Soup, canned, condensed*, 8 oz., except as noted:

asparagus, cream of, with milk (*Campbell's* Creamy Natural) 170
asparagus, cream of, with water (*Campbell's*) 90
barley and mushroom (*Rokeach*), 1 cup 85
bean with bacon (*Campbell's*) 120
bean, black (*Campbell's*) 110
beef (*Campbell's*) 80
beef broth or bouillon (*Campbell's*) 16

Soup, canned, condensed **(cont.)**

beef consomme with gelatin (*Campbell's*)	25
beef noodle (*Campbell's*)	70
beef noodle (*Campbell's* Homestyle)	80
beef, sirloin (*Campbell's* Golden Classic)	70
broccoli, with milk (*Campbell's* Creamy Natural)	140
cauliflower, with milk (*Campbell's* Creamy Natural)	200
celery, cream of (*Campbell's*)	100
cheese, cheddar (*Campbell's*)	130
cheese, nacho, with milk (*Campbell's*)	180
chicken alphabet or barley (*Campbell's*)	70
chicken broth (*Campbell's*)	35
chicken broth and noodles (*Campbell's*)	60
chicken broth and rice (*Campbell's*)	50
chicken, cream of (*Campbell's*)	110
chicken and dumplings (*Campbell's* Chicken 'n Dumplings)	80
chicken gumbo or chicken and stars (*Campbell's*)	60
chicken mushroom, creamy (*Campbell's*)	120
chicken noodle (*Campbell's/Campbell's* Homestyle/Noodle-O's)	70
chicken rice (*Campbell's*)	60
chicken vegetable (*Campbell's*)	70
chicken vegetable, with wild rice (*Campbell's* Golden Classic)	80
chili beef (*Campbell's*)	140
clam chowder, Manhattan (*Campbell's*)	70
clam chowder, Manhattan (*Snow's*), 7.5 oz.	70
clam chowder, New England, with milk (*Campbell's*)	150
clam chowder, New England, with milk (*Gorton's*), ¼ can	140
clam chowder, New England, with milk (*Snow's*), 7.5 oz.	140
corn chowder, with milk (*Snow's*), 7.5 oz.	150
fish chowder, with milk (*Snow's*), 7.5 oz.	130
minestrone (*Campbell's*)	80
mushroom, beefy (*Campbell's*)	60
mushroom, cream of (*Campbell's*)	100
mushroom, golden (*Campbell's*)	80
noodle and ground beef (*Campbell's*)	90
noodle, curly, with chicken (*Campbell's*)	80
onion, cream of, with water and milk (*Campbell's*)	140
onion, French (*Campbell's*)	60
oyster stew, with milk (*Campbell's*)	150
pea, green (*Campbell's*)	160
pea, split, with egg barley (*Rokeach*), 1 cup	132
pea, split, with ham and bacon (*Campbell's*)	150
pepper pot (*Campbell's*)	90
potato, with water and milk (*Campbell's* Creamy Natural)	190
potato, cream of, with water and milk (*Campbell's*)	110
Scotch broth (*Campbell's*)	80

Soup, canned, condensed **(cont.)**

seafood chowder, with milk (*Snow's*), 7.5 oz.	140
shrimp, cream of, with milk (*Campbell's*)	160
spinach, with milk (*Campbell's* Creamy Natural)	160
tomato, with milk (*Campbell's*)	160
tomato, regular or zesty, with water (*Campbell's*)	90
tomato bisque (*Campbell's*)	120
tomato, cream of, with milk (*Campbell's* Homestyle)	180
tomato rice (*Campbell's* Old Fashioned)	110
tortellini and vegetable (*Campbell's* Golden Classic)	80
turkey noodle or vegetable (*Campbell's*)	70
vegetable (*Campbell's*)	80
vegetable beef (*Campbell's*)	70
vegetable, vegetarian (*Campbell's*)	80
wonton (*Campbell's*)	45

Soup, frozen, 6 fl. oz., except as noted:

asparagus, cream of (*Kettle Ready*)	62
asparagus, cream of (*Myers*), 9.75 oz.	152
bean, savory, with ham (*Kettle Ready*)	113
beef, hearty, vegetable (*Kettle Ready*)	85
black bean, with ham (*Kettle Ready*)	154
broccoli, cream of (*Kettle Ready*)	94
broccoli, cream of (*Myers*), 9.75 oz.	174
cauliflower, cream of (*Kettle Ready*)	93
cheddar cheese, cream of (*Kettle Ready*)	158
cheddar cheese and broccoli, cream of (*Kettle Ready*)	137
cheese and broccoli (*Myers*), 9.75 oz.	325
chicken, cream of (*Kettle Ready*)	98
chicken, gumbo or noodle (*Kettle Ready*)	94
chicken, noodle (*Kettle Ready*)	94
chicken, noodle (*Myers*), 9.75 oz.	87
chili, traditional (*Kettle Ready*)	161
chili, jalapeño (*Kettle Ready*)	173
clam chowder, Boston (*Kettle Ready*)	131
clam chowder, Manhattan (*Kettle Ready*)	69
clam chowder, New England (*Kettle Ready*)	116
clam chowder, New England (*Myers*), 9.75 oz.	152
clam chowder, New England (*Stouffer's*), 8 oz.	180
corn and broccoli chowder (*Kettle Ready*)	102
minestrone, hearty (*Kettle Ready*)	104
mushroom, cream of (*Kettle Ready*)	85
onion, French (*Kettle Ready*)	42
pea, split, with ham (*Kettle Ready*)	155
pea, split tortellini, in tomato (*Kettle Ready*)	122
seafood bisque, (*Myers*), 9.75 oz.	163
spinach, cream of (*Myers*), 9.75 oz.	174

Soup, frozen **(cont.)**

spinach, cream of (*Stouffer's*), 8 oz.	210
vegetable, garden (*Kettle Ready*)	85
vegetable beef (*Myers*), 9.75 oz.	120

Soup, mix*, 6 fl. oz., except as noted:

beef (*Lipton Cup-a-Soup*)	44
beef, hearty and noodles (*Lipton*), 7 fl. oz.	107
broccoli, creamy (*Lipton Cup-a-Soup*)	62
broccoli, creamy, and cheese (*Lipton Cup-a-Soup*)	70
broccoli, golden (*Lipton Cup-a-Soup Lite*)	42
cheddar, creamy, with noodles (*Fantastic Noodles*), 7 oz.	178
cheese (*Hain* Savory Soup & Sauce Mix)	250
cheese and broccoli (*Hain* Soup & Recipe Mix)	310

chicken or chicken flavor:

broth (*Lipton Cup-a-Soup*)	20
cream of (*Lipton Cup-a-Soup*)	84
creamy with vegetables (*Lipton Cup-a-Soup*)	93
creamy, with white meat (*Campbell's* Cup 2-Minute Soup)	120
with sweet corn (*Lipton Cup-a-Soup* Country Style)	133
Florentine (*Lipton Cup-a-Soup Lite*)	42
hearty (*Lipton Cup-a-Soup* Country Style)	69
hearty, supreme (*Lipton Cup-a-Soup*)	107
noodle (*Campbell's* Quality Soup & Recipe), 1 cup	100
noodle (*Lipton Cup-a-Soup*)	48
noodle, hearty (*Lipton Cup-a-Soup Lots-a-Noodles*), 7 fl. oz.	110
noodle, with meat (*Lipton Cup-a-Soup*)	46
noodle, with white meat (*Campbell's* Cup 2-Minute Soup)	90
'n rice (*Lipton Cup-a-Soup*)	47
supreme (*Lipton Cup-a-Soup*)	107
vegetable (*Campbell's* Cup 2-Minute Soup)	90
vegetable (*Lipton Cup-a-Soup*)	47

lentil (*Hain* Savory Soup Mix)	130
minestrone (*Hain* Savory Soup Mix)	110
minestrone (*Manischewitz*)	50
mushroom (*Hain* Savory Soup & Recipe Mix)	210
mushroom, cream of (*Lipton Cup-a-Soup*)	71

noodle:

(*Campbell's* Quality Soup & Recipe), 1 cup	110
(*Lipton Cup-a-Soup* Ring Noodle)	47
beef (*Cup O'Noodles*), 1 cup	290
beef flavor (*Oodles of Noodles/Top Ramen*), 1 cup	390
chicken (*Cup O'Noodles*), 1 cup	300
chicken (*Oodles of Noodles/Top Ramen*), 1 cup	400
chicken, country (*Cup O'Noodles* Hearty), 1 cup	300
chicken, with chicken broth (*Campbell's* Cup 2 Minute Soup)	100
chicken, with chicken broth (*Lipton Ring-O-Noodle*), 1 cup	71

Soup, mix, noodle (cont.)

Oriental or pork (*Oodles of Noodles/Top Ramen*), 1 cup	390
shrimp or savory seafood (*Cup O'Noodles*), 1 cup	300
vegetable or vegetable beef (*Cup O'Noodles* Hearty), 1 cup	290
onion:	
(*Campbell's* Quality Soup & Recipe), 1 cup	50
(*Hain* Savory Soup, Dip & Recipe Mix)	50
(*Lipton Cup-a-Soup*)	27
beefy (*Lipton*), 1 cup	29
creamy (*Lipton Cup-a-Soup*)	70
golden, with chicken broth (*Lipton*), 1 cup	62
mushroom (*Campbell's* Quality Soup & Recipe), 1 cup	50
Oriental (*Lipton Cup-a-Soup* Lite)	45
pea, green (*Lipton Cup-a-Soup*)	113
pea, split (*Hain* Savory Soup Mix)	310
pea, split (*Manischewitz*)	45
pea, Virginia (*Lipton Cup-a-Soup* Country Style)	148
potato leek (*Hain* Savory Soup Mix)	260
tomato (*Hain* Savory Soup & Recipe Mix)	220
tomato (*Lipton Cup-a-Soup*)	103
vegetable:	
(*Hain* Savory Soup Mix)	80
(*Lipton*), 1 cup	39
(*Manischewitz*)	50
curry, with noodles (*Fantastic Noodles*), 7 oz.	150
garden (*Lipton Lots-a-Noodles Cup-a-Soup*), 7 fl. oz.	123
harvest (*Lipton Cup-a-Soup* Country Style)	91
miso, with noodles (*Fantastic Noodles*), 7 oz.	152
noodle with meatballs, (*Lipton Cup-a-Soup* Country Style)	95
spring (*Lipton Cup-a-Soup*)	33
tomato, with noodles (*Fantastic Noodles*), 7 oz.	158
vegetable beef, with sirloin (*Campbell's* Cup 2 Minute Soup)	110
Sour cream, see "Cream"	
Souse loaf (*Kahn's*), 1 slice	90
Soy bean "milk", fluid, 4 oz.	37
Soy sauce:	
(*Kikkoman*), 1 tbsp.	10
(*La Choy/La Choy* Lite), 1 tsp.	<1
Soybean, dried:	
boiled, ½ cup	149
roasted, ½ cup	405
Soybean, green:	
raw, shelled, ½ cup	188
boiled, drained, ½ cup	127
Soybean, sprouted, mature seeds:	
raw, ½ cup	45

Soybean, sprouted **(cont.)**

steamed, ½ cup	38
stir-fried in vegetable oil, 4 oz.	142

Soybean curd, see "Tofu"

Soybean kernels, roasted and toasted, 1 oz.	129

Spaghetti, see "Pasta"

Spaghetti, canned, 7⅜ oz., except as noted:

in tomato sauce, with cheese (*Franco-American*)	190
in tomato sauce, with cheese (*Heinz*), 7¾ oz.	160
in tomato sauce, with meat (*Heinz*), 7½ oz.	170
in tomato and cheese sauce (*Franco-American SpaghettiOs*), 7½ oz.	170
with franks (*Van Camp's Skettee Weenee*), 1 cup	243
with franks, sliced, beef, in tomato sauce (*Franco-American SpaghettiOs*)	220
with meatballs, in sauce (*Buitoni*), 7.5 oz.	190
with meatballs, in tomato sauce (*Franco-American*)	220
with meatballs, in tomato sauce (*Franco-American SpaghettiOs*)	210

Spaghetti dinner, frozen:

and meatballs (*Banquet*), 10 oz.	290
and meatballs (*Swanson*), 12½ oz.	370

Spaghetti entree, frozen:

with Italian sausage (*The Budget Gourmet*), 10 oz.	400
with Italian style meatballs (*Swanson* Homestyle Recipe), 13 oz.	460
with meat sauce (*Banquet* Casserole), 8 oz.	270
with meat sauce (*Healthy Choice*), 10 oz.	310
with meat sauce (*Stouffer's*), 12⅞ oz.	370
with meatballs (*Stouffer's*), 12⅝ oz.	380

Spaghetti sauce, see "Pasta sauce"

Spaghetti squash, baked or boiled, drained, ½ cup	23
Spaghettini entree, packaged (*Hormel Top Shelf*), 1 serving	240

Spareribs, see "Pork entree"

Spice Leaf:

(*Kahn's* Family Pack), 1 slice	70
beef (*Kahn's* Family Pack), 1 slice	60

Spinach:

fresh, raw, trimmed, 1 oz. leaf or ½ cup chopped	6
fresh, boiled, drained, ½ cup	21
canned, chopped or whole (*Del Monte*), ½ cup	25
canned, slice or chopped, curly (*Allens*), ½ cup	28

frozen:

(*Green Giant Harvest Fresh*), ½ cup	25
leaf or chopped (*Birds Eye*), 3.3 oz.	20
creamed (*Birds Eye* Combinations), 3 oz.	60
creamed (*Green Giant*), ½ cup	60
creamed (*Stouffer's*), 4½ oz.	170
in butter sauce, cut (*Green Giant*), ½ cup	40

Spinach au gratin, frozen (*The Budget Gourmet*), 6 oz. 120
Spinach souffle, frozen (*Stouffer's*), 4 oz. 140
Spiny lobster, mixed species, raw, meat only, 4 oz. 128
Split peas, boiled, ½ cup 116
Spot, fresh, raw, meat only, 4 oz. 139
Squash, see specific squash listings
Squash, summer, all varieties, boiled, drained, sliced, ½ cup 18
Squash, winter:
fresh, all varieties, baked, cubed, ½ cup 39
frozen, cooked (*Birds Eye*), 4 oz. 45
Squid, raw, meat only, 4 oz. 104
Steak sauce:
(A.1), 1 tbsp. 12
(*Heinz 57*), 1 tbsp. 15
(*Lea & Perrins*), 1 oz. 40
(*Steak Supreme*), 1 tbsp. 20
Strawberry:
fresh, trimmed, ½ cup 23
frozen, in light syrup, halved (*Birds Eye* Quick Thaw Pouch), 5 oz. ... 90
frozen, in light syrup, whole (*Birds Eye*), 5 oz. 80
frozen, in syrup, halved (*Birds Eye* Quick Thaw Pouch), 5 oz. 120
Strawberry flavor drink mix (*Nestlé Quik*), ¾ oz. 80
Strawberry fruit drink (*Wylers* Fruit Slush), 4 fl. oz. 157
Strawberry nectar (*Libby's*), 6 fl. oz. 110
Strawberry topping:
(*Kraft*), 1 tbsp. 50
(*Smucker's*), 2 tbsp. 120
Stuffing, ½ cup, except as noted:
all varieties (*Pepperidge Farm*), 1 oz. 110
frozen, chicken or cornbread (*Green Giant Stuffing Originals*) 170
frozen, mushroom (*Green Giant Stuffing Originals*) 150
frozen, wild rice (*Green Giant Stuffing Originals*) 160
mix*, beef, chicken flavor, long grain and wild rice, mushroom and
onion, or with rice (*Stove Top*), ½ cup 180
mix*, cornbread, pork, savory herbs, San Francisco, or turkey (*Stove
Top*), ½ cup 170
Sturgeon, mixed species, meat only:
baked, broiled, or microwaved, 4 oz. 153
smoked, meat only, 4 oz. 196
Succotash:
canned (*S&W* Country Style), ½ cup 80
frozen (*Frosty Acres*), 3.3 oz. 100
Sucker, white, meat only, raw, 4 oz. 104
Sugar, beet or cane:
brown, 1 cup packed 821
granulated, 1 cup 770

Sugar (cont.)

granulated, 1 tbsp.	46
granulated, 1 packet, approx. .2 oz.	23
powdered or confectioners, 1 cup, unsifted	462
powdered or confectioners, 1 tbsp., unsifted	31

Sugar, turbinado (*Hain*), 1 tbsp. 50

Sugar apple, 1 medium, 2⅞" diam. × 3¼", approx. 9.9 oz. ... 146

Summer sausage (see also ''Thuringer cervelat''):

(*Eckrich*), 1-oz. slice	80
(*Hillshire Farm*), 2 oz.	180
(*Hormel* Perma-Fresh), 2 slices	140
(*Hormel* Tangy, Chub, or Thuringer), 1 oz.	90
(*Oscar Mayer*), .8-oz. slice	73
beef (*Hormel* Beefy), 1 oz.	100
with cheese (*Hillshire Farm*), 2 oz.	200

Sunflower seeds (*Frito-Lay's* Kernels), 1 oz. 180

Sunflower seed butter, 1 tbsp. 93

Swedish sausage (*Hickory Farms*), 1 oz. 100

Sweet potato:

raw, trimmed, cubed, ½ cup	72
baked in skin, 1 medium, 5" × 2" diam.	118
boiled, without skin, mashed, ½ cup	172

canned, ½ cup:

in water, cut (*Allens*)	70
in light syrup (*Joan of Arc/Princella/Royal Prince*)	110
in syrup, whole or cut (*Allens*)	90
in heavy syrup (*Joan of Arc/Princella/Royal Prince*)	130
in extra heavy syrup (*S&W* Southern)	139
in pineapple orange sauce (*Joan of Arc/Princella/Royal Prince*)	210
candied (*Joan of Arc/Princella/Royal Prince*)	240
candied (*S&W*)	180
mashed (*Joan of Arc/Princella/Royal Prince*)	90
frozen, candied (*Mrs. Paul's*), 4 oz.	190
frozen, candied, with apples (*Mrs. Paul's* Sweets 'n Apples), 4 oz.	160

Sweet and sour sauce:

(*Kikkoman*), 1 tbsp.	18
(*La Choy*), 1 tbsp.	30

Swiss chard, boiled, drained, chopped, ½ cup 18

Swiss steak, see ''Beef dinner''

Swordfish, meat only, baked, broiled or microwaved, 4 oz. 176

Syrup, see specific listings

Szechwan sauce, hot and spicy (*La Choy*), 1 oz. 48

T

Food and Measure	Calories

Tabbouleh mix* (*Near East*), ½ cup 170
Taco dinner mix:
(*Old El Paso*), 1 taco 87
(*Tio Sancho* Dinner Kit):
   sauce, 2 oz. 62
   seasoning, 1.25 oz. 104
   shell, 1 piece 64
Taco dip:
(*Wise*), 2 tbsp. 12
and sauce (*Hain*), 4 tbsp. 25
Taco John's:
beans, refried, 9.5 oz. 331
burrito, bean, 5 oz. 249
burrito, beef, 5 oz. 355
burrito, combo, 5 oz. 302
burrito, smothered, with green chili, 12.3 oz. 405
burrito, smothered, with Texas chili, 12.3 oz. 518
burrito, super, 8.3 oz. 434
chili, Texas, 9.5 oz. 430
chimi, 12 oz. 487
churro, 1.2 oz. 122
enchilada, 7 oz. 369
nachos, 4 oz. 407
nachos, super, 11.25 oz. 657
Potato Ole Large, 6 oz. 414
taco, burger, 6 oz. 332
taco, *Bravo,* super, 8 oz. 485
taco, regular, 4.3 oz. 228
taco, soft shell, 5 oz. 276
taco salad, super, 12.3 oz. 450
tostada, 4.3 oz. 228

Taco sauce (see also "Salsa"):

(*Lawry's* Sauce'n Seasoner), ¼ cup	40
chunky (*Lawry's*), ¼ cup	22
hot or mild (*Del Monte*), ¼ cup	15
hot or mild (*Ortega*), 1 oz.	12
mild (*Enrico's* No Salt Added), 2 tbsp.	14
mild, medium or hot (*Old El Paso*), 2 tbsp.	10
Western style (*Ortega*), 1 oz.	8

Taco seasoning:

(*Old El Paso*), 1 pkg.	100
mix (*Lawry's* Seasoning Blends), 1 pkg.	118
mix (*Tio Sancho*), 1.51 oz.	132
mix, meat (*Ortega*), 1 oz. dry	90

Taco shell:

(*Old El Paso*), 1 piece	55
(*Old El Paso Super Size*), 1 piece	100
(*Ortega*), 1 piece	50
(*Tio Sancho*), 1 piece	64
(*Tio Sancho Super*), 1 piece	94
corn (*Azteca*), 1 piece	60
miniature (*Old El Paso*), 3 pieces	70
salad shell, flour (*Azteca*), 1 piece	200
Taco starter (*Del Monte*), 8 oz.	140
Tahini mix (*Casbah*), 1 oz. dry	25

Tamale, canned:

(*Old El Paso*), 2 pieces	190
(*Wolf* Brand), scant cup, 7.5 oz.	328
beef (*Hormel/Hormel* Hot 'N Spicy), 2 pieces	140
with sauce (*Van Camp's*), 1 cup	293
Tamale, frozen, beef (*Hormel*), 1 piece	140
Tamale dinner, frozen (*Patio*), 13 oz.	470
Tamalito, canned, in chile gravy (*Dennison's*), 7½ oz.	310
Tamarind, fresh, 1 medium, 3″ × 1″, approx. .2 oz.	5

Tangerine:

fresh, 1 medium, 2⅜″ diam., 4.1 oz.	37
canned (*Del Monte* Mandarin Oranges), 5½ oz.	100
canned, in light syrup (*Dole*), ½ cup	76
canned, in light syrup (*Empress*), 5½ oz.	100

Tangerine juice:

fresh, ½ cup	53
chilled (*Dole Pure & Light* Mandarin Tangerine), 6 fl. oz.	97
chilled or frozen*, (*Minute Maid*), 6 fl. oz.	91
Taro, cooked, sliced, ½ cup	94
Taro chips, ½ cup	57
Taro leaves, steamed, ½ cup	18
Taro shoots, cooked, sliced, ½ cup	10

Tarragon, ground, 1 tsp. 5
Tartar sauce, 1 tbsp.:
(*Hellmann's/Best Foods*) 70
all varieties (*Sauceworks*) 70
Tea:
brewed (*Nestea*), 6 fl. oz. 0
brewed, caffeine-free (*Celestial Seasonings*), 8 fl. oz. 4
iced:
    (*Shasta*), 12 fl. oz. 124
    with lemon and sugar (*Nestea*), 8 fl. oz. 70
    instant, lemon flavored (*Lipton*), 6 fl. oz. 55
    instant, sugar sweetened (*Lipton*), 6 fl. oz. 37
    instant, unsweetened (*Nestea* 100%), 8 fl. oz. 2
    instant, unsweetened, lemon flavor (*Nestea*), 8 fl. oz. .. 6
Tempeh, 1 oz. 56
Teriyaki sauce:
(*Kikkoman*), 1 tbsp. 15
(*Kikkoman* Baste and Glaze), 1 tbsp. 27
(*La Choy* Sauce & Marinade), 1 oz. 30
thick and rich (*La Choy*), 1 oz. 41
Thuringer cervelat (see also "Summer sausage"):
(*Hillshire Farm*), 2 oz. 180
(*Hormel Old Smokehouse/Hormel* Viking Chub), 1 oz. 90
(*Hormel Old Smokehouse,* chub or sliced), 1 oz. 100
Thyme, ground, 1 tsp. 4
Tilefish, meat only, baked, broiled, or microwaved, 4 oz. 167
Toaster muffins and pastries, 1 piece:
all varieties (*Toaster Strudel* Breakfast Pastries) 190
apple cinnamon (*Pepperidge Farm* Toaster Tarts), 2 oz. 170
apple spice or banana nut (*Toaster Muffins*) 130
banana nut (*Thomas' Toast-r-Cakes*) 111
blueberry (*Thomas' Toast-r-Cakes*) 108
blueberry, wild, Maine (*Toaster Muffins*) 120
bran (*Thomas' Toast-r-Cakes*) 103
cheese or strawberry (*Pepperidge Farm* Toaster Tarts), 2 oz. 190
corn (*Thomas' Toast-r-Cakes*) 120
corn, old fashioned or raisin bran (*Toaster Muffins*) 120
Tofu:
raw, firm, ½ cup 183
flavored, country herb or Chinese 5-spice (*Nasoya*), 5 oz. 150
pasteurized (*Frieda* of California), approx. 4.2 oz. pkg. 86
salted and fermented (fuyu), 1 oz. 33
Tomato, green:
fresh, 1 medium, 2⅗" diam., approx. 4.75 oz. 30
pickled, kosher (*Claussen*), 1 oz. 5

Tomato, red, ripe:

fresh, raw, 1 medium, 2⅗" diam., approx. 4.75 oz.	26
fresh, boiled, ½ cup	32

canned, ½ cup:

whole (*Hunt's*)	20
whole, peeled, with liquid (*Del Monte*)	25
whole, peeled, or Italian-style pear (*Contadina*)	25
crushed (*Hunt's*)	25
crushed, in puree (*Contadina*)	30
Italian-style or with jalapeños (*Contadina*)	35
Mexican-style (*S&W*)	40
puree (*Contadina*)	40
stewed (*Contadina*)	35
stewed (*Del Monte*)	35
wedges, with liquid (*Del Monte*)	30
Tomato-beef cocktail (*Beefamato*), 6 fl. oz.	80
Tomato and chili cocktail (*Snap-E-Tom*), 6 fl. oz.	40
Tomato-clam juice cocktail (*Clamato*), 6 fl. oz.	96

Tomato juice, canned, 6 fl. oz.:

(*Campbell's*)	35
(*Hunt's*)	30
(*Welch's*)	35

Tomato paste, canned:

(*Contadina*), 2 oz. or approx. ¼ cup	50
(*Del Monte*), ¾ cup	150
(*Hunt's*), 2 oz.	45
Italian (*Contadina*), 2 oz. or approx. ¼ cup	65

Tomato sauce (see also "Pasta sauce"):

(*Contadina*), ½ cup	30
(*Contadina* Thick and Zesty), ½ cup	40
(*Del Monte/Del Monte* No Salt Added), 1 cup	70
(*Hunt's*), 4 oz.	30
(*Hunt's* Special), 4 oz.	35
Italian style (*Contadina*), ½ cup	30
marinara, canned or in jars (*Buitoni*), 4 fl. oz.	70
marinara, refrigerated (*Contadina Fresh*), 7.5 oz.	100
with onions (*Del Monte*), 1 cup	100

Tongue:

fresh, beef, simmered, 4 oz.	321
fresh, veal, braised, 4 oz.	229
canned, pork, cured (*Hormel,* 8 lb.), 3 oz.	190

Toppings, dessert, see specific listings

Tortellini, refrigerated, 4.5 oz.:

egg, with cheese or meat (*Contadina Fresh*)	380
egg, with chicken and prosciutto (*Contadina Fresh*)	370

Tortellini (cont.)

spinach, with cheese or meat (*Contadina Fresh*) 380
spinach, with chicken and prosciutto (*Contadina Fresh*) 340

Tortellini dishes, frozen:

beef, with marinara sauce (*Stouffer's*), 10 oz. 360
cheese (*The Budget Gourmet* Side Dish), 5.5 oz. 180
cheese, in Alfredo sauce (*Stouffer's*), 8⅞ oz. 600
cheese, marinara (*Green Giant* One Serving), 5.5 oz. 260
cheese, with tomato sauce (*Stouffer's*), 9⅝ oz. 360
cheese, with vinaigrette dressing (*Stouffer's*), 6⅞ oz. 400
Provencale (*Green Giant* Microwave Garden Gourmet), 1 pkg. 210
veal, in Alfredo sauce (*Stouffer's*), 8⅝ oz. 500

Tortellini dishes, packaged:

cheese with shrimp and seafood (*Hormel Top Shelf*), 10 oz. 278
in marinara sauce (*Hormel Top Shelf*), 10 oz. 211

Tortilla, 1 piece:

corn (*Azteca*) 45
corn (*Old El Paso*) 60
flour (*Azteca*), 9″ diam. 130
flour (*Azteca*), 7″ diam. 80
flour (*Old El Paso*) 150

Tortilla chips, see "Corn chips and similar snacks"

Tortilla entree, frozen, (*Stouffer's* Grande), 9⅝ oz. 530

Tostaco shell (*Old El Paso*), 1 piece 100

Tostada shell:

(*Old El Paso*), 2 pieces 110
(*Ortega*), 1 piece 50
(*Tio Sancho*), 1 piece 67

Tree fern, cooked, chopped, ½ cup 28

Trout, meat only:

fresh, mixed species, raw, 4 oz. 168
fresh, rainbow, baked, broiled or microwaved, 4 oz. 171

Tumeric, ground, 1 tsp. 8

Tuna:

fresh, bluefin, meat only, baked, broiled or microwaved, 4 oz. 209
fresh, skipjack, meat only, raw, 4 oz. 117
fresh, yellowfin, meat only, raw, 4 oz. 123

canned in oil, drained 2 oz.:

    chunk light or chunk white (*Bumble Bee*) 110
    chunk light (*Star-Kist*) 150
    chunk or solid white, Albacore (*Star-Kist*) 140
    solid light (*Star-Kist* Prime Catch) 150
    solid white, albacore (*Bumble Bee*) 100
    solid white, albacore (*S&W* Fancy) 160

canned in water, drained, 2 oz.:

    chunk light (*Star-Kist*) 60

Tuna (cont.)

chunk light (*Star-Kist* Select 60% Less Salt) 65
chunk white (*Star-Kist/Star-Kist* Select 60% Less Salt) 70
solid white, albacore (*Bumble Bee*) 60
solid white, albacore (*Star-Kist*) 70
Tuna entree, frozen (*Banquet*), 7 oz. 540
Tuna noodle casserole, frozen (*Stouffer's*), 10 oz. 310
Tuna sandwich, frozen (*Mrs. Paul's Microwave*), 3.25-oz. sandwich ... 200
Turbot, European, meat only, raw, 4 oz. 108
Turkey, fresh:
fryer-roaster, roasted:
 meat and skin, 4 oz. 195
 breast, with skin, ½ breast, 12.1 oz. 526
 breast, meat only, ½ breast, 10.8 oz. 413
 leg, with skin, 1 leg, 8.6 oz. 418
 leg, meat only, 1 leg, 7.9 oz. 355
 wing, with skin, 1 wing, 3.2 oz. 186
 wing, meat only, 1 wing, 2.1 oz. 98
young hen, roasted:
 meat and skin, 4 oz. 247
 breast, with skin, 4 oz. 220
 leg, with skin, 1 leg, 15.8 oz. 955
 wing, with skin, 1 wing, 6.1 oz. 414
young tom, roasted:
 meat and skin, 4 oz. 229
 breast, with skin, 4 oz. 214
 leg, with skin, 4 oz. 234
 wing, with skin, 4 oz. 251
Turkey, frozen or refrigerated:
breast, raw:
 (*Longacre* Cook-N-Bag), 1 oz. 27
 (*Longacre* Ready-to-Cook), 1 oz. 39
 with gravy (*Norbest*), 4 oz. 115
 steaks, cubed (*Norbest*), 4-oz. steak 135
 strips and tips or tenderloin (*Norbest Tasti-Lean*), 4 oz. ... 135
breast, cooked:
 (*Longacre* Cook-N-Bag), 1 oz. 38
 barbecued, hickory smoked or honey roasted (*Louis Rich*), 1 oz. .. 35
 barbecue or oven-prepared, quarter (*Mr. Turkey* Chub), 1 oz. 34
 oven-roasted and dark, roasted (*Louis Rich*), 1 oz. 30
cutlets, raw (*Norbest Tasti-Lean*), 4 oz. 135
dark meat, hickory smoked, roasted (*Louis Rich*), 1 oz. 35
dark meat, skinless, roasted (*Swift Butterball*), 3.5 oz. 195
drumsticks (*Louis Rich*), 1 oz. cooked 55
hindquarter roast (*Land O' Lakes*), 3 oz. 140
thigh (*Louis Rich*), 1 oz. cooked 65

Turkey, frozen or refrigerated **(cont.)**
white and dark, with skin, roasted (*Swift Butterball*), 3.5 oz. 195
whole, cooked, boneless or boneless, smoked (*Norbest*), 1 oz. 42
wings (*Louis Rich* Drumettes), 1 oz. cooked 50
wings, regular and portions (*Louis Rich*), 1 oz. cooked 55
Turkey, boneless and luncheon meat (see also "Turkey bologna,"
    etc.):
breast:
    (*Butterball Deli* No Salt Added), 1 oz. 45
    (*Butterball* Cold Cuts), 1-oz. slice 30
    (*Butterball Slice 'n Serve*), 1 oz. 35
    (*Hormel* Perma-Fresh), 2 slices 60
    (*Longacre* Catering or Gourmet), 1 oz. 35
    (*Longacre* Premium), 1 oz. 30
    (*Louis Rich*), 1 oz. 45
    (*Mr. Turkey*), 1 oz. 31
    golden (*Boar's Head*), 1 oz. 35
    golden, skinless (*Boar's Head*), 1 oz. 30
    honey-roasted (*Louis Rich*), 1-oz. slice 30
    oven roasted (*Louis Rich*), 1-oz. slice 30
    oven roasted (*Oscar Mayer*), .75-oz. slice 22
    roast (*Louis Rich*), 1 oz. 40
    with skin (*Norbest* Blue or Orange Label), 1 oz. 28
    skinless (*Longacre* Gourmet or Premium), 1 oz. 30
    skinless (*Norbest* Blue, Orange, or Yellow Label), 1 oz. 26
    sliced (*Louis Rich*), 1 oz. 40
smoked:
    (*Butterball* Cold Cuts), 1-oz. slice 35
    (*Hormel* Perma-Fresh), 2 slices 60
    (*Louis Rich*), .7-oz. slice 20
    (*Mr. Turkey*), 1 oz. 31
    (*Oscar Mayer*), .75-oz. slice 20
    hickory (*Butterball Slice 'n Serve*), 1 oz. 35
breast and thigh (*Norbest* Blue Label), 1 oz. 31
loaf (*Louis Rich*), 1-oz. slice 45
luncheon loaf, spiced (*Mr. Turkey*), 1 oz. 51
roll, white meat (*Norbest* Orange Label), 1 oz. 29
smoked (*Butterball* Cold Cuts), 1-oz. slice 35
smoked (*Louis Rich*), 1-oz. slice 30
steaks or tenderloin (*Louis Rich*), 1 oz. 40
Turkey, canned:
chunk (*Hormel*), 6¾ oz. 230
white or white and dark meat (*Swanson*), 2½ oz. 90
Turkey, ground:
raw (*Norbest*), 1 oz. 45
cooked (*Longacre*), 1 oz. 60

Turkey, ground (cont.)

cooked (*Louis Rich* 85% Lean), 1 oz.	60
cooked (*Louis Rich* 90% Lean), 1 oz.	50

Turkey bologna:

(*Butterball* Cold Cuts), 1-oz. slice	70
regular or mild (*Louis Rich*), 1-oz. slice	60

Turkey dinner, frozen:

(*Banquet*), 10.5 oz.	390
(*Banquet Extra Helpings*), 19 oz.	750
(*Swanson*), 11½ oz.	350
(*Swanson Hungry-Man*), 17 oz.	550
breast, Dijon (*The Budget Gourmet*), 11.2 oz.	340
breast, roast (*Stouffer's Dinner Supreme*), 1¾ oz.	330
breast, sliced (*The Budget Gourmet*), 11.1 oz.	290
breast, sliced, with mushroom gravy (*Le Menu*), 10½ oz.	270
with dressing and gravy (*Armour Classics*), 11.5 oz.	320

Turkey entree, frozen:

(*Tyson Gourmet Selection*), 11.5 oz.	380
a la king, with rice (*The Budget Gourmet*), 10 oz.	390
casserole (*Pillsbury Microwave Classic*), 1 pkg.	430
casserole with gravy & dressing (*Stouffer's*), 9¾ oz.	360
with dressing and potatoes (*Swanson* Homestyle Recipe), 9 oz.	290
glazed (*The Budget Gourmet* Slim Selects), 9 oz.	270
pie (*Banquet*), 7 oz.	510
pie (*Banquet* Supreme Microwave), 7 oz.	430
pie (*Morton*), 7 oz.	420
pie (*Stouffer's*), 10 oz.	540
pie (*Swanson* Pot Pie), 7 oz.	390
pie (*Swanson Hungry-Man*), 16 oz.	750
sliced and gravy (*Banquet Family Entree*), 8 oz.	150
sliced and gravy (*Freezer Queen Family Supper*), 7 oz.	230
sliced, in mild curry with rice pilaf (*Right Course*), 8¾ oz.	320
tetrazzini (*Stouffer's*), 10 oz.	380

Turkey frankfurters:

(*Butterball*), 1 link	140
(*Longacre*), 1 oz.	66
(*Mr. Turkey*, 10 lb.), 1.6-oz. link	106
cheese (*Mr. Turkey*), 1.6-oz. link	109

Turkey gravy:

canned (*Franco-American*), 2 oz.	30
canned (*Heinz*), 2 oz.	30
with chunky turkey (*Hormel Great Beginnings*), 5 oz.	138
mix* (*Lawry's*), 1 cup	102
mix* (*McCormick/Schilling*), ¼ cup	22

Turkey ham:

(*Butterball Slice 'n Serve/Butterball* Cold Cuts), 1 oz.	35

Turkey ham (cont.)
(*Louis Rich* unsliced, round or water added), 1 oz. 35
chopped (*Louis Rich*), 1-oz. slice 40
honey cured (*Butterball* Coldcuts), 1-oz. slice 35
honey cured (*Louis Rich*), .75-oz. slice 25
roll (*Norbest*), 1 oz. 31
sliced (*Butterball* Deli Thin), 1 oz. 35
sliced (*Longacre*), 1 oz. 33
smoked, regular or chub (*Mr. Turkey*), 1 oz. 32
Turkey pastrami:
(*Butterball* Cold Cuts), 1-oz. slice 30
(*Butterball Slice 'n Serve*), 1 oz. 35
(*Louis Rich* Round), 1-oz. slice 35
(*Louis Rich* Square), .8-oz. slice 25
(*Mr. Turkey*), 1 oz. 28
Turkey patty, cooked (*Louis Rich*), 2.9-oz. patty 220
Turkey pie, see "Turkey entree"
Turkey salami:
(*Butterball Deli/Slice 'n Serve*), 1 oz. 50
(*Louis Rich*), 1-oz. slice 55
cotto (*Louis Rich*), 1-oz. slice 50
sliced (*Longacre*), 1 oz. 52
Turkey sausage:
(*Butterball*), 1 oz. 50
(*Louis Rich*), 1 oz. 50
(*Norbest Tasti-Lean,* Chub or Links), 1 oz. 53
breakfast (*Mr. Turkey*), 1 oz. 58
breakfast, ground, cooked (*Louis Rich*), 1 oz. 55
Polish (*Louis Rich* Polska Kielbasa), 1 oz. 50
smoked (*Mr. Turkey*), 1 oz. 47
Turkey sticks, cooked (*Louis Rich*), 1 stick 80
Turkey summer sausage (*Louis Rich*), 1-oz. slice 55
Turmeric, ground (*Spice Islands*), 1 tsp. 7
Turnip:
fresh, boiled, drained, cubed, ½ cup 14
canned (*Stokely*), ½ cup 20
Turnip greens:
fresh, raw, trimmed, 1 lb. 85
fresh, boiled, drained, chopped, ½ cup 15
canned, chopped (*Allens*), ½ cup 21
frozen, chopped (*Frosty Acres*), 3.3 oz. 20
frozen, chopped or with turnips (*Seabrook*), 3.3 oz. 20
Turnip root:
canned, diced (*Allens*), ½ cup 16
frozen, diced (*Southern*), 3.5 oz. 17

Turnover, frozen, 1 piece:
apple (*Pepperidge Farm*) 300
blueberry, cherry, peach, or raspberry (*Pepperidge Farm*) 310

V

Food and Measure	Calories

Vanilla extract, pure (*Virginia Dare*), 1 tsp. 20
Vanilla flavor drink mix:
(*Pillsbury* Instant Breakfast), 1 pouch 140
Veal, retail cuts:
cubed for stew (leg and shoulder), lean only, braised or stewed,
  4 oz. 213
ground, broiled, 4 oz. 195
ground, broiled, 1 cup, approx. 4.1 oz. 200
leg (top round):
  lean with fat, braised or stewed, 4 oz. 239
  lean with fat, braised or stewed, diced, 1 cup, approx. 4.9 oz. 295
  lean with fat, roasted, 12.6 oz. (1 lb. raw boneless) 574
  lean with fat, roasted, 4 oz. 181
  lean only, braised or stewed, 4 oz. 230
  lean only, braised or stewed, diced, 1 cup, approx. 4.9 oz. 284
  lean only, roasted, 12.4 oz. (1 lb. raw boneless, with fat) 528
  lean only, roasted, 4 oz. 170
loin:
  lean with fat, braised or stewed, 4 oz. 322
  lean with fat, roasted, 8.1 oz. (1 lb. raw with bone) 498
  lean with fat, roasted, 4 oz. 246
  lean only, braised or stewed, 4 oz. 256
  lean only, roasted, 8.5 oz. (1 lb. raw with bone and fat) 364
  lean only, roasted, 4 oz. 198
rib:
  lean with fat, braised or stewed, 4 oz. 285

Veal, rib (cont.)

lean with fat, roasted, 8.5 oz. (1 lb. raw with bone)	548
lean with fat, roasted, 4 oz.	259
lean only, braised or stewed, 4 oz.	247
lean only, roasted, 7.6 oz. (1 lb. raw with bone and fat)	381
lean only, roasted, 4 oz.	201

shoulder, whole:

lean with fat, braised or stewed, 4 oz.	259
lean with fat, braised or stewed, diced, 1 cup, 4.9 oz.	319
lean with fat, roasted, 4 oz.	209
lean only, braised or stewed, 4 oz.	226
lean only, braised or stewed, diced, 1 cup, 4.9 oz.	279
lean only, roasted, 4 oz.	193

shoulder, arm:

lean with fat, braised, 4 oz.	268
lean with fat, roasted, 10 oz. (13.6 oz. raw steak with bone).	518
lean with fat, roasted, 4 oz.	208
lean only, braised, 4 oz.	228
lean only, roasted, 9.6 oz., (13.6 oz. raw steak with bone and fat)	447
lean only, roasted, 4 oz.	186

shoulder, blade:

lean with fat, braised or stewed, 4 oz.	255
lean with fat, braised, diced, 1 cup, 4.9 oz.	315
lean with fat, roasted, 8.6 oz. (1 lb. raw with bone)	452
lean with fat, roasted, 4 oz.	211
lean only, braised or stewed, 4 oz.	224
lean only, braised or stewed, diced, 1 cup, 4.9 oz.	277
lean only, roasted, 8.3 oz. (1 lb. raw with bone and fat)	406
lean only, roasted, 4 oz.	194

sirloin:

lean with fat, braised, 4 oz.	286
lean with fat, braised, diced, 1 cup, 4.9 oz.	353
lean with fat, roasted, 9.5 oz. (1 lb. raw with bone)	542
lean with fat, roasted, 4 oz.	229
lean only, braised, 4 oz.	231
lean only, braised, diced, 1 cup, 4.9 oz.	286
lean only, roasted, 8.9 oz. (1 lb. raw with bone and fat)	423
lean only, roasted, 4 oz.	191

Veal dinner, frozen:

Marsala (*Le Menu Light Style*), 10 oz.	260
parmigiana (*Armour Classics*), 11.25 oz.	400
parmigiana (*Swanson*), 12¼ oz.	450
parmigiana (*Swanson Hungry-Man*), 18¼ oz.	560

Veal entree, frozen:

parmigiana (*Swanson* Homestyle), 10 oz.	330
parmigiana, breaded (*Banquet Cookin' Bags*), 4 oz.	230

Veal entree (cont.)

parmigiana, breaded (*Freezer Queen Deluxe Family Suppers*), 7 oz. .. | 300
parmigiana, patty (*Banquet Family Entrees*), 8 oz. .... | 370

Vegetable entree, canned:

chow mein, meatless (*La Choy*), ¾ cup .... | 35
stew (*Dinty Moore*), 8 oz. .... | 170

Vegetable juice, 6 fl. oz.:

("*V-8*" Regular or Spicy Hot) .... | 35
("*V-8*" No Salt Added) .... | 40
(*Veryfine* 100%), 6 fl. oz. .... | 32
hearty or hot and spicy (*Smucker's*), 8 fl. oz. .... | 58

Vegetables, mixed (see also specific listings):

canned, ½ cup, except as noted:

(*Del Monte*) .... | 40
(*Green Giant* Garden Medley) .... | 45
Chinese (*La Choy*) .... | 12
chop suey (*La Choy*) .... | 9

frozen, ½ cup, except as noted:

(*Birds Eye*), 3.3 oz. .... | 60
(*Green Giant*) .... | 40
(*Green Giant Harvest Fresh*) .... | 40
Chinese style (*Birds Eye* Stir Fry), 3.3 oz. .... | 35
in Dijon mustard sauce, without added chicken or fish (*Birds Eye Custom Cuisine*), 4.6 oz. .... | 70
with herb sauce, without added chicken or shrimp (*Birds Eye Custom Cuisine*), 4.6 oz. .... | 90
Italian (*Birds Eye* International), 3.3 oz. .... | 100
Japanese (*Birds Eye* International), 3.3 oz. .... | 90
Japanese (*Birds Eye* Stir Fry), 3.3 oz. .... | 30
Oriental style (*Birds Eye* International), 3.3 oz. .... | 70
pasta primavera (*Birds Eye* International), 3.3 oz. ...... | 120
in butter sauce (*Green Giant*) .... | 60
with onion sauce (*Birds Eye* Combinations), 2.6 oz. .... | 100
with Oriental sauce, authentic, without added beef (*Birds Eye Custom Cuisine*), 4.6 oz. .... | 90
stew (*Frosty Acres*), 3 oz. .... | 42
stew (*Ore-Ida*), 3 oz. .... | 60
with tomato-basil sauce, without added chicken (*Birds Eye Custom Cuisine*), 4.6 oz. .... | 110

Vegetables, pickled (*Vlasic* Hot and Spicy), 1 oz. .... | 4
Venison, roasted, meat only, 4 oz. .... | 179
Vienna sausage, canned, drained (*Hormel*), 4 links .... | 200

Vinegar:

apple cider, white or wine, 1 fl. oz. .... | 4
basil, garlic, or raspberry (*Great Impressions*), 1 tbsp. ...... | 7

W

Food and Measure	Calories

Waffles, frozen (see also "Pancake and waffle mix"), 1 piece:

apple cinnamon (*Aunt Jemima*), 2.5 oz.	176
apple cinnamon, strawberry, or blueberry (*Eggo*)	130
blueberry (*Aunt Jemima*), 2.5 oz.	175
buttermilk (*Aunt Jemima*), 2.5 oz.	179
buttermilk or homestyle (*Eggo*)	120
oat bran (*Eggo Common Sense*)	110.
oat bran, with fruit and nut (*Eggo Common Sense*)	120
plain or raisin and bran (*Eggo Nutri-Grain*)	130
Walnut topping, in syrup (*Smucker's*), 2 tbsp.	130

Walnuts, shelled, 1 oz.:

black, dried (*Planters*)	180
English or Persian (*Planters*)	190

Waterchestnut, Chinese:

fresh, 4 medium, 1¼"–2" diam., approx. 1.7 oz.	38
canned (*La Choy*), 1.28 oz.	18
Watercress, fresh, trimmed, chopped, ½ cup	2

Watermelon, fresh:

¹⁄₁₆ of 10" diam. melon, 1" thick	152
diced, ½ cup	25

Welsh rarebit:

canned (*Snow's*), ½ cup	170
frozen (*Stouffer's*), 10 oz.	350

Wendy's:

breakfast:

breakfast sandwich, 4.6 oz.	370
danish, apple, 3.4 oz.	360
danish, cheese, 3.4 oz.	430
danish, cinnamon-raisin, 3.4 oz.	410
French toast, 2 slices or 4.8 oz.	400

Wendy's, breakfast **(cont.)**

omelet, ham and cheese, 4.2 oz.	290
omelet, ham, cheese and mushroom, 4 oz.	250
omelet, ham, cheese, onion, and green pepper, 4.5 oz.	280
potatoes, breakfast, 3.6 oz.	360
sausage, 1 patty or 1.6 oz.	200

sandwiches:

bacon Swiss burger, 9.2 oz.	710
Big Classic, 9.5 oz.	580
Big Classic, with cheese, 10.2 oz.	640
cheeseburger, Kid's Meal or small	320
cheeseburger, single, 4.8 oz.	410
cheeseburger, single, with everything, 8.6 oz.	490
chicken sandwich, 7.7 oz.	430
hamburger, Kid's Meal or small	260
hamburger, plain, single, 4.2 oz.	350
Philly Swiss burger, 7.1 oz.	510

chicken nuggets and chill:

nuggets, crispy, cooked in vegetable oil, 6 pieces	310
nuggets, crispy, cooked in animal/vegetable oil, 6 pieces	290
chili, new, 9 oz.	230
chili, regular, 8.3 oz.	240

baked potato, hot stuffed:

plain, 8.8 oz.	250
bacon and cheese, 12.3 oz.	570
broccoli and cheese, 13 oz.	500
cheese, 12.3 oz.	590
chili and cheese, 14.1 oz.	510
sour cream and chives, 10.9 oz.	460

salads and side dishes:

chef salad, take-out, 11.7 oz.	180
French fries, regular, cooked in vegetable oil, 3.7 oz.	300
French fries, regular, cooked in animal/vegetable oil, 3.7 oz.	310
garden salad, take-out, 9.8 oz.	102
taco salad, prepared, 28 oz.	660
dessert, dairy, frosty, small, 8.6 oz.	400
dessert, pudding, butterscotch or chocolate, ¼ cup	90

Western dinner, frozen:

(*Banquet*), 11 oz.	630
(*Morton*), 10 oz.	290
style (*Swanson*), 11½ oz.	450

Wheat, whole-grain:

durum, 1 cup	650
hard red winter, 1 cup	628
soft red winter, 1 cup	556
soft white, 1 cup	571

Wheat bran, toasted (*Kretschmer*), 1 oz. 57
Wheat cake (*Quaker* Grain Cakes), .32-oz. piece 34
Wheat germ:
(*Kretschmer*), 1 oz., approx. ¼ cup 103
honey crunch (*Kretschmer*), 1 oz., approx. ¼ cup 105
Wheat pilaf, mix (*Casbah*), 1 oz. dry or ½ cup cooked 100
Whelk, meat only, raw, 4 oz. 156
Whiskey, see "Liquor"
White sauce, mix, prepared with milk, ½ cup 155
Whitefish, mixed species, meat only:
raw, 4 oz. 153
smoked, 4 oz. 122
Whiting:
fresh, baked, broiled, or microwaved, meat only, 4 oz. 130
frozen (*Booth*), 4 oz. 100
frozen, individually wrapped (*Booth*), 4 oz. 80
Wiener, see "Frankfurter"
Wild rice, cooked, ½ cup 83
Wine:
dessert, 3½ fl. oz. 140
table, dry, red, 3½ fl. oz. 75
table, dry, white or champagne, 3½ fl. oz. 80
Wine, cooking:
Burgundy or Sauterne (*Regina*), ¼ cup 2
marsala (*Holland House*), 1 fl. oz. 9
sherry (*Regina*), ¼ cup 20
vermouth (*Holland House*), 1 fl. oz. 2
Winged bean, boiled, drained, ½ cup 12
Wolf fish, Atlantic, raw, meat only, 4 oz. 109
Wonton skin (*Nasoya*), 1 piece 23
Worcestershire sauce:
(*Heinz*), 1 tbsp. 11
(*Lea & Perrins*), 1 tsp. 5
white wine (*Lea & Perrins*), 1 tsp. 3

Food and Measure Calories

Yams:
fresh, baked or boiled, drained, ½ cup 79
canned and frozen, see "Sweet potato"
Yam, mountain, Hawaiian, steamed, cubed, ½ cup 59
Yam bean tuber, boiled, drained, 4 oz. 52
Yardlong bean, boiled, drained, sliced, ½ cup 25
Yeast, baker's:
(*Fleischmann's* Active Dry/Rapid Rise), ¼ oz. 20
fresh or household (*Fleischmann's*), .6-oz. pkg. 15
Yellow squash, see "Crookneck squash"
Yellowtail, mixed species, raw, meat only, 4 oz. 166
Yogurt, 8 oz., except as noted:
plain (*Dannon* Lowfat) 140
plain (*Dannon* Nonfat) 110
plain (*Yoplait* Nonfat), 6 oz. 120
all flavors, lowfat (*Dannon* Fresh Flavors) 200
all flavors, except vanilla (*Dannon* Hearty Nuts & Raisins) .. 260
all flavors (*New Country/New Country* Supreme), 6 oz. 150
all fruit flavors:
    lowfat (*Dannon* Fruit-on-the-Bottom) 240
    lowfat (*Dannon* Extra Smooth) 130
    lowfat (*Yoplait* Light), 6 oz. 90
    nonfat (*Yoplait* Fat Free), 6 oz. 150
    (*New Country* Supreme), 6 oz. 150
    (*Yoplait* Original), 6 oz. 190
berries or tropical fruit (*Yoplait* Breakfast Yogurt), 6 oz. . 210
strawberry-banana (*Yoplait* Breakfast Yogurt), 6 oz. 220
vanilla, with wheat, nuts and raisins (*Dannon* Hearty Nuts & Raisins) 270
vanilla (*Yoplait* Custard Style), 6 oz. 180

Yogurt, frozen, ½ cup, except as noted:
all flavors:

(*Crowley*), 3 fl. oz.	80
except chocolate and nonfat, soft serve (*Dannon*)	100
nonfat, soft serve (*Dannon*)	90
soft serve (*Bresler's* Gourmet), 1 oz.	29
soft serve (*Bresler's* Lite), 1 oz.	27
chocolate (*Dannon*)	120
cherry, black, nonfat (*Sealtest Free*)	110
cherry, black or red raspberry (*Breyers*)	120
chocolate almond (*Elan*)	160
chocolate, nonfat (*Sealtest Free*)	110
chocolate or vanilla (*Breyers*)	120
peach or strawberry (*Breyers*)	110
peach, raspberry or strawberry, nonfat (*Sealtest Free*)	100
strawberry-banana (*Breyers*)	110
vanilla, nonfat (*Sealtest Free*)	100
Yogurt drink, all flavors (*Dan'up*), 8 oz.	190

Yogurt and fruit bar, see "Fruit bar, frozen"

Z

Food and Measure	**Calories**

Ziti, frozen, in marinara sauce (*The Budget Gourmet* Side Dish),
6.25 oz. 220
Zucchini:

fresh, raw, trimmed, sliced, ½ cup	9
fresh, boiled, drained, sliced, ½ cup	14
canned, in tomato sauce (*Del Monte*), ½ cup	30
frozen (*Seabrook*), 3.3 oz.	16
frozen, breaded (*Stilwell Quickkrisp*), 3.3 oz.	200